THE DETECTION OF
HUMAN REMAINS

ABOUT THE AUTHOR

Edward W. Killam is a private legal investigator and security consultant with Alliance Services, 7540 Baseline Road, Boulder, Colorado 80303. He has a Bachelor of Science Degree from Cornell University, an A.A.S. in Police Science from Mesa College and a Master's Degree in anthropology from Colorado State University. Prior to private practice, he was employed as a police officer, most recently as a Detective Sergeant for the Aspen, Colorado Police Department. He is also currently an instructor for the Colorado Mountain College Law Enforcement Training Academy.

THE DETECTION OF
HUMAN REMAINS

By

EDWARD W. KILLAM

CHARLES C THOMAS • PUBLISHER
Springfield • Illinois • U.S.A.

Published and Distributed Throughout the World by

CHARLES C THOMAS • PUBLISHER
2600 South First Street
Springfield, Illinois 62794-9265

© *1990 by* CHARLES C THOMAS • PUBLISHER
ISBN 0-398-05662-5 (cloth)
ISBN 0-398-06201-3 (paper)
Library of Congress Catalog Card Number: 89-20558

With THOMAS BOOKS *careful attention is given to all details of manufacturing
and design. It is the Publisher's desire to present books that are satisfactory as to their
physical qualities and artistic possibilities and appropriate for their particular use.*
THOMAS BOOKS *will be true to those laws of quality that assure a good name
and good will.*

Printed in the United States of America
2SC–R-3

Library of Congress Cataloging-in-Publication Data

Killam, Edward W.
    The detection of human remains / by Edward W. Killam.
      p. cm.
    Based on the author's thesis (M.A.)—Colorado State University.
    Includes bibliographical references.
    ISBN 0-398-05662-5.— ISBN 0-398-06201-3 (pbk.)
    1. Forensic anthropology. 2. Criminal investigation.
3. Anthropometry. I. Title.
GN69.8.K55 1990
363.2'52—dc20   89-20558
                                               CIP

To David Yates and Clifton Browning
Special Agents
Federal Bureau of Investigation,
Glenwood Springs, Colorado

Good Men Gone

FOREWORD

Serial murders and mass murders are becoming ever more common (Levin & Fox, 1985). It is also becoming apparent that this kind of violence brings with it the call for novel and sophisticated methods for handling the "crime scene." The discovery, retrieval, identification, and postmortem examination of bodies that are part of a mass disaster (whether of natural, accidental, or criminal origin) pose challenging technical requirements for coroners, medical examiners, and police crime scene investigators (Leyton, 1986; Damore, 1981; Michaud & Aynesworth, 1983).

Of particular importance is the discovery and initial processing of human remains. Recent history of some mass murders in the United States suggests that the processes used to discover and retrieve bodies that are the result of serial killings, or of individual killings that are being concealed, are less than elegant. Some of the murders resulting from so-called satanic perversions pose challenges for discovery of the human remains deriving from such viciousness and demand sophisticated analysis of the scene or scenes of the atrocity. Failure to meet adaptively these galvanizing events may well result in the prosecution of many such cases rendered more difficult than necessary and too often less adequate that the seriousness of the crime or incident warrants.

Every possible kind of scientific and technical "know-how" must be employed in the investigation of mass and serial murders to insure that complete and valid evidence is guaranteed for the prosecuting attorneys. Killers like Ted Bundy, finally executed on January 24, 1989 and estimated to have murdered 40 to 50 young women, have exploited our legal system and showed nothing but contempt for their victims. It was the search for one of Bundy's victims that first interested the author, then an officer with the Aspen, Colorado Police Department, in methods for finding human remains.

Edward W. Killam, in this present volume, has addressed himself to one critical aspect of the problem: the detection of human remains. He has also emphasized a widely neglected specialty with critical implications for the retrieval of bodies; that is, field archeology. It is apparent from the rather chaotic and unrefined methods used to recover bodies in many recent mass killings that better methods are demanded. (The John W. Gacy and the Juan Corona mass murders in the 1970s are cases in point.) Some mass murderers commit such enormities that our present thinking patterns have not been adequate to design appropriate investigative procedures in response; in the early 1980s the 150 or more murders carried out by Henry Lee Lucas and the more than 40 murders attributable to Gerald Stano are beyond our present capacity to respond totally (Leyton, 1986).

Archaeologists who work in the field (at "digs") have remarkably effective methods for garnering from sites large amounts of relevant information about human remains found and about the processes that went into the hiding of the remains. With minor adaptations their field research modality can and ought to be applied to the recovery of human remains of legal interest (e.g. Morse et al., 1983).

The present volume is unique in being the first of its kind. The author presents in a detailed but understandable form the various methods for finding buried, concealed or discarded bodies. He, as an experienced private legal investigator, is keenly aware of the courtroom implications of every step in the detection and recovery of evidence. His book is a valuable "how-to-do-it" manual for investigators charged with finding human remains of forensic science interest.

The volume is a needed and competent addition to the forensic science literature. It should be of interest to police investigators, prosecuting and defense attorneys, coroners, medical examiners, civil defense authorities, and others faced with the detection and retrieval of human remains lost from criminal or other causes.

References

Damore, L.
    1981 *In his Garden: The Anatomy of a Murderer.* Arbor House, New York.
Levin, J. and J.A. Fox
    1985 *Mass Murder: America's Growing Menace.* Plenum Press, New York.
Leyton, E.
    1986 *Compulsive Killers: The Story of Modern Multiple Murder.* Washington Mews Books, New York Univ. Press, New York.
Michaud, S. G. and H. Aynesworth
    1983 *The Only Living Witness.* Linden Press, Simon and Schuster, New York.

Morse, D., J. Duncan, and J. Stoutamire (editors)
    1983 *Handbook of Forensic Archaeology and Anthropology.* Florida State University Foundation, Inc., Rose Printing, Tallahassee, FL.

CHARLES G. WILBER, PH.D.
Director, Forensic Science Laboratory,
Colorado State University,
Fort Collins, Colorado
Former Deputy Coroner,
Larimer County, Colorado

PREFACE

This work is intended as a guide to the various methods for locating human remains. Most of the information is applicable to both archaeological and forensic situations. My intended audience are those who become actively involved in the hunt for human bodies, such as historic and prehistoric archaeologists and the law enforcement community, including coroner or medical examiner investigators and search and rescue teams. I also believe it will be of benefit to criminal justice prosecutors who need to prepare search warrants and court orders or must qualify and question expert witnesses.

This work contains guidelines for the investigation of missing-person or homicide cases which require comprehensive body search planning. The core is a guide to methods for locating surface and buried bodies. The methods considered include ground contact, proximate and remote sensing techniques. The categories of methods are non-intrusive pedestrian searches, surface-penetrating ground searches, geophysical prospecting techniques, remote-sensing methods, aerial photography and interpretation, and parapsychological techniques. The underlying operational principles, advantages and disadvantages and possible applications of each method are discussed.

I have six broad objectives in preparing this work. The first is to assemble basic information on search methods and condense that information into a single source which can be a ready reference for practitioners. A number of these search methods may be known to archaeologists but not law enforcement, and vice versa. Some of these methods, or at least their application to body-search situations, may be new to both groups.

Secondly, I hope to provide sufficient information for practitioners to try and use the "do-it-yourself" techniques. I hope the information presented gives the reader sufficient confidence to try such techniques as oblique infrared photography, probes and gas vapor detectors, metal detectors, etc. This work should assist in choosing and purchasing the necessary equipment for these methods. Other techniques are beyond the "do-it-yourself" category and require the use of specialized equipment or professional expertise.

My third objective is to provide supervisors with guidelines for recognizing a situation that needs outside consultants. The information presented will enable a knowledgeable consumer to ask questions of experts before making a hiring decision. There will also be enough information for the employer to judge the results of the expert's work and decide whether the search should be continued with current methods. A search supervisor or case investigator may have to explain his decisions to superiors, the press, and the victim's family. He may have to justify his budget expenditures in light of the search results. Accordingly, my fourth objective is to provide the data necessary to balance time, manpower, and costs against expected results. Beyond justifying his choices, a search supervisor must be able to explain why other techniques were not used, such as refusing to use psychics and dowsers or suspending a magnetic search because of sunspot activity. In some situations, an investigator may have unwanted search methods thrust upon him, e.g. a family willing to supply search volunteers. The investigator will need the sophistication to accept such assistance gracefully and maximize its benefits without compromising other search efforts already underway.

My fifth objective is to assist a supervisor in compiling his own set of standard operating procedures (S.O.P.) for a search effort. A body search S.O.P. should contain investigative and interrogation suggestions which can narrow down the search areas. It should provide information on choosing search techniques based upon the totality of environmental circumstances and the equipment and expertise available. It should also specify the order in which search methods will be used so that early searches do not confound later efforts. For instance, aerial photography should be used before foot searches so that the search area is not scared by search vehicles and ground teams. The S.O.P. should present at least the basic guidelines for conducting searches without damaging the search area or destroying valuable physical evidence.

My last objective is to provide a list of references for investigators who want additional information. I have tried to emphasize the best comprehensive texts I have encountered so that the professional can build his personal reference library. I have also tried to include sources of advice and assistance found outside books and journals. I hope this work encourages communication among the geophysicists and archaeologists found on college campuses, the law enforcement and search and rescue personnel in the field, and the manufacturers and vendors of search equipment. One of the hallmarks of the forensics field is the rapidly changing technologies, which means an investigator must be constantly receptive to new information and suggestions. Better communication and mutual assistance among academia, law enforcement, and private industry can be beneficial to all concerned with the successful conclusion of a search problem.

ACKNOWLEDGMENTS

This work began as my thesis prepared in partial fulfillment of the requirements for the Degree of Master of Arts in the Department of Anthropology at Colorado State University. My thanks go to the members of my graduate committee: Diane L. France, Calvin H. Jennings, Jeffrey L. Eighmy and Charles G. Wilber. Archaeologists Calvin Jennings and Jeffrey Eighmy and forensic anthropologist Diane France also reviewed Chapters 1, 2 and 3 of this book.

My thanks for assistance in preparation of this work go to geologist John W. Lindemann who reviewed and added to chapters 5 and 6. Geophysicist G. Clark Davenport also helped me prepare chapters 5 and 6, providing me with advice and photographs. I also thank Heinz W. Siegel, General Manager of the Geological Instrument Supply Company of Denver, CO who provided technical information and photographs of geophysical instruments and techniques.

I am indebted to Donald H. Heimmer of Geo-Recovery Systems, Inc. of Englewood, CO for his review and comments on chapter 7 and to archaeologist James Grady of The University of Colorado at Denver for his review of chapter 8. If any errors remain in this book, they are the sole responsibility of the author, not the reviewers who did all they could to straighten out my facts.

My additional thanks go to artist Mark H. Minter who made all the drawings and to Kathleen Smith who endured my dictation and typed all the drafts of my thesis. I am also grateful to all the authors and publishers who allowed me to include portions of their work. Finally I wish to thank my wife, Gail L. Hanson, for preparing the final book manuscript and enduring my seemingly endless revisions.

273460

CONTENTS

The Detection of Human Remains

THE DETECTION OF
HUMAN REMAINS

Chapter 1

FORENSIC ANTHROPOLOGY

"Whoever thou art that findest me lying, respect my remains: they are those of a man who consecrated all his life to being useful, and who has died as he lived, virtuous and honest. Not fear, but indignation, made me quit my retreat, on learning that my Wife had been murdered. I wished not to remain longer on an Earth polluted with crimes."

Suicide note of Jean Marie Roland de la Platiere. Appears by permission of Philosophical Library Publishers from *Dictionary of Last Words* by Edward S. LeComte, 1955.

The detection and recovery of buried bodies is not a concern just to law enforcement. It has long been a focus of anthropological and archaeological study as well. Anthropology is a broad academic and research area commonly defined as "the study of man" (Guralnik, 1970). It is classically divided into four major subfields: cultural anthropology, linguistics, archaeology, and physical anthropology.

Cultural anthropologists specialize in man's cultural patterns and social institutions, such as family structures, religions beliefs, etc. Funeral and burial practices are within the realm of cultural anthropology. Linguistics is the study of language, their origins, structures, and relationships. Archaeology concerns itself primarily with the life ways and cultures of ancient peoples, based largely upon the excavation and recovery of buried objects, including human remains.

Physical anthropology treats man as a biological species and has a number of specialties within its domain. These include primatology which is the study of living primates, osteology or the study of the bones and skeleton, and paleontology directed at fossil primates, including man. It also includes the study of human genetic variation and forensic anthropology, the examination of skeletal material in forensic situations. Typically, the archaeologist is highly trained in excavation techniques and the physical anthropologist is more skilled in the actual interpreta-

3

tion of skeletal remains. A good forensic anthropologist will bring all the fields of anthropology (cultural, archaeology, etc.) to bear upon the legal problem at hand. He will be knowledgeable in the field of taphonomy, the study of events after death, from decomposition to fossilization (Haglund, 1989).

Those physical anthropologists engaged in forensic examinations can assist in the identification, or at least description, of the deceased individual and perhaps reconstruct some of the circumstances surrounding death. The fundamental techniques and capabilities of physical anthropology are well covered in the classic texts of the field: Bass (1987b), Krogman and Iscan (1986), and Stewart (1979). The forensic anthropologist commonly becomes involved in a case when the body has become partially or completely skeletonized. The skeleton is the most durable system of the human body and is available long after the rest is gone.

Physical anthropologists first carefully describe the condition of all remains brought to them, including an inventory of the bones present. From this inventory, they can determine the minimum number of individuals represented, thus determining possible commingling of remains. They can also make a species determination, separating human from animal bones (Brues 1958).

Presuming a reasonably complete recovery of the skeleton, a physical anthropologist can usually determine the "Big Four" about the deceased: stature, age at death, sex and racial stock or affiliation (Krogman & Iscan, 1986). The estimation of stature is based upon measurement of the long bones of the body and subsequent calculations based on the maturation and then degeneration of the human skeleton over time. The bones mature and grow until the twenties and then begin irreversible degeneration. This pattern of change with age, though subject to wide variation among individuals, is well known (Bass, 1987a).

If the deceased was an adult, the probable sex can be determined by examination of the pelvis, skull and other bones. The skeletal differences between male and female generally become apparent after the age of 12 to 15 years. Racial affiliation is based upon statistical differences in skeletal features between the major racial groups. There are a host of problems involved in racial determination, among which is admixture, or the mixing of racial traits. The skeletal definition of racial type may also not correspond with social definitions, i.e. bone shape is not always correlated with skin color. Another difficulty is the basic nature of human variation; that there is often more variation in the skeleton *within* a racial type than there is *between* racial groups (France & Horn, 1988).

The anthropologist, after the examination of the remains is completed, may be able to provide "accessory information" to investigators (Krogman & Iscan, 1986). This accessory information may include the approximate time since death or time of burial. He may also be able to describe the cause or manner of death if it is registered in the bones. The anthropologist will also describe individualities or anomolies in the skeleton which may assist in the identification of the deceased. These may include pathologies and the remnants of orthopedic injuries. The identification of the deceased can often be made when the conventional identification techniques based on soft tissues, such as facial recognition or fingerprints, are no longer possible. Methods of identification used by anthropologists include facial reconstruction, photographic superimposition, and comparison of the skeleton with antemortem medical and dental records.

FORENSIC ARCHAEOLOGY

Archaeology, another subfield of anthropology, also has direct applications to law enforcement and other legal problems. Criminalists can learn from archaeologists, as it is the business of archaeology to detect and recover evidence. Archaeologists, like criminalists, are concerned with ecofacts which are natural objects with no evidence of human use, such as soils, pollens, plants, and animal bones. They are also interested in artifacts which are objects of human manufacture and use (Eddy, 1984). In modern murder cases, burial rites are often stark without the coffins, artifacts or tombs more commonly associated with archaeologists, but "both forensic pathologists and archaeologists deal with the examination of the dead and ponder on the circumstances, both broad and narrow, that are summarized in death" (Boddington et al., 1987:3).

Two recent books, Morse, Duncan and Stoutamier (1983) and Skinner and Lazenby (1983), are attempts to integrate the excavation techniques of archaeology into field criminalistics. Criminalistics, or in modern nomenclature terms, forensic science, is that endeavor which applies the principles of biology, chemistry, physics and other scientific disciplines to law enforcement. Criminalistics and anthropologists have had a long history of cooperation going back at least to Alphonse Bertillon and his "science of identification" (O'Brien & Sullivan, 1976). Despite the fact that archaeological techniques have only recently been used by crime scene technicians, the need for such expertise has long been recognized. Even before World War II, Krogman (1939) was teaching investigators about physical anthropology and later (Krogman, 1943, 1962) specifically suggested that archaeologists assist forensic exhumations.

There are profound advantages to having a forensic anthropologist at the scene of a body recovery. First, his archaeology training may help in the search for a buried body by applying techniques used for locating archaeological sites. Secondly, the anthropologist can assist in the complete recovery and preservation of evidence. Snow (1982:118) noted that: "Systematic recovery of the materials from burial and surface sites is best accomplished by suitably modifying methods long employed by archaeologists to solve similar problems."

Furthermore, information he obtains or observations he makes during the recovery will assist him in interpreting the condition of the skeletal remains he will later examine. Finally, by being involved in the case from its inception, the expert may also testify as to the recovery techniques used and the chain-of-evidence custody (Berryman, 1986). Morse, Stoutamire and Duncan (1976) noted that police investigators were generally competent to sketch, photograph and collect evidence on the ground's surface, but rarely had they taken the same techniques underground. There are still simply too many cases where "surface skeletons are collected with a garden rake and buried bodies with a backhoe" (Morse et al., 1984:53).

Very narrowly, then, forensic archaeology was defined by Morse, et al. (1983:1) as "the application of simple archaeological recovery technique in death scene investigations involving a buried body or skeletal remains." The synthesis of archaeology and criminalistics should increase the amount of information derived from the crime scene processing part of an investigation. For instance, the collection of pollen, soil, seeds and insects by police officers is based on their importance and relevance first discovered by archaeologists. As another example, the discovery of a body buried more than 40 years is not generally of forensic interest, but the tentative dating of such a burial can most rapidly be done by an archaeologist/anthropologist who can derive information not only from the skeleton itself but from the associated grave goods such as buttons, buckles, coins, coffin nails, etc. (Morse, Crusoe & Smith, 1976). There are additional specific skills of the archaeologists which could be adapted to police work, such as evidence recovery techniques and specialized photography (Barker, 1977). Criminalistics have even adopted some of the jargon of archaeology, such as the description of body positions (Sprague, 1968).

A grasp of some principles of archaeology is helpful and applicable to criminalistics, for example, stratigraphy. The process of stratigraphy is the continual deposition of discarded things upon the earth's surface. With time, there is a gradual buildup of these deposits. The opposing force is erosion which tends to move objects from high points to low. The extension of stratigraphy is stratigraphic succession or the principle of superposition. Since new depositions are on top of pre-existing levels, the relative age of levels can be determined. The older materials will tend to be at the bottom and the younger ones on top, in the absence of disturbance. Thus, to penetrate to older deposits, the excavator must mimic erosion in digging down through the upper layers to those underneath.

Stratification has two important applications to criminalistics. The first is in trying to locate graves themselves. Graves are detectable because of a disruption in the natural stratigraphy of the soils. Digging into the ground interrupts the depositional process (Hester & Grady, 1982). Phrased another way, "one can never dig in the ground and put the dirt back exactly as nature had put it there originally" (Bass & Birkby, 1978:6). The alterations to the soil layers brought about by digging make the grave site detectable almost indefinitely. The investigator's ability to detect the site is limited only by his technological expertise, equipment, and time available for the effort.

The second use of the law of superposition is the relative dating information obtainable from the sequence of deposits. To use a simple example, a cigarette butt found on top of the grave must have been deposited on the day the grave was finished or since but not before. Objects may be found in any of the four discernable layers of a grave: substrate, body layer, fill or surface. Each layer may yield physical evidence which must be interpreted in light of the layer from which it came.

Another useful principle is that of uniformitarianism. Uniformitarianism suggests that the physical processes now underway affect all matter and those processes have always been essentially the same. That is, "similar causes produce similar effects" (Hole & Heizer, 1973). The application to archaeology and forensics is that physical and chemical processes affecting objects in the ground now also had similar effects in the past. Thus, it may be possible to approximately date burials by examining the degree of deterioration of articles found within the grave (Morse & Daily, 1985).

Uniformitarianism is also extended to behavioral processes. With some modifications, human behavior must always have been essentially the same because of the biological restrictions of our bodies. Behavior, of course, is also influenced by cultural restrictions. Human behavior impacts the way a body is prepared for burial and the choice of a burial location.

As an outgrowth of behavioral uniformitarianism, it is expected that man, or society, when confronted with a problem will always seek a satisfactory solution which requires the least effort. Consider that the disposal of a dead body is a practical problem, both for a society when it is sedentary and for an individual criminal attempting to conceal evidence of a crime. Burial of the body is a common solution to both problems. To accomplish the burial, the criminal will want to expend the least amount of physical effort balanced against the need to hide the body where he hopes it will not be found.

The principle of least effort also enables investigators to make conclusions from the nature of the grave itself. If the grave is very deep or very large, it perhaps indicates that there was more than one person involved in the grave digging or that the person had plenty of time in which to accomplish the inhumation. Conversely, a shallow grave with a body compressed into a fetal position indicates a hurried, pressured or solitary suspect was involved.

TYPES OF BURIALS

All the search methods described in this work have or can be used in an effort to find human remains. They are principally designed to detect bodies buried on land. Though only land searches are covered, many of the methods are also applicable to underwater searches. For instance, ground-penetrating radar, normally pulled on a wheeled cart, could be put in a waterproof housing and used over freshwater lakes when towed behind a boat. Likewise, some metal detectors are specifically designed for use in underwater search and salvage operations.

Just as there is no clear-cut distinction between land and water search methods, there is little difference between searching for a buried body versus a surface body. Both can be discovered by aerial photography, air-scenting dogs, foot searches, etc. Human remains that start out on the surface may become buried by natural processes (Wolf, 1986). A flood or drowning victim may be covered by silt or debris. A body left in the forest will eventually be covered by ground litter or new plant growth. Heavy rains may mix bone and soil so that the heavier bones sink beneath the surface (Morse et al., 1983). Such self-burials may be partial or complete, and just as bodies may become buried by natural mechanism, so they may be uncovered by natural events such as erosion or digging by animals.

Inhumations, or the deliberate burial of bodies by other humans, have long been objects of study by archaeologists. Collins (1975) noted that there are two broad categories of buried human remains important to the archaeological record. There are those that were intentionally deposited and those that were not. Both are culturally and biologically informative. Examples of the first are deliberate interments versus the second type, adventitious remains in which bodies are preserved in place after accidental death.

Primary interments are burials in which the bones lie in an anatomical relationship approximating the normal bone articulation when the person was alive. The presumption is that no changes have occurred in the position of the body since the soft tissue disappeared (Hester et al., 1975). Secondary interments may also be found in either archaeological or forensic context. In these situations, bones are collected after the decomposition of soft flesh and are then buried. In such cases it is not likely that the bones are still in the normal anatomical position and the remains may be fragmentary. Multiple interments are most common in the archaeological record or military situations in which several bodies are located in one grave. The bodies may have been buried all at once or additional bodies added to the burial ground over time. Such circumstances can occur in a forensic context when mass or serial murderers are involved.

Regardless of the type of burial, each grave has four layers of interest. They are the substrate or natural soils below the grave itself, the buried body and its associated artifacts, the fill above the body, and the surface of the grave exposed to the world (Hole & Heizer, 1973). Of these four layers, the top three are typically used in grave detection. As examples, the surface depression may be seen during a foot search, the mixed grave fill may be differentiated from the substrate by ground-penetrating radar, and decomposition gases from the body may be picked up by a methane gas detector.

If a body is deeply buried, below about 4 feet, it is essentially in long-term storage and changes are relatively slow. "Looking for a buried body is not an emergency situation . . . " (McLaughlin, 1974:28). Surface-laying or shallow-buried bodies, on the other hand, may deteriorate rapidly depending upon climate and other environmental conditions. Since an investigator cannot know the burial conditions beforehand, all searches should be conducted as soon as possible after formulating a good search plan. There is always enough time to plan and carry out a thorough search. A preparation delay will always be better than having to search an area a second time because of an inadequate first search.

Investigators and searchers sometimes forget the fact that a grave is also a crime scene which must be handled and processed with appropriate care. The body of the victim and the grave are an enormous potential source of physical evidence to link the suspect to the crime. Investigators must be sure that the search, excavation and subsequent recovery of human remains are done with all the necessary permission. Depending upon the circumstances involved, parties with an interest in an exhumation may include the landowner or tenant, the next of kin (or surviving spouse), the coroner or medical examiner's office, the county or state health department, and the civil and criminal courts. Exhumations in civil matters may require a court order, and criminal exhumations will surely require a valid consent(s) to search and/or a search warrant (Feegel, 1972).

Chapter 2

COMPREHENSIVE SEARCH PLAN

"Yeah, tonight I'm sittin' alone,
diggin' up bones.
I'm diggin' up bones.
I'm diggin' up bones.
Exhumin' things that's better left alone."

> "Diggin' Up Bones" performed by
> Randy Travis on his *Storms of Life* album
> from Warner Bros. Music. Appears by
> permission of Sawgrass Music Division
> of Musiplex Group, Inc.

A comprehensive plan for the recovery of human remains can be divided into five major steps as follows:

  I. Planning, Phase One
  II. Reconnaissance
  III. Planning, Phase Two
  IV. Search Operation
  V. Excavation/Recovery

The phase one planning step is the accumulation of all available information that is pertinent to the search. The information collected comes from four major categories. The first is all information about the incident precipitating a search, usually beginning with the report of a missing person. This category of information contains everything known about the victim, the disappearance incident, and, when applicable, anything known about the suspect(s). It also includes predictions about the search areas based upon knowledge of the victim and suspect.

The second category of information to be gathered is the environmental conditions found in the search areas. This includes ground conditions and atmospheric conditions. The third area of information is the resources available to the search agency. This includes manpower and equipment immediately available as well as consultants and specialized equipment which can be brought in.

The fourth area of information could be called, for want of a better term, the political environment. This category may determine how much effort can realistically be devoted to the search. Typical facts contained here may be the identity of the victim and pressure from the victim's family, pre-existing and concurrent case loads, evidence for or absence of foul play, jurisdictional issues, etc.

The exhaustive collection of information in these four data categories (victim/suspect, environment, resources, and politics) establishes the base from which a comprehensive search plan can be formulated. Setnicka (1980:78–81) provided an outline of the sources of planning information along with suggestions on questioning witnesses, collecting evidence, etc. That outline is included in this work as Appendix 1. It is certainly not unreasonable for the phase one planning to take at least a whole day before any field work is actually undertaken.

The second major step (II) in a search operation is the reconnaissance of selected search areas. The investigator does not simply follow a hunch and begin digging. First, the prudent search director does a site evaluation before even visiting the area. This off-site investigation is intended to answer questions about the physical location and jurisdiction of the search area. Questions to be addressed are the ownership status of the land and means for obtaining legal permission for a search effort. Other questions to be answered are accessibility for men and equipment and basic topography based upon available maps.

After all available off-site information has been gathered, the investigator can do a preliminary reconnaissance of the search area. This reconnaissance does *not* include trampling the grave site and destroying physical evidence. The reconnaissance, done from afar, should confirm information about ownership, topography, and access. It should identify likely areas for physical evidence collection. During the first visit the investigator should record nearby buildings, roads, utility lines, fences, and other features which may influence how the search is conducted. The reconnaissance will also record the type of vegetation cover that may restrict search methods. Non-destructive search techniques such as remote sensing (Chapter 6) and aerial photography (Chapter 7) may be used during this period.

This preliminary reconnaissance by the investigator is indispensable in formulating the final field operation plan. Whenever possible, this reconnaissance should be done quietly and with minimal manpower so as to not to draw curious press, neighbors or other bystanders to the scene. A useful aid to both the off-site and on-site search area evaluation can be found in the Forensic Geology checklist and Forensic Geophysics checklist found in Davenport et al. (1986) and included in this book as Appendices 2 and 3.

The second phase planning (Step III) takes place after the preliminary reconnaissance and is dependent upon the results of the previous step. During this planning phase, the actual search strategy is formulated, a logistics system set up, and resources assembled. Also during this stage, legal authority for the search operation is obtained.

The fourth step is the actual search itself. The field techniques may include non-intrusive foot search (Chapter 3), intrusive ground searches (Chapter 4), and geophysical techniques (Chapters 5 and 6). When the search is completed, the final step of the operation is the excavation of suspected grave sites and the eventual recovery of the human remains.

The decision to proceed with a search operation using a particular technique does not depend only upon the scientific merit and reliability of the method but also upon less tangible factors uncovered in the planning steps. Typical factors considered in choosing a search technique include the size of search area, type of terrain and expected type of burial, such as duration of interment, depth, etc. Other factors include manpower, equipment, and expertise readily available as well as the advantages and limitations of each method. Another important consideration is the cost of the search techniques relative to the agency or search budget available. The search director must decide how much time can be devoted to the search and the likelihood of success under existing environmental conditions. Sometimes a postponement of the search is the logical decision even in the face of political pressure to do something right away. The decision to do nothing *now* can be the most difficult decision to make and defend. A summary of the factors to be considered in choosing search methods is contained in Appendix 4.

PRELIMINARY INVESTIGATION

Information gathering is the critical first step after the report of a crime or missing person has been received. Traditionally, there are three sources of information for an investigation, i.e. information received from people, documents, or physical evidence (objects). All three may be involved in the search for human remains. For instance, documents on file at the county assessor's office will contain descriptions of all properties owned by the suspect, which are logical first places to start the search. Soil samples recovered from the suspect's boots, vehicle, or shovel may narrow the search area to a particular soil type.

For most searches, information from witnesses is likely to give the best leads. The people likely to have valuable information, besides the suspect, are people who know the victim or know the suspect. All potential witnesses need to be interviewed with tact and consideration for the emotional atmosphere surrounding the search.

If investigators have the luxury of a confession from the defendant or an accomplice, it does not mean that other interviews should be less thorough. The information in hand may be deliberately or inadvertently inaccurate so that a complete search still becomes necessary. The suspect or informant should be questioned carefully about where the body was buried, not just in general terms, but in specifics as to directions and distance from nearby landmarks. Whenever possible, the witness should be provided with aerial photographs, maps, and sketching materials to pinpoint the burial site. The witness should also be questioned about how the burial was done and how deep the grave is estimated to be. The witness must be questioned about the condition of the body such as injuries, clothing, coverings, and other objects which may be in the grave. Whenever possible, the complete interview should be tape recorded and transcribed.

In missing-person cases, whether foul play is suspected or not, the most important witnesses become those who knew and last saw the victim. Investigators on the case will need to obtain detailed information on the victim's physical description, clothing, habits, health, etc. The questioning should not be limited to the reporting party but to all friends, relatives, and recent companions of the victim. Search and rescue team members may have particular expertise in this type of questioning. A good preliminary list of questions is contained in Setnicka (1980:66–70) and is included in this book as Appendix 5.

SEARCH AREA SELECTION

Before any search operation can begin, there must be a selection of the search area(s). The prediction of where remains might be found is based largely upon information gathered about the victim, suspect(s), and incident. Certainly most human remains are found accidentally (Krogman & Iscan, 1986) and only rarely is one led to the scene by the suspect or an informant (Gerberth, 1983). Most surface remains are found accidentally by civilians rather than as a result of organized search efforts, and most buried remains are discovered by highway, sewer or other construction operations (Wolf, 1986).

As discussed in Chapter 1, all human actions are subject to behavior restrictions. In choosing an action, each person is subject to cultural as well as physical or biological limitations (Hole & Heizer, 1973). A killer trying to get rid of a body is subject to physical constraints such as how long and far he can carry the weight of his victim. He is also burdened by cultural restrictions based upon the fear of discovery. The suspect will seek a location for the body or a manner of disposal achievable within these restrictions.

The fear of discovery is an overwhelming factor in criminal behavior. From introductory crime prevention courses we know that burglars, and in fact all criminals, fear time, light, and noise. The longer the crime takes, the greater the likelihood of discovery. The more light present, the more likely it is that the criminal act will be seen by witnesses. The more noise that is created, the greater the probability of detection. These same fears burden a killer suddenly encumbered with a body. In defense, he will seek to dispose of the body quickly in a relatively secluded area, probably at night.

The location and manner of body disposal may yield valuable information about the murderer's personality. Dump-site analysis may assist in profiling the suspect, because the choice of site and arrangement of the body may be meaningful to the suspect. Murderers may be categorized as organized or disorganized based upon profile characteristics (Ressler & Burgess, 1985). Disorganized killers are more likely to leave the body in view, probably right at the death scene. Organized murderers who plan their crimes, however, are more likely to transport the body and conceal it. The organized killer's choice of a disposal location may be far from his home or work. He may return to the site to check for mistakes or to see if the body has been discovered. The murderer may even engineer a scenario in which he is instrumental in the discovery or recovery of the body (Ressler, 1987).

Greene (1987) held that there are two types of body disposals in homicide situations. The first is the "quick dump" in which no burial is involved. It is likely that the dumping of the body may be in an area unknown or only slightly known to the perpetrator. The suspect is aware that the body will be found shortly but hopes there will be insufficient evidence to connect him to the scene.

The second type of discard is the planned or premeditated concealment of the body, usually by burying. In this case, the perpetrator will likely choose an area he knows well, where he feels relatively assured that he will not be interrupted or seen. The area chosen may be on land owned or controlled by the defendant or his relatives. It may be a former residence or an area the suspect knows from childhood, or it may be public lands where the suspect has frequently hiked, hunted, or fished. Greene also studied suicide victims and learned that 90 percent of them will be found downhill and within one-quarter mile of where they were last seen alive.

Snyder (1977) contended that the suspect is the best source of information for predicting where remains may be found. Even if the suspect will not confess nor cooperate, information may be obtained indirectly. Snyder recommended the use of a polygraph to narrow the search area. The suspect could be shown a map which has been divided into areas. The suspect, while attached to the polygraph instrument, can be asked about each zone of the map. Any areas in which a reaction is obtained can be further subdivided to narrow the search area. Aerial photographs or even road maps could be used in a similar fashion. Snyder also recommended a thorough examination of the suspect's property for any evidence of excavation, construction, or new concrete work. A suspect may dump a body in a pre-existing hole such as a mine shaft or open well (Levine et al., 1984). Similarly, lakes, deep rivers, and the ocean have been traditional disposal points, i.e. "concrete boots."

In our highly mobile society, it's likely that the body was transported to its burial site by vehicle. Experts have universally noted the tendency of bodies to be found close to roads or other vehicle access. McLaughlin (1974:28) wrote that most bodies will be found within 50 feet of a road because "most people are not physically capable of carrying or dragging a body any great distance." This assumes that just one suspect was involved in disposing of the body. If the perpetrator had help, the body could be carried considerably farther. Since the criminal is likely to take the "path of least resistance" from the road to the grave site, it is important that searchers not use the same easy path or they may destroy tracks or trace evidence sticking to vegetation (Skinner & Lazenby, 1983).

An analysis of body dump sites presented by Streed (1989) confirmed that victims are usually recovered near roadways. The sites chosen by the suspects indicate the urgency to dispose of the evidence. Most sites were within a 30- to 45-minute drive from the point where the victim was picked up to the place where the body was discarded. Bodies were usually found off the right, passenger side of the road, outbound from the city or town. Normally, the suspect drove out from the city on a major artery for about five minutes, then turned off on to a secondary road. The body was often dumped within 45 seconds driving time on the secondary road. The site frequently offered a panoramic view of the area as though the killer was demonstrating his dominance over the situation.

Cherry and Angel (1977) emphasized that a downhill search is very important, not only because that direction is easier for the suspect to drag the victim, but also because rain, wind, animal activity and gravity will cause a separation of skeletal parts after the connecting tissue of the body has decomposed. The separated parts will tend to spread downhill and away from the rest of the body. Any body found on an incline signals the need for a careful downhill search for further evidence. Consideration should also be given to the suspect's technical capabilities. For instance, a suspect with access to a furnace may try to burn the body, or a suspect employed in the construction industry may have access to a backhoe or other excavation equipment.

In summation, the prudent criminal will attempt to minimize the time he spends with the victim's body. He will also attempt to reduce the physical work involved in disposing of it. He will try to avoid witnesses. Within time and work constraints, he will try to decrease the likelihood that the body will be quickly found by covering or burying it. So where are graves likely to be found? The body will probably be found near a road or parking area. It is likely to be found downhill or at least at the same level as the road. Rarely will it have been dragged uphill. The grave will probably be made where the soil is easy to dig, not in soil full of rocks or tree roots. The grave is likely to be located in a secluded place, not within view of neighboring houses. The discard might have been done at night so it is someplace the suspect could get to in the dark or with only a flashlight. Disposal is likely to have been made on land controlled by or at least familiar to the suspect, to which he may have had legal access. The drop point may be near the crime scene, especially if the disposal was done in haste. The criminal might take advantage of preexisting disposal sites such as bodies of water, open holes, or latrines. The suspect may hope to disguise the grave by burying the body at a landfill, construction site, or cultivated field where subsequent earth-work will obscure surface signs.

ADVANTAGES AND DISADVANTAGES OF EACH METHOD

After all available information has been gathered from witnesses, site reconnaissance and weather forecast, the investigator should consider the advantages and disadvantages of each search method in light of prevailing conditions. The advantages and disadvantages of each method are condensed into Appendix 6.

In considering the various methods, the investigator must keep in mind the expected characteristics of the target and the parameters of the search site. The target characteristics include the dimensions of the grave, its contents and expected contrast between the grave and the surrounding area. The investigator will then have to consider the possible "noise" or interference from man-made or natural conditions which may rule out some of the search techniques.

At the conclusion of this planning phase, the investigator will have chosen a handful of methods suitable for use. The next decision to make is the order in which the search methods will be used. This decision is made by referring again to the advantages and disadvantages of each search system. Some methods, such as heavy equipment, are destructive and will preclude or at least hinder subsequent search methods. Those techniques should be a last resort. Other techniques, such as aerial photography, are not only non-destructive but even non-contact and should begin as soon as a search area has been identified. Many of the techniques can be used concurrently to save time and effort. For instance, foot searchers looking for visual signs of a grave could be equipped with metal detectors. The proper use of a metal detector means that the searchers must move slowly so they will search more carefully. The two methods are also compatible because the searcher is using his eyes to detect visual signs while his ears listen for audible alerts from the metal detector. As other examples, a single instrument can be used to collect both electric resistivity and self-potential data, and electromagnetic-profiling instruments simultaneously scan the search area for soil electrical conductivity, soil magnetic susceptibility and the presence of metal objects.

The experienced investigator, even if he expects immediate success based on his preliminary work, is advised to have a secondary or contingency plan. It is embarrassing to assemble volunteers and equipment, conduct a search and excavation, only to find an empty hole. At that point, the search director had better have an idea of what to do next.

OPERATIONAL PLAN

Having chosen his search area and methods, the search director must now formulate an operational plan. He will have to plan for the acquisition, use and return of necessary equipment and supplies. He needs to determine the type and amount of support services for the search. He must assure adequate documentation of the search and recovery effort and plan for the examination and analysis of the recovered remains.

A critical part of the search plan will be specifying the thoroughness of the survey. In many of the methods discussed, e.g. probing, soil analysis, gravity surveying, etc., the investigator must specify how close together the survey points will be. With other methods (e.g. magnetic surveying, ground-penetrating radar, visual search, etc.), the investigator will establish parallel search lines. In each case, too great a spacing between observations may mean that the grave is missed, whereas observation points too close together means wasted time and effort. Theoretically, a maximum amount of information will be obtained when the observation points are infinitely close to each other. This is obviously impractical. Therefore, a balance must be struck between the amount of information desired and the limitations of time, cost and terrain (Parasnis, 1979). A time management decision will have to be made. Is it better to do a slow, thorough, detailed search once or face the possibility of having to search the area all over again? For each technique and set of terrain conditions, there is probably an optimum point or line spacing which will provide a maximum probability of detecting a grave-sized target. That spacing will have to be adjusted as search conditions vary, but starting recommendations are contained in this text.

PRESERVATION OF REMAINS

It would be a mistake for any investigator to speculate to the press or family about the preservation of a buried body. Pathologists and archaeologists both have noted the enormous variety in states of preservation of bodies, even from the same burial site. It is necessary, however, for the investigator to make some private estimation of the degree or stage of decomposition as a factor to be considered in choosing certain search techniques. For instance, active decomposition is necessary to produce the scent detected and traced by dogs.

The degree of preservation varies with intrinsic and extrinsic factors (Henderson, 1987). Intrinsic factors pertain to the body itself and the nature of bone and other body parts. For bone alone, the likelihood of preservation depends upon the bone chemistry, bone shape, size and density. For instance, the fragile skull is more likely to be broken than the tubular tibia. The small pisiform is more likely to be lost than the large femur. The size, density, and chemical nature of bone are dependent upon the genetics, age, and health of the deceased. Other intrinsic factors include antemortem injuries to or infections within the deceased, both of which will accelerate decomposition.

Extrinsic factors include those variables beyond the body itself. They include the immediate environment of the burial such as the geography and geology of the site, such as moisture content, soil type, temperature, atmosphere, etc. Extrinsic factors also include the flora and fauna of the grave site including bacteria, fungi, insects, scavenging mammals, plant root systems, etc. Human activities, such as burial practices, also influence the degree of preservation.

Feegel (1973) identified a number of conditions which affect the rate of decay. His work was addressed to cemetery exhumations but applies as well to other types of forensic burials. Feegel considered length of burial an important factor as well as soil conditions which included soil type, drainage characteristics, and subsurface temperature. Obviously cold and dry conditions will preserve a body longer than one subjected to temperature variation and water seepage. Feegel also noted the importance of the container, if any, in which the body resides. A coffin or casket of any type profoundly alters the decomposition rate because of the differences in entrapped microorganisms, water retention, and available air. Even a cloth wrapping or bagging affects the decomposition rate. A plastic covering may shut out insects, water, and air, whereas a cloth covering may hold water but still protect the body from insects.

Mant (1987) identified additional factors based upon his observations of exhumations performed after World War II. He noted that the physical state of the body at the time of the death was an important factor. Healthy, well-nourished bodies resisted decay when compared with sick, thin, or injured bodies. Another important factor was the interval between the time of death and the actual burial as well as the environment during the hiatus. The longer the body was exposed to warm air, the greater the decomposition rate. Bodies quickly buried in the winter time were the best preserved. Mant also observed that deeply buried bodies were better protected. Below a depth of four feet, a stable, cool thermal equilibrium is reached and bodies may be well preserved for a long time. At that depth the body is protected from animal access, plants, insect activity and warmth, all of which speed decomposition.

All these various factors interact, potentiating or mitigating the rate of decay. Since the precise burial conditions are unknown prior to the body being excavated, it is not possible to predict the condition of the remains before recovery. Regardless of its condition, the body will always be able to provide, upon examination and analysis, some information about the deceased and perhaps the circumstances of death.

Chapter 3

NON-INTRUSIVE FOOT SEARCH METHODS

"Other gravedigger: Who builds stronger than a mason, a shipwright,
  or a carpenter?
Gravedigger: Ay, tell me that and unyoke . . .
Other gravedigger: Mass, I cannot tell.
Gravedigger: Cudgel thy brains no more about it, for your dull ass will
  not mend his pace with beating. And when you are asked this
  question next, say 'A grave-maker.' The houses he makes last till
  doomsday."

Hamlet, Act V, Scene I
by William Shakespeare

The tactical planning, or phase two planning, discussed in Chapter 2 is particularly important when foot searches are used because so many searchers and agencies are commonly involved. It's advisable to bring local search and rescue officials into the planning phase early. They will have more search experience and a cadre of trained ground searchers. Additionally, they may have useful equipment, supplies, and terrain knowledge. They probably have access to search and rescue dogs, search aircraft (Civil Air Patrol), etc.

Covering the search area by pedestrians is a contact-sensing method in which the searcher is in direct contact with the ground. The ground search or survey is the backbone of wilderness search and rescue and a fundamental technique of archaeology. The archaeological survey is one or more individuals travelling by foot through a defined area, attempting to locate archaeological sites by means of their own eyesight. The same definition applies to a forensic crime scene search. The site being sought includes the grave and the immediate area contiguous to it.

The success in finding an individual grave, or archaeological site, depends upon several factors (Schiffer et al., 1977). These include: (1) the abundance of surface evidence; (2) the clustering of evidence; (3) the obtrusiveness of the evidence or its probability of detection; (4) the visibility or obstructions to detection; and (5) accessibility, i.e. whether the area can be legally and thoroughly traversed. These factors, of course, have also influenced the choice of search methods. Under reasonable conditions, any burial placed within two years prior to the investigation should manifest some surface evidence of its presence (Wyckoff, 1986). Pedestrian surveys are most likely to be successful in cultivated fields, deserts, thin woodlands, or areas of sparse vegetation. They may be less productive in heavy forests which have rapid buildup of leaf litter or pine duff.

A foot search operation can be divided into three main phases: planning and background studies, preliminary reconnaissance, and the actual search operation. As always, the planning stage may be the most critical to the efficient and successful conduct of the search. Each stage in the process gathers information needed for the next phase. A large foot search is a complex undertaking, so operational assignments must be made in the traditional areas of command, planning, operations, support and communications. Part of the initial phase is notifying or recruiting searchers in cooperation and coordination with mutual assistance agencies.

The second phase of the operation is for the command and operations directors to visit the search area. They may confirm or alter a tentative search plan and set up search grid markers. After a visit, they will be in a better position to estimate the number of searchers, equipment, and supplies needed. Logistical plans need to be made as completely as possible before the search commences.

The third phase is the search operation itself. Before the search begins, searchers must be properly trained on what to look for and how to comply with search procedures so that every area is thoroughly and efficiently covered. The survey methods will have to be adjusted to field conditions. Searchers need to be rotated among crews to maintain interest and acuity. Likewise, they will need adequate rest, food, and water.

Each search situation must be evaluated for the appropriate search response. A full, massive manpower search is not always warranted. Search and rescue tactics for the foot search may be divided into three types (Setnicka 1980). A Type I search may be considered a hasty search using a minimum number of personnel. A "blitz team" of rescuers is sent directly to the known site of any emergency situation immediately after receipt of the incident report. The forensic equivalent is dispatching an investigative team to a known burial location or to confirm a specific informant tip. A Type II search tactic is a "measured response" or a search of moderate size which is conducted promptly but under most favorable conditions, such as waiting for daylight. A measured response might mean a thorough reconnaissance involving three to seven searchers walking widely spaced search lines.

A Type III or complete search is an intensive search of an area for clues. In search and rescue operations it generally means an effort involving 30 or more searchers walking in lines. In choosing the type of search to be conducted, there is always a trade-off between the time it takes to cover a given search area and the probability of successfully detecting the remains. The more time and searchers assigned to a given area, assuming they search methodically, the more likely it is that all available evidence or signs will be discovered.

SEARCH PATTERNS

Conducting an outdoor search for a grave is not the same as conducting a crime scene search. The grave search may cover vast areas and is aimed only at the detection of the site. The crime scene search is usually conducted in a limited area with the focus upon collection of evidence down to microscopic size. Accordingly, not all crime scene search patterns are readily transferable to a pedestrian survey operation, though the spiral search pattern is commonly recommended for outdoor use (Swanson et al., 1977). It is generally described as a one-person technique in which the searcher moves in decreasing concentric circles within a limited area. That search pattern is always executed from the outside toward the inside so that no evidence is inadvertently trampled during the search. A foot search should be a non-intrusive tactic, that is, the searchers pass over the surface of the ground attempting to minimize disturbances from the search itself. In the same way, a search using air-scent dogs is not intrusive since there is no penetration of the ground surface.

As a result of the planning and reconnaissance phases of the operation, a decision has been reached about the intensity of the search to be conducted. Intensity is determined by the spacing of search personnel and the speed at which they move. A single grave site may only be an arm's length in size or it may be a disturbed area as much as several meters long. In searching for archaeological sites which may be 10 to 75 meters across, Schiffer et al. (1977) recommended a spacing of two meters between searchers. With that spread, there is a high discovery probability for all evidence within the survey unit. Morse et al. (1983) recommended that the search area, no matter how large, be subdivided so that a distinct section can be searched in one day's effort. This will help keep morale high by giving a sense of completion to each day's work, even if the remains are not discovered. Whenever possible, the sections should follow natural or pre-existing man-made boundaries.

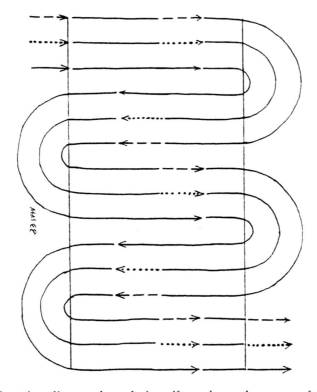

Figure 3.1. The strip or line search results in uniform, thorough coverage of the search area so long as the spacing remains uniform and the line moves slowly. (Adapted from Swanson, Chamelin & Territo, 1977.)

The common method for making a saturation search of an area is the line or strip search (May 1973). Searchers are spaced close enough together so that they can see all the area between adjacent searchers. The line is then swept slowly through an area until the search boundary is reached (Figure 3.1). The searchers proceed down their respective lanes at a slow-walking pace. The end persons on the line carry flagging tape to mark the boundaries of the searched area. Within their individual lanes, searchers may freely zigzag to cover their ground area thoroughly. The operation's leader normally stations himself near the middle or perhaps behind the line so that he may constantly monitor its progress.

Any member of the search line may stop the line to mark evidence with a pin flag, but only the leader may move the line again after the find has been evaluated. The searchers should be encouraged to look back often so they get an alternate view of the area being covered. To maintain effectiveness of the line, searchers should keep abreast with searchers on their left and right and maintain a uniform distance from adjacent searchers as well. Often, the leader will designate the left or right end of the line as the reference for spacing and speed. If pin flags are carried by searchers, they should be color coded so that all flags carried by searcher A are blue, searcher B has red, searcher C has yellow, etc. (Figure 3.2).

Two variations of the skirmish line search can be used for more thorough coverage. The first is the interlocking line search in which two

Figure 3.2. All searchers should be equipped with pin flags or other means of marking evidence. The markers should be color coded so that each searcher can identify his own finds. (Photograph by the author.)

rows of searchers face each other (Figure 3.3). The searchers walk towards each other, pass shoulder to shoulder in the middle, and then continue forward, completing a double search of the prescribed area. This is a good system to use on those rare occasions when there are more volunteers than are actually needed for the area to be covered.

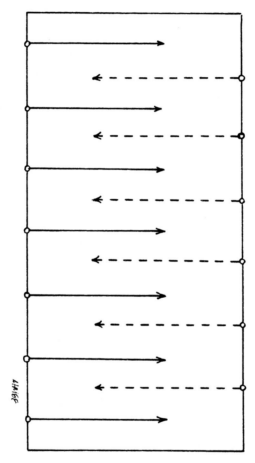

Figure 3.3. The interlocking line search provides even more complete coverage of the search area when there are extra searchers available.

The other variation is the grid search which is the most thorough of the line searches because the ground is inspected from a different viewpoint and lighting angle (Geberth, 1983). After having completed the strip search pattern, the searchers reform the line and search perpendicularly across the same area (Figure 3.4). It is more time consuming than the interlocking grid but offers the highest probability of finding all evidence. If a still finer search is needed, the grid and interlocking search patterns can be combined so that the interlocking system is used in one direction and then conducted again on the perpendicular (MacInnes, 1972).

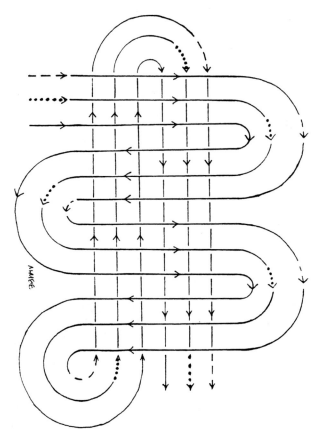

Figure 3.4. The grid search is the most thorough search pattern because the ground is viewed from two different angles as the searchers walk. (Adapted from Swanson, Chamelin & Territo, 1977.)

Transects and line searches are easy to operate and control in gentle terrain. In mountainous country or land full of obstructions such as fences, streams, etc., searchers are best conducted by following topographical features or pre-existing boundaries. Under such conditions, a zone search may be profitably employed (Figure 3.5). In this search context, a zone search is an administrative technique for subdividing the search area into manageable units. The size and shape of the search units are adjusted in response to the terrain and size of search parties. Within each unit, the search can be conducted by any thorough search pattern.

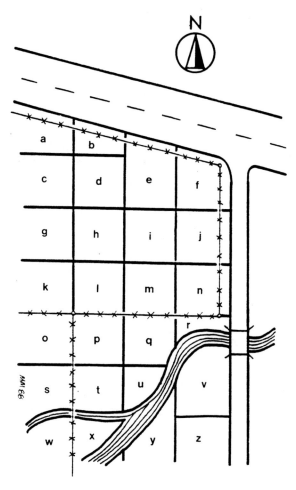

Figure 3.5. The division of the search area into zones is a management tool for sectioning the total area into manageable portions.

May (1973) estimated that a saturation search in rugged terrain can be accomplished at the rate of approximately one man-hour per acre. This is a slow and tedious but thorough ground search. At that rate, it takes 640 man-hours or 80 man-days to search one square mile. In metric units at the same rate, it takes 250 man-hours or 30 man-days to search one square kilometer. This is based upon the search line moving at one mile per hour, or 1.6 kilometers per hour, being in motion 50 percent of the time. It also assumes approximately 16 feet or five meters spacing between searchers.

The object of any search pattern is to make the most efficient use of available manpower, in the time available, for the highest probability of detection. Any search pattern is better than the "mill around" method in which unsupervised searchers flit from one likely looking area to another without coordination.

VISUAL SIGNS

Before embarking on a field operation, searchers need to be told what to look for. Human remains might be located on the surface, in a shallow grave, or buried in a deep hole. Deliberate burials will leave surface evidence and are commonly revealed as a depression where the fill soil has settled or as a mound where the surplus dirt has been piled up (Geberth, 1983). Graves may also be detected by differences in plant growth, animal signs, or other surface objects or indicators.

Vegetation Differences

The vigor of plant growth is an indication of soil and subsurface conditions. Vegetation difference can be detected from the ground during a foot search and by aerial photography. Alterations in the plant community are caused both by the physical action of digging in the ground and by changes in the soil profile that remain after the grave is completed. The presence of a grave, depending upon the circumstances, may result in better plant growth conditions (positive indicators) or worse plant growth conditions (negative indicators). Plant growth factors are covered in more detail in Chapter 8, "Aerial Photography."

The basic assumption is that before a grave was dug, there was a uniform level of vegetation on the ground's surface (Figure 3.6). The physical act of digging destroyed those plants that were located where the hole is now. In addition, the fill from the hole was likely dumped on the adjacent plants, damaging them as well (Figure 3.7). Assuming a horizontally placed burial, the area of damaged vegetation could be six feet wide and eight feet long (Morse et al., 1983). The size of the damaged area is related to the length, width, and depth of the hole.

When the grave is refilled, it will be completely bare of plant growth.

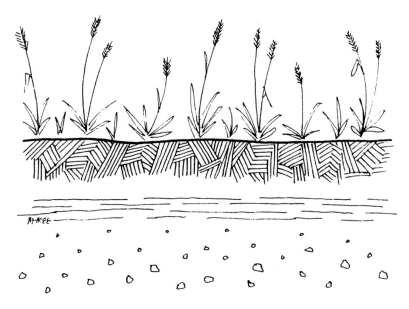

Figure 3.6. Prior to any digging, the ground has a uniform level of vegetation and a constant profile of topsoil and layers of subsoils. (Adapted from McLaughlin, 1974.)

Adjacent and around the grave will be broken, trampled, or otherwise damaged plants, perhaps still partly covered with extra fill dirt (Figure 3.8). With the passage of time, the plants will recover and the damaged area will begin to blend in. The blending may be especially rapid in areas that were inhabited by weeds or other annual plants. If the terrain was brush or perennial plants, the damage will be visible for a longer period of time. Another variable in the plant regeneration cycle is, of course, the climatic conditions in the area (Morse et al., 1983).

It may be difficult to predict whether a grave will, in the long run, assist or hinder plant growth. A deeper grave, for instance, hurts large plants by damaging the deep root systems. On the other hand, a deep grave may help plant growth by providing a looser area for root penetration and a trap for ground moisture (Figure 3.9). On the other hand, a shallow burial, in which the body is wrapped in a root-tight covering may restrict root penetration and thus limit plant growth. After a year or more, a burial, within the plant root zone, should increase plant growth because organic materials are released from the decomposing body as natural fertilizer (Rodriguez & Bass, 1985).

Figure 3.7. Digging penetrates through the soil layers and the mixed soils are usually dumped next to the open hole. (Adapted from McLaughlin, 1974.)

Soil Disturbances

"One can never dig in the ground and put the dirt back exactly as nature had put it there originally" (Bass & Birkby, 1978:6). Differences between the grave fill and the surrounding soil are preserved and may be seen as differences in chemistry, color, texture, compactness, moisture retention, volume, organic content, and pH level (Wolf, 1986). Some of these differences may be seen on the surface by the naked eye while others require probing or soil sampling.

There is usually a soil color difference between the grave fill and the undisturbed matrix. This is caused by the mixing of surface soil with subsoil layers of a different type (Morse et al., 1984). Accordingly, the fill may be lighter or darker than its surroundings. Because the stratigraphy of the soils has been upset, the mixed fill will never again be the same consistency as the original soil. The color differences will lessen over time as the new grave surface is exposed to the same weathering conditions as the rest of the surface (Rodriguez & Bass, 1985).

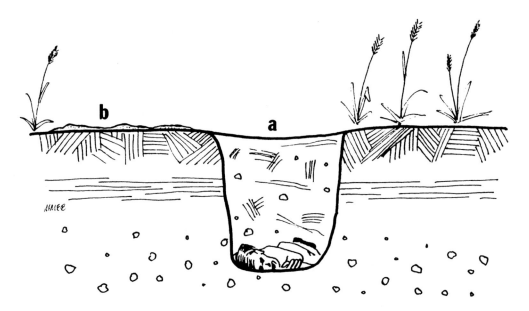

Figure 3.8. The completed grave leaves two areas of plant damage: the grave area itself (a) and the adjacent ground where the fill was piled up (b). (Adapted from McLaughlin, 1974.)

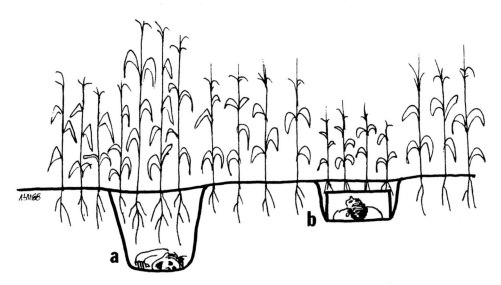

Figure 3.9. The totality of circumstances determine whether a grave will ultimately favor (a) or retard (b) plant growth. (Adapted from Wilson, 1982.)

In addition to color, there will be a difference in texture between the primary soil (undisturbed stratigraphy) and secondary soil (mixed top and subsoils). The disturbed soil will be softer as a result of layer mixing and the breakup of soil clumps by the mechanical actions of digging (Brooks & Brooks, 1984). The fill will also have an increased organic component from the plants and ground litter mixed in with it. The pre-existing soil texture may partially determine how deep a grave is dug. In loose soil that is easy to work, a grave may be four to six feet deep, whereas in rocky or hard soil, the same amount of work and time may only result in a grave two to three feet deep (Morse et al., 1983).

As anyone who has dug a hole knows, it is not usually possible to refill a hole so that its surface is level. Dirt is always left over due to inflation of the soil with air. Additionally, the body placed in the grave occupies some of the space formerly filled with soil. Thus, a fresh grave is commonly revealed by a mound of dirt. This is somewhat offset by soil lost in the leaf litter or spread around the area during back filling. The size of the mound may be correlated with the depth of the grave, in that the higher the mound, the deeper the grave is likely to be. With time, the soil compacts again. The amount of settling varies with time and moisture. Most settling will occur in the first few months and as a result of snow or rain.

The amount of settling also depends upon the type of soil and the depth of the hole. Loam soils are likely to settle the most and sand the least (McLaughlin 1974). Eventually, the grave surface will become lower than the surrounding ground. It will slope downward and inward toward the center. Often, cracks will appear around the periphery or margin of the grave. Complete compaction requires deep water penetration. In shallow graves, a secondary depression may occur over the abdomen area of the body as decomposition causes the abdominal cavity to collapse (Morse et al., 1983). A secondary depression is likely to be seen in a grave shallower than two feet deep. A single depression likely means the body is more than two feet below the surface. A grave ultimately may show a constellation of features visible on the surface (Figure 3.10).

Active farming will eventually destroy vegetation, texture and compaction differences. The damage, however, will be limited to the plow depth. Differences below that will remain, though they may not be visible on the surface. A grave may be impossible to detect in a newly plowed field because of the large dirt clods. After the ground has been disked, the clods will be smaller and more evenly distributed. If the soil is harrowed, the chance of seeing a depression is better yet because of the fineness of the surface texture. With each agricultural working, differences become

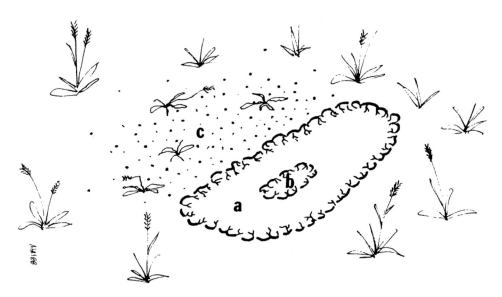

Figure 3.10. A recent grave may show a constellation of features including a primary depression (a), a secondary depression over the abdomen (b) and an adjacent area of contamination and damaged vegetation (c). (Adapted from Morse, Duncan & Stoutamire, 1983).

less clear and depressions may be completely gone after one full agricultural season (Morse et al., 1983). Farmers often have a good memory of field conditions, so they should be questioned about any holes or depressions they noticed in the spring when the ground was first worked.

Animal Signs

Animal scavengers may cause extensive damage to human remains, especially when the remains are on the surface or only buried to a shallow depth. Scavengers are the leading cause of scattered remains just as insects are a dominant factor in decomposition rates (Rodriguez, 1987). It is also possible, however, for animal activity to aid in the detection and recovery of human remains. Any fresh animal digging should be investigated, as Rodriguez and Bass (1985) found that raccoons and opossums, as well as dogs, will dig to reach shallow burials. Fragments of human bones, hinting as deeper burials, have been found in the back dirt of rodent burrows (Ubelaker, 1984). Examining prairie dog and other burrowing rodent mounds is a standard part of archaeological searches. Birds and rodents may carry off hair or bits of clothing to use as nesting material. These bits of evidence may be recovered from nests or burrows. Scavenger birds will also congregate near a body. A familiar example in the West is magpies flocking about a road-killed deer.

Coyotes and dogs may carry body parts or bones from their concealed or buried location out into the open where they may be seen and found. Rodriguez found that dogs and coyotes will usually not carry the bones far but will cache them in nearby ravines, creek beds, or concentrated patches of foliage such as brush piles, thickets, and fallen trees (Rodriguez 1987). Canids prefer to lie and chew where they have their backs to cover. Binford (1981) similarly found that wolves commonly dragged large animal parts to the periphery of the feeding area, usually about 20 feet from the main body. Many searches have been initiated when a pet dog brings home a human bone.

Rodriguez and Bass (1983) documented the important role of insects in the decomposition of human remains. Different insect species tend to be present at different stages of decay. Rodriguez also recounted instances where the presence of carrion insects on the ground's surface, along with stained soils, indicated the former location of a body that had been moved. Beyond animal signs, foot searchers should be constantly alert for any physical evidence of human activity such as off-road vehicle damage, discarded tools, empty cartridge casings, etc.

AIR–SCENT DOGS

Air-scent trained dogs, sometimes called avalanche dogs, may be used before, contemporary with, or after a conventional foot search. Dogs are an impressive law enforcement tool and can be used in a variety of roles. They must be trained, however, for each specific task they are to undertake. "Scent work" encompasses various tasks in which the dog uses its superior olfactory powers. Subcategories of scent work include drug detection, bomb search, man-tracking, and air scenting (Johnson, 1977). In drug and explosives detection, the dog is taught to recognize a particular odor(s) and then react to it as a signal to its handler. Even humans have the ability to detect odors but are usually unable to locate its source by smell alone.

Tracking is the capacity of a dog to follow a ground scent or a specific path followed by a person (May, 1973). Track-trained dogs are rarely used in search and rescue work, since the minimum requirement is a scent article from the missing person and a known and preferably recent point of departure. If these are available, the dog tracks by following the peculiar body odor or "perfume" of the individual. Additionally, the dog may be able to track by following the scent of the disturbed area. Apparently, a different odor is given off by crushed vegetation and ground that enables the dog to distinguish it from an undisturbed surface. This "track scent" may be followed even if the human odor has faded. Track scent is increased by moisture, so the tracking dog may be most successful in fog, light snow, and after a rain.

Air-scent trained dogs work differently and are the ones commonly used in search and rescue work. They don't need to start with the specific scent of the victim. Instead, they search for the airborne scent of *anyone* within the search area. The missing person, alive or dead, will continually release scent which travels downwind. Following a search pattern, the dog will eventually scent the person and follow the scent upwind to the source (Figure 3.11). An air-scent dog is disinterested in ground contamination but rather focuses on air scent. A well-trained dog can ignore disturbances caused by previous search efforts.

The same principle is used by dogs in searching for buried human remains. Gas products of decomposition, carbon dioxide, hydrogen sul-

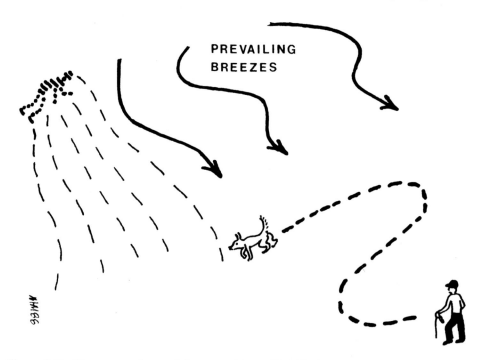

Figure 3.11. The gas products of decomposition will drift downwind where they can be detected and traced back to their source by an air-scent trained dog.

fide and methane are produced by the body (Mueller, 1986). These gases rise through the soil and are carried by the prevailing air currents. The invisible vapors form a cone-shaped pattern downwind from the source. The scents will travel at the speed of the wind and tend to pool and remain in low or sheltered areas (Greene, 1982). These gases are water soluble, so ground moisture and rain helps the air-scenting dog.

The rate of human decomposition is variable and dependent largely upon temperature. Air-scent dogs should be used at 30-, 60-, 90- and 120-day intervals if there was no success the first time. This will allow sufficient time for decomposition to produce gases and for these gases to be released into the air (Greene, 1987). Greene reported that an air-scent dog was able to find a murder scene one month after the incident, based on the smell of decomposing blood on the ground. Likewise, a dog was able to locate a fully skeletonized body after it lay in the open for a year because there was still some decomposition underway. A well-trained dog may be able to distinguish between human and other dead animals such as wildlife or livestock.

Air-scent dogs are commonly used for avalanche rescues. For international search and rescue work, air-scent dogs are rated A, B, and C, depending upon their levels of training and experience. C is the highest rating and requires a record of proven success, the fortitude to work difficult terrain under adverse weather conditions, and the ability to endure lengthy search efforts. The breed of dog is not critical so long as it has the stamina for field work. A dog that performs to C standards is capable of doing the search work of at least 30 searchers (MacInnes, 1972).

Another common use of air-scent dogs is in disaster rescue work. After the 1985 earthquake in Mexico City, 13 air-scent dog teams from the United States assisted recovery efforts (Mueller, 1986). There are search and rescue dog units throughout the United States. The nearest team should be known by local search and rescue officials. The National Association for Search and Rescue, P.O. Box 3709, Fairfax, Virginia 22038 (703-352-1349) maintains a current roster of trained dog-handler teams.

Before air-scent dogs are used, the search area is cleared of other searchers and their equipment. If a scent article from the victim is available, it can help the dog discriminate the victim's scent, though the dog does not need to be "fired" by such a scent article. After a short time, the air has had an opportunity to clear so that the victim's scent should predominate. The search area is subdivided or zoned just as in a regular foot search. This allows search efforts to go on elsewhere without interference. If additional dog teams are available, they can be assigned to different zones or actually work in a line fashion so long as the dogs are separated by a wide distance, approximately 100 yards or 90 meters (MacInnes, 1972).

The actual tactics for searching the designated zone should be left to the dog handler. Generally, the dog will be worked "off lead," allowed to range free within sight of the handler. After receiving the "search" command from the handler, the dog may appear casual, charging about as if playing in wide zigzag patterns. It will work into the wind, starting from the lee side of the search area. If the dog detects a scent out of the ordinary, it will focus its full attention, follow the air scent to its source and signal its location, usually by sitting down or, in avalanche work, starting to dig (Setnicka, 1980). The dog is normally allowed to diverge from the search line to follow a scent. If the scent lead is unsubstantiated, then the dog will be brought back to the search pattern, given time to settle down and then started again.

Because dogs rely little upon their sight, they may be used at night when other search efforts must be curtailed. Lights are attached to the dog's harness so that his handler can keep track of his movements and position. Though lighting conditions are unimportant, scent conditions are. The dog should be kept away from auto fumes or other strong smells. Likewise, loud noises, such as sirens, should be avoided as they may disrupt the dog's concentration. A dog may be worked up to eight hours in a day, depending upon the dog and the search conditions. Dogs need to be rested occasionally, since they suffer from "nose fatigue." This is the desensitizing of the olfactory sensors after continual use (May, 1973).

Greene (1987) reported that dogs may also be useful in locating a submerged body. A dog can smell the decomposition odors on the surface of the water and may even be able to taste the smells in a flowing stream. Greene and other authors noted, however, that air-scent work requires specific training and that other trained dogs, patrol, tracking, hunting, etc., are rarely successful. She believed that, given adequate time without restrictions, a dog will be successful in detecting buried human remains at a 90 percent success rate. It is not unusual for a dog to detect the scent of a body from half a mile away and the record is two miles on flat Alaska tundra (Greene, 1982). Greene reported an actual 86 percent search success rate after all other conventional search efforts had failed. A dog may also locate secondary sites such as evidence or previous locations of the body before it was moved to its final resting spot.

There are several factors that affect search success. In avalanche situations, these include snow density, burial depth, moisture, air temperature, and wind conditions. The same factors apply to earth burials. The record for detecting an avalanche burial is 24 feet down (Greene 1982). Avalanche recoveries to a depth of 15 feet, or 5 meters, are widely reported (MacInnes, 1972; Setnicka, 1980; Pella & Martinelli, 1975). Search results in snow indicate that there is insufficient scent coming from a frozen body, so detection by dogs may not be possible until the body begins to thaw and decompose.

The best conditions for using an air-scent dog are moist ground, loose soil texture, light breeze to move the scent, and a cool air temperature. The worst weather conditions are hot and dry with calm air or heavy rain or snowfall which tend to wash the scent from the air (May, 1973). Poor results are also likely in extremely cold temperatures with strong winds or in areas heavily contaminated by other search efforts or smells (Pella & Martinelli, 1975).

There are many more advantages to using air-scent dogs such as the speed with which a dog can cover a large search area. The dog replaces manpower which can be used elsewhere. Additionally, the dog is highly mobile and can search areas difficult to search by foot, such as boulder fields, heavy scrub, or downed timber. Also, the dog, with its superior smelling ability, can detect bodies buried or otherwise hidden from human searchers. Lastly, the dog can re-search an area quickly and easily weeks or months later without the problems of mounting another major search effort.

Chapter 4

INTRUSIVE GROUND SEARCH METHODS

"Six feet of earth make all men of one size."

> An old proverb from *Death in Early America* by Margaret M. Coffin. Copyright © 1976 by Margaret M. Coffin. A Lodestar book from E.P. Dutton, a division of NAL Penguin Inc.

The previous chapter covered techniques for the methodical search of the ground's surface for signs of a burial. The methods in that chapter caused minimal damage to the site, since the soil was not penetrated by search efforts. Any intrusion into or disturbance of a burial site will necessarily result in an undesirable loss of evidence and information. The techniques contained in this chapter are arranged from minimal intrusion, i.e. probing, to massive alteration, i.e. earth-moving equipment. Profoundly disruptive search techniques should never be used until less intrusive ones have been exhausted or are impractical under the totality of search conditions. Even a probing search, which involves minimal damage, should not be conducted until a search for visual signs has failed (Morse et al., 1983).

PROBING

Probing is a process of sticking a sharpened rod into the ground in a regular search pattern. The probing is intended to detect ground softness associated with a grave site and then to further outline the grave shape. It is not to be used for locating the body itself within the grave, for puncturing the body with the probe will damage the remains and possibly confuse the postmortem examination. Once the probe holes are made, further confirmatory tests can be done, such as subsurface soil temperature, soil pH, and combustible gas vapor detection.

The probing tool itself may be of a manufactured type used in agricul-

43

tural soil testing, sometimes called a "soil examination stick" (Imaizumi, 1974). The soil-sampling stick is approximately four feet long with a wooden or metal T-shaped handle on one end. It may be made in sections which are fastened together (Figure 4.1). The other end of the rod contains a sharpened groove which collects a soil sample as the rod is stuck into the ground and then turned around and removed. Home-made probes may be easily fabricated from 5/16″ diameter stainless steel rods. They should be approximately four to five feet long with a ground, sharpened point. A T-handle at the other end can be made of 10″ long, 5/16″ square stock (Morse et al., 1983). For use in archaeological exploration, Hole and Heizer (1973) describe the use of a rod of 1/2″ spring steel to which a ball bearing has been welded to the tip in place of a sharpened point. Another good design is that described by Lagal (1972) and shown in Figure 4.2.

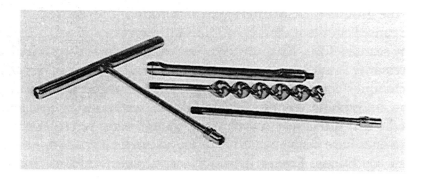

Figure 4.1. A commercial soil sampling tool may be made in one piece or segmented for easier storage. (Photograph courtesy of GISCO.)

The first step in conducting a probe search is to establish the boundaries of the search area. Within the daily search area, a grid should be prepared with stakes and string to establish search lanes. The search supervisor should clearly mark the areas which have already been covered. Probing is very thorough but also slow. It is hard work, so supervisors will have to plan for new shift personnel, occasional job rotation and frequent rest periods. All probing efforts are done slowly and it's easier to work in a uphill direction. The line of searchers may become unmanageable if there are more than 20 probers working together.

The probing search patterns I am recommending are based on those used in avalanche rescue. In a coarse probing pattern, searchers stand

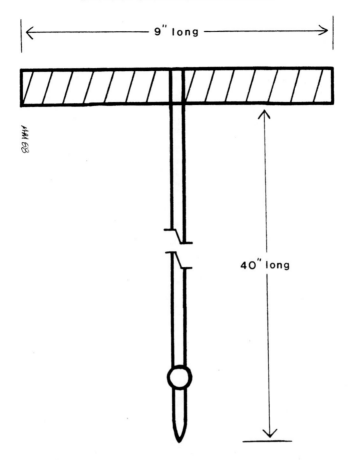

Figure 4.2. This homemade probe may be fabricated in a welding shop from a ³/₈″ stainless steel rod. The rod should be cut 1″ from the tip and a ½″ ball bearing welded in place. The handle is made from ⅞″ conduit covered with plastic grips. (Adapted from Lagal, 1982.)

with their hands on their hips, elbows touching the elbows of adjacent searchers. This should establish a center-to-center search pattern approximately 75 cm apart (Figure 4.3). Each searcher is straddling approximately 50 cm of ground with another 25 cm between the feet of adjacent probers. During a coarse probe, each search will insert his probe at the center of his straddled area. If there is no contact, he will take one full step forward (approximately 70 cm) and probe again (Pella & Martinelli, 1975). Using this coarse probing pattern, searchers in a snow avalanche situation should have a 75 percent chance of locating a buried body (MacInnes, 1972). The discovery of a grave, which is larger than just the body, should be even higher.

A fine probe pattern is used when greater thoroughness is necessary or

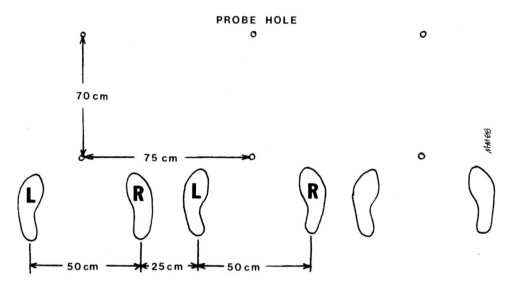

Figure 4.3. The coarse probing pattern is used in avalanche rescue where there is hope that the victim may still be found alive. It is a relatively rapid search technique which gives good coverage of the search area. (Adapted from MacInnes, 1972.)

when a possible grave has been detected and its outline needs to be defined. The searchers begin by lining up in the same way as for a coarse search. Instead of a single probe between the feet, each searcher makes three probe insertions: in front of the left foot, between the feet, and in front of the right foot (Figure 4.4). After each series of three probes, the searcher takes a half-step forward and repeats the search pattern (Pella & Martinelli, 1975). In an avalanche situation, the fine search pattern theoretically yields a 100 percent chance of finding the victim, presuming the probe penetrates deep enough to reach the victim (MacInnes, 1972).

Using the coarse probe pattern, the average spacing of probe holes is 75×70 centimeters which yields the equivalent of 1.9 probes per square meter. Using the fine probe pattern, the average distance between holes is 25×30 centimeters for an average of 13 probes per square meter. The probing work should be conducted silently so that the line can hear commands of the supervisor who will move the line at a uniform pace, maintaining the integrity of the search pattern.

During probing, searchers will attempt to detect the difference between disturbed and undisturbed soil. The searchers will need practice to get the "feel" of local soil conditions (Boyd, 1979). The feel of the soil will vary depending upon the depth of the probe and the pressure applied.

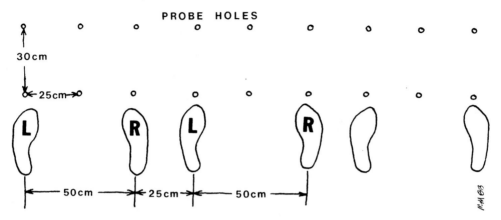

Figure 4.4. The fine probing pattern is employed in avalanche rescue when the search objective is body recovery. It is a thorough search which should find the victim if the probes penetrate deep enough. (Adapted from MacInnes, 1972.)

In all conditions, the probe should sink deeper and easier into disturbed soil. If a soft spot is found, the coarse search pattern switches to a fine search pattern until the outlines of the disturbed area are marked. The probe should not be pushed too deep into the soil for fear of damaging evidence. The probe should be inserted only deep enough to confirm a difference in soil texture (Figure 4.5).

The search efforts should not be abandoned just because a soft spot is found. Several types of soil disturbances may give the feel and general shape of a grave. These include rotting tree stumps, rodent burrows, trash burial pits, etc. The probing search should continue while verification tests, such as vapor detectors, are used to explore the suspect area.

COMBUSTIBLE GAS VAPOR DETECTORS

A combustible gas vapor detector is used to augment a probe search. The detector can confirm the presence or absence of a body within a suspected grave. This determination can be made without excavation of the site and with no additional damage beyond the pre-existing probe hole. The most commonly used vapor detector is the catalytic combustion detector, so named because of its method of operation. That instrument, and its kin, may also be called a "sniffer," "combustible gas indicator," "explosimeter," "vapor detector," "combustible gas analyzer," or "flammable vapor detector" (Boudreau, 1977; Swift, 1986). There are many types of gas vapor analyzers which could be used in forensic work.

Figure 4.5. The probe should only be inserted into the ground deep enough to detect soil-compaction differences. Evidence could be damaged if the probe point strikes the buried body. (Photograph by the author.)

They are commonly employed in the detection of accelerants at suspected arson scenes. For use in the field, a unit must be portable so that it can be carried and operated by one man. It must be sensitive enough to detect gas in quantities of a few parts per million in air. It should be relatively easy and rapid to operate, and it ought to be moderately priced. All of these specifications are met by catalytic combustion detectors which are available from several manufacturers. For a list of available equipment and manufacturers, see Boudreau (1977) and Jackson (1984).

Gas Formation

As a human body decomposes, the putrefaction of tissue forms gaseous products including hydrogen sulfide, hydrogen phosphide, methane, carbon dioxide, ammonia, and hydrogen. The foul odor of a rotting body is attributed to a combination of hydrogen sulfide, hydrogen phosphide, and ammonia (McLaughlin, 1974). Methane gas is the principal combustible gas which is detected by instruments, though others can be detected as well. Since methane is also produced from animal, plant, and waste product decay, the tests are not specific for human remains.

The temperature of a body is important. Below approximately 35° F., little gas is produced because the biological processes of decay are retarded at cold temperatures. At these temperatures, however, the ground may be frozen so that probing efforts could not be conducted successfully anyway. Between 35° and 40° F., the body will be sufficiently warm so that detectable quantities of gases are produced. Above 45° F., a lot of gas will be produced from the body in easily detectable quantities. Gas from a buried body may be produced for up to ten years (McLaughlin, 1974).

The vapors arising from a buried body will move toward the surface in a V-shaped pattern originating from the body core. Thus, the highest concentration of gas will be directly over the body. To be sure of detecting the gas, tests will have to be made in several probe holes within the suspected grave site. Several tests are conducted because it is possible that probe holes may be too deep or too wide to detect the vapors (Figure 4.6). The same system of probe hole and vapor testing could be done indoors or in situations where the ground's surface is covered by concrete, asphalt paving, etc. In this case, a hole must be drilled in the surface and then the detector probe inserted.

Vapor detectors have been successfully used in actual forensic cases (McLaughlin, 1974) and in simulated experiments. Morse et al. (1976) reported that instruments verified the presence of a "sharp increase" of methane gas over and near the buried bodies of dogs, even ten months after burial.

Gas Detectors

Gas detectors were originally intended to detect dangerous working conditions. The search for reliable gas detectors goes back at least 300 years to the digging of the first underground coal mines. Portable com-

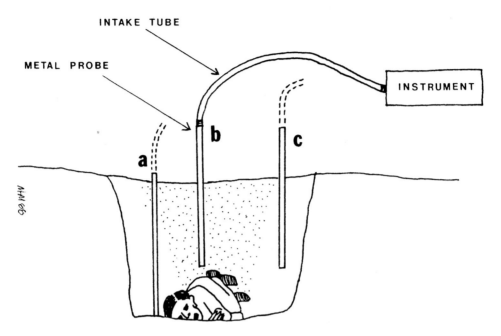

Figure 4.6. Several combustible gas detector tests are made in the suspected grave area since the intake probe may be inserted too deep (a) or too wide (c). The highest concentration of gas will be directly over the body core (b). (Adapted from Boyd, 1979 and Geberth 1983.)

bustible gas detectors are still based on the design first introduced by Oliver W. Johnson and P.S. Williams in 1928. It is the combustible gas detector which is most applicable to forensic investigations. Specific toxic gas detectors which have been tuned to detect ammonia and hydrogen sulfide could also sense these products of body decomposition (Cooney, 1978).

A catalytic combustion detector is generally equipped with an elongated probe which can be inserted into suspected combustible gas areas. The device takes an instantaneous or "grab" sample of the air. The vapor is drawn through the probe into the instrument by either a hand pump or battery-powered electric pump. The vapor sample is passed over a platinum-plated coil of wire which has been heated to approximately 550° C (King, 1983). Platinum is used because gas vapor can burn on its surface at temperatures well below its normal ignition temperature (Zatek, 1970). The platinum is the catalyst which causes any combustible gas to oxidize on its surface. The heat from the oxidation raises the electrical resistance of the wire coil. The change in resistance is measured electronically and is reflected on the instrument's meters. The detector's signal strength is determined by the concentration of combustible gas vapor in the air and to a lesser degree by the type of vapor present (Brannigan, 1980).

The detector instrument may show test results on either a parts per million gas-to-air concentration scale or on a less sensitive explosive scale (Hillard & Thomas, 1976). Some instruments may have both meters, or some may have a single meter equipped with a selector switch to choose the measurement parameter. The meters may be analogue (scaled with a needle) or of a digital type. The parts per million concentration scale is used principally in instruments designed to detect toxic gases. This scale is more sensitive because many gases are toxic at well below explosive concentrations. The maximum allowable concentration (M.A.C.), also known as the threshold limit value (T.L.V.), is often below 1 percent of volume (or 10,000 parts per million) of a gas/air mixture (Hartz, 1959).

The other type of meter has a scale measured in terms of a gases' lower explosive limit (L.E.L.), which is the concentration at which the gas/air mixture first becomes potentially explosive (King, 1983). This usually falls within the range of 1 to 10 percent by volume of gas/air mixtures. The L.E.L. is considered to be synonymous with the lower flammable limit (L.F.L.) which is the minimum concentration of vapor and air below which a flame does not occur on contact with a source of ignition (Zatek, 1970).

As an example of the two types of measurement, methane has an L.E.L. of 5.0 percent. At that level on the parts per million scale, the instrument would read 5.0 percent, whereas on the L.E.L. scale it would read 100 percent. The variation in L.E.L.s for various gases means that the instrument must be individually calibrated for the gas to be detected. Such recalibration is not necessary when results are reported in percentages or concentrations of the gas/air ratio.

Newer devices may employ a catalytic mass instead of a platinum wire and may sense temperature differences by means other than an increase in electrical resistance. These newer devices use solid-state sensors (semiconductors). In operation, the gas within a sample diffuses through a porous metal disk and contacts the heated surface of a silicon chip. As the concentration of combustible gas in the sample increases, the chemical reaction on the chip surface reduces the semiconductor's resistance. This change is quantified and reported by the instrument (Swift, 1986). The semiconductor instruments are extremely sensitive, but results may easily be distorted by changes in temperature or humidity. Therefore, they are best used in stable laboratory situations, not in the field.

All combustible gas detectors, whether platinum wire or semiconductor type, need to be calibrated before use. McLaughlin (1974) stated that before a detector can be used, a temperature-sensing probe must be inserted into the ground hole for a reading of subsurface soil temperature. This temperature reading is necessary to set the gas sensitivity level of the instrument. This setting is good all day in a given area, since the subsurface temperature varies little. Additionally, the detector instrument should be calibrated to read "0" when a sample of uncontaminated air is drawn through the device (McKinnon, 1976). Zero readings should be obtained on both the actual concentration scale as well as the L.E.L. scale.

Most devices come from the manufacturer already calibrated on a methane/air mixture (Firth et al., 1973). Correction factors must be applied when the devices are used for other gases. Over time, the device can be damaged and lose sensitivity as it is exposed to dust, silicone, leaded gasoline, or hydrogen sulfide gases (King, 1983). When in use, therefore, the instrument must be periodically checked to be sure that it is still properly tuned. In heavy use, the calibration checks should be done daily. During such a check, gas/air concentrations of known quantity are passed through the instrument. The responses are then compared with the manufacturer's supplied performance information. If necessary, adjustments to the calibration are made. Most instrument manufacturers are able to supply pressurized tanks containing samples of known methane/air mixtures.

There are two weaknesses inherent in the use of vapor detectors. The first has just been mentioned . . . that the device can lose sensitivity. Unless periodically recalibrated, positive concentration levels might be under-recorded and overlooked. The second weakness is that the instrument can only test for vapors which pass through the detector; thus, the air sample grabbed must have been close enough to the body to contain the gases produced by decomposition.

SOIL STRATIGRAPHY

Soil is the natural material that covers the land. Its characteristics will vary with the influences of climate and living things acting upon the parent rock material. The type of surface may vary from exposed bedrock to silt mud. Pedology is the study of soils, a science whose origin is linked to agriculture (Cornwall, 1966).

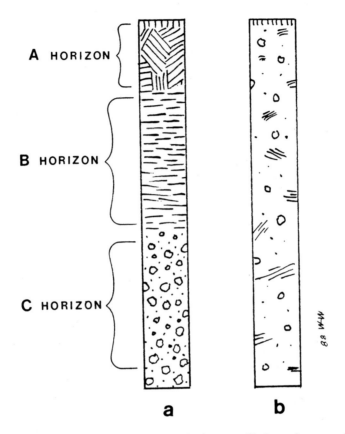

Figure 4.7. The soil sample from an undisturbed area will show the naturally occurring stratigraphy (a). All three horizon levels A, B, and C will only rarely be seen in a single sample. Grave backfill will be mixed soil without the natural layering of soil types (b).

Where soils form on level to slightly sloping terrain, distinctive layers known as horizons will occur. A basic system divides soil layers into A, B and C horizons (Figure 4.7a). Certainly more comprehensive classifications are available but in this case are unnecessary. The basic A, B and C horizons have (can have) distinct chemical and physical characteristics and therefore sampling for any purpose must be within comparable horizons, i.e. don't compare "C" characteristics with "A" characteristics in a given grid. "A" horizon is the surface, usually an organically enriched part of a soil profile. It is generally darker in color, may have a slightly lower pH due to organic acids and is generally the home of the soil fauna. Thickness is highly variable and largely dependent upon climate and topography. Desert soils and/or soils on steep topography have minimal "A" horizons.

"B" horizon is generally thought of as a transitional horizon between "A" and "C." It really is "C" altering/transforming to "A." It is generally organically poor and therefore of a color approaching source material, i.e. lighter. The chemistry of "B" horizon is highly variable depending on mineral composition, grain size, porosity, permeability, climate, position of water table, etc. "B" horizon thickness is also highly variable and it can be meters thick. Most burials would be in the "B" horizon.

"C" horizon or regolith is essentially weathering/altering bedrock and is recognizable as such. It tends to be heterogeneous in grain size and contains fragments, boulders or cobbles of bedrock. "C" horizon is organically poor (devoid in most cases) and most nearly reflects the chemistry of bedrock. Thickness is variable dependent upon climate, topography, nature of bedrock, etc. Mountain soils often consist of "C" horizon with a thin "A" horizon on top.

Soil is a transitory being; it is rock on its way to the sea. Soil falls within the continuum of residual to transported and in a given area it may be important to recognize its character. Soil profiles (A, B, or C) may manifest themselves differently in residual or transported material. For instance, the residual soils of tropical temperate regions of the earth show well-developed, classical horizons. The alluvial fans of desert regions (all transported) can be mixed and show no profile at all. Glacial soils also tend to be chaotic. Soil disturbances are very difficult to recognize in areas where soil horizons are poorly developed or nonexistent.

"A vertical section through a soil from the surface with its vegetation, down to unaltered bedrock, is termed its profile" (Cornwall, 1966:81). Since local profiles vary so much, every effort should be made to understand the natural soil stratigraphy in the search area. This can be done initially by contacting the county, state, or federal Soil Conservation Service and obtaining copies of soil survey results. A second method is to study nearby gullies, creek banks, road cuts or other places in which the natural soil profile is exposed. This will help the investigator anticipate subsurface conditions (Wyckoff, 1986).

CORING AND DRILLING

There may be situations in which probing, even combined with the use of the vapor detector, does not locate a grave site. This is most likely to occur when a grave has been undisturbed for years so that the backfill compaction differs very little from the surrounding soil. In such a situation, it may be necessary to take larger or deeper soil samples to locate the burial area. Certainly, probing is a preferable first step, since the intrusion holes are less than one inch in size. Soil-coring techniques will cause more damage because the hole they leave is two to three inches in diameter. The use of a hand-held or tractor-mounted power auger causes even more damage, as it leaves a hole 6″ to 12″ in diameter, depending upon the bit size chosen.

Before coring or drilling begins, a search grid should be reestablished and the search area divided into one-meter squares. The coring should be done at least at each one-meter interval. Kintigh (1988) conducted mathematical simulation studies to predict the likelihood of striking a target by coring. His study involved archaeological sites, but the principles remain the same . . . that the probability of detection depends upon target size and search grid dimensions. McManamon (1984) also examined augering and coring techniques in archaeology and calculated relative time costs for the methods.

In very soft or sandy soils, coring may be done with a hand-operated soil sampler or coring rod. The coring tool is pushed or hammered into the ground and then removed with the soil sample inside. The sample may then be examined in the field or removed from the tool and transported to a soil analysis laboratory for further examination. In hard soils or for deeper sampling, a core-sampling tool is used with a drill rig outfitted with a percussion driver. The sampling tool itself is a split pipe with a hollow core. At the back it is screwed to the drill pipe, and at its forward edge it is attached to a sharpened bit which cuts out the core sample (Figure 4.8). As the hollow core sampling tube is forced into the ground, a soil sample is collected and then extracted intact when the tool is removed from the ground.

In operation, the drilling rig is parked over the point where the soil is to be sampled. The bit/tube/drilling pipe is hammered into the ground with a captive weight device mounted on the drilling tower. The length of the pipe is measured as it goes into the ground and samples are removed for collection and examination at periodic intervals. The longi-

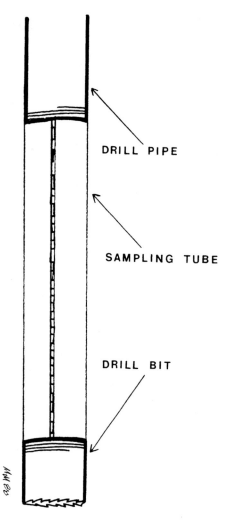

Figure 4.8. A soil-sampling tube is driven or drilled into the ground to collect an intact sample of the soil stratigraphy in the search area.

tudinal split in the coring tool allows it to be opened into two sections so the contents can be emptied. Within the coring tool will be compressed soil representative of the horizon layers. To chart the stratigraphic layers, the sample is cut in half down the center and then the inside face examined (Loker, 1980). The inside of the sample is used because the outside of the core sample will be smeared by contact with the sampling tube. In a grave backfill situation, the stratigraphy should be mixed and markedly different from the naturally occurring stratigraphy nearby (Figure 4.7b).

Figure 4.9. Some power augers can be operated by one man, whereas others are designed for two men. Drill shaft extensions enable deep holes to be drilled in soft soil. (Photography courtesy of GISCO.)

A power auger resembles a large drilling bit from a brace and bit set. The motor-driven screw cuts into the ground and removes the hole contents to the surface (Figure 4.9). An auger does not allow soil stratigraphy to be examined intact, nor can its depth be so accurately controlled. Though less controlled than a coring operation, the auger may be faster in soft soils. Both the auger and the coring tool can be defeated by subterranean rocks. Coring samples and the hole debris from an auger should be examined for trace evidence such as bits of cloth. The visual examination can be aided with a magnifying glass. Both tools are likely to bring up chunks of organic material such as roots, wood or bone. A rapid preliminary identification of bone can be made by exposing it to ultraviolet light.

Ultraviolet Fluorescence

The nature of ultraviolet light is discussed in greater detail in Chapter 8, "Aerial Photography." It is sufficient to note now that ultraviolet light occurs at the lower end of the visible range of electromagnetic radiation. When certain materials are subjected to shortwave electromagnetic radiation, they will emit another kind of radiation in turn. This newly emitted radiation will have a longer wavelength, often within the visible spectrum.

Ultraviolet light may be used as the exciting radiation to cause this fluorescence. When a fluorescent material is exposed to ultraviolet light, the individual atoms in the material become excited so that electrons travelling in orbits around the nucleus jump to another more distant orbit. In turn, an electron in the outer orbit drops to replace the electron that moved away. The movement of these electrons produces energy which is detectable to the human eye as visible light (Murray & Tedrow, 1975). The phenomenon of induced light emission is called luminescence, of which there are two types. In fluorescence, the lumination ceases after the exciting radiation is removed. In phosphorescence, the material continues to emit light for some time, even after the exciting radiation is gone (Eastman Kodak, 1972).

The organic constituents of bone are fluorescent under ultraviolet excitation. Knight (1969) reported that all fresh-cut limb bones show ultraviolet fluorescence, though thin bones such as the skull or ribs may not. This fluorescence is visible in bones up to 100 years old. Ultraviolet fluorescence is eventually lost from the outside of the bone, but a central zone of fluorescence remains even after that time. The rate at which fluorescence decreases is influenced by the environment and is related to time but in such an inexact way that fluorescence is only of limited use in aging recovered bone. Wood, plastic, and other bone-like appearing material will not exhibit the same kind or intensity of fluorescence, making it a useful first test.

SOIL ANALYSIS

Parts of a soil analysis can be done in the field, such as preliminary testing for pH and texture. A more complete analysis, however, requires the services of a soil laboratory. A laboratory will generally request a sample of approximately one-half pound (approximately 250 grams), though some analyses can be done on only 10 grams of material. Soil samples should be taken with a clean tool and should be kept in solid blocks or cores for submission to the laboratory. If mineralogical analysis is not being done, stones may be removed from the sample. Soil samples should be submitted in screw-top jars (Cornwall, 1966) or wrapped in aluminum and then placed in sealed plastic bags (Limbrey, 1975). The samples should be air dried in the sun if there will be a delay in getting them to the lab. All soils contain moisture, and, unless they are dried first, algae or mold will begin to grow which will confound later analysis. The soil samples should not be touched with the hands, and, while drying, they should be protected from contamination by dust or other material. All samples should be labeled on the outside of the container so that they can be retraced to the grid location from which they came.

If soil gases are to be analyzed, additional small samples are put into rubber-topped bottles or tubes which are sealed in the field. The bottles must be hermetically sealed, because most soil gases are volatile. The lab will warm the soil sample and then extract a portion of the "head" gas with a hypodermic needle inserted through the cap. The air sample is then analyzed for organic gases. The presence of a grave site or buried body may be indicated through soil analysis in several ways. It may be detected by a difference in texture or visual soil components, soil organic content, soil pH, chemical composition, or soil gases.

Textural and Visual Indicators

An indication of a disturbed site is a disruption of the normal organic material covering the soil (Murray & Tedrow, 1975). In forested area, there is usually a 1″ or 2″ undisturbed layer of leaves and twigs which have not yet decomposed. Beneath that is a layer of humus. If the humic layer is gone, that's an indication of a disturbance. It generally takes years to regenerate the humus layer to its original state. There are many types of humus, depending upon the microscopic appearance and origins of the material. The conversion of raw plant and animal remains to soil is a process partly chemical but largely biological; the work of the soil fauna and flora (Cornwall, 1966). The visible agents include insects and worms and the invisible ones, fungi and bacteria. Worms and insects are generally only found in the upper 20 cm of the soil profile (Limbrey, 1975). Finding their remains deeper may indicate that the soil has been overturned.

Another obvious indication of burial is finding bone, cloth, or other odd fragments in the soil samples. Such an examination for physical evidence can be aided with a hand-held 10-power lens or a binocular microscope. Flesh rarely survives for any period of time, but skin, hair, bone, and artifacts may be preserved and recovered. The decomposition of organic material may be retarded under extremely acid conditions or under waterlogged conditions. Decomposition occurs within a range of temperatures and is most rapid in the range of 10 degrees to 40° C. Organic breakdown occurs most rapidly with moisture above a relative humidity of 63 percent. Decomposition occurs fastest with pH conditions above 2.5 to the upper limits of soil organism salt tolerance. Fungi in particular have a wide tolerance of soil pH conditions. Decomposition also occurs most rapidly with air present, though both aerobic and anaerobic microorganisms assist the decay process.

As mentioned previously, naturally occurring soils tend to form stratigraphic layers. Each horizon may differ in texture, which is a measure of its relative composition of soil particles. Texture may best be described as the "feel of the soil to the fingers" (Limbrey, 1975). Soil particle sizes are classed as sand, silt or clay, in decreasing size. The percentage of each constituent determines the soil classification (Figure 4.10). Sand is coarse and gritty, silt is smooth and flour-like, while clay is sticky and plastic (Wyckoff, 1986).

The texture of the grave backfill will be mixed, as opposed to the layering of naturally deposited soils seen in a test core or exposed soil profile. Additionally, the soil from a grave may appear darker than the surrounding matrix. This may be a function of its altered chemical composition, mixing of soil types, and increased moisture retention.

Organic Content

Soil organic content varies and is usually expressed as a percentage of the soil constituents. In its final form, organic matter is "an amorphous, dark brown-colored coloidal substance coating the mineral grains" (Cornwall, 1966:78). Organic content may vary from less than 1 percent to over 90 percent in some bogs (Murray & Tedrow, 1975). In average mineral soil, organic content hovers around 3 percent. The remainder of the solid material in soil is mineral. The rest of the soil ingredients are voids between the soil particles filled with water and air. The organic nature of soil is transitory and changes with time, water content, and

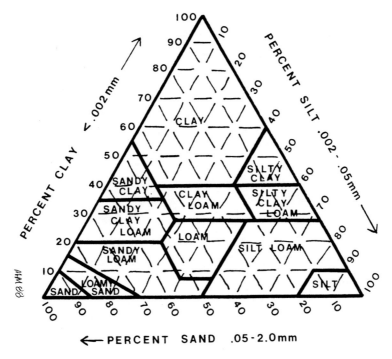

Figure 4.10. This chart shows the American system of naming soil textural classes based upon the percentages of clay, silt, and sand in the sample. (Adapted from Murray & Tedrow, 1975.)

temperature. A profound difference between organic matter percentage from a test core and a nearby core, however, is suspicious. It could be only a submerged rotting tree stump, but the deviation should be noted and examined. "Any real anomaly of which no immediate explanation is forthcoming, is worth a little study" (Cornwall, 1966:186). A rotting tree stump is mentioned by several authors as the condition most resembling a grave. It too will be a depression containing dark, high humus soil in a roughly circular configuration.

Soil pH

The pH value is a measure of the free hydrogen ion concentration in a solution. The greater the concentration of hydrogen ions, the greater the acidity. pH ranges from 0 to 14; a lower value indicates greater acidity. Soils normally range from a pH of 3.5 to 8.5, with eastern soils generally measuring between 3.8 and 5.5, western soils between 5.0 and 6.5, and desert soils with a pH range of 6.0 to 8.0 (Murray & Tedrow, 1975).

In the early stages of decomposition, acids are produced from the decomposition of sugars in the body. In the later stages, a high percentage of alkaline substances are released with the breakdown of albuminous tissue. These alkaline substances permeate the soil surrounding the body and produce a strong reaction to pH testing (Imaizumi, 1974; Murray & Tedrow, 1975). Rodriguez and Bass (1985) confirmed with soil tests taken both before and after exhumation of buried bodies, that soil pH was raised between .5 and 2.1 units. The increase in alkalinity was detected both at the base of the burial trench and one-quarter inch above the cadaver. The search for a grave is really a search for an anomaly, i.e. an unexplained difference in pH between a soil sample and adjacent samples.

Plant growth and crop marks are also affected by pH values. In a low pH, acid soil, phosphorus is apparently not available, so plant growth tends to be thin and of poor color. In high pH, alkali soils, there is an improved availability of nutrients and plant growth tends to be more robust. These differences in soil pH may contribute to the positive plant or crop marks shown over grave sites (Wilson, 1982).

pH may be roughly tested in the field by putting distilled water and a pinch of soil on a clean watch glass. After having an opportunity to soak, litmus paper can be dipped into the liquid and then the color compared with a color-scale chart on the box. In the laboratory, more accurate tests can be conducted. The most precise is a pH meter, though less precise colormetric techniques are adequate for most purposes. In one colormetric technique, a sample of soil and distilled water is mixed with a chemical (barium sulfate) to enhance sedimentation. An indicator liquid is then added and the whole sample shaken. The color is then compared to a standard chart. The technique is accurate to a + or − .5 pH unit and can be done on nearly trace amount of soil, though a normal sample size is 2.5 grams. Experiments by Dudley (1976) showed that pH values are stable and no change in pH results occurred when moist soils were stored in plastic bags for 14 days before testing.

Chemical Composition

Before any tests of suspected grave soil are done, background values for a given search area must be established. All the soil horizons must be sampled and analyzed, then questioned soils are compared to the known standards. In normal soils, silica, iron, and alumina make up 80 percent to 90 percent of the total soil chemical composition (Murray & Tedrow, 1975). Fresh bone is a complex of mineral and organic materials, the mineral being chiefly calcium phosphate. As a body decomposes, the organic portion is broken down into simple compounds such as carbon monoxide, ammonia, and water. The mineral constituents of the bone are the most resistant to change. The rate of decomposition depends upon the acidity of the soil, drainage, aeration, climate, and the pre-existing chemical composition of the soil. The phosphates from the bones are the most enduring. Thus, phosphates in the soil are indicative of "contemporary animal matter" (Cornwall, 1966).

The search for archaeological remains is often the search for anthrosols or "settlement-affected soils" (Eidt, 1977). Anthrosols may be subdivided into anthropogenic soils and anthropic soils. Anthropogenic soils are those intentionally altered by man, as by fertilization and plowing. Anthropic soils are those changed unintentionally as a by-product of man's activities, such as burials or trash dumping (Eidt, 1985). Anthrosols are detected by higher levels of inorganic phosphate. Phosphorous in the form of phosphate is sought because of its "universal association with human activity" (Eidt, 1977:1327). Phosphorous is not normally leached out from the soils like carbon, nitrogen, calcium, sulfur or other common elements. The phosphorous levels decline very slowly over time, so they tend to accumulate in the soil. Native soils devoid of human habitation show only minute amounts of phosphates. High soil phosphates without another explanation are considered chemical evidence of human activity. Procedures for testing phosphate levels in the field by non-chemists are outlined by Eidt (1977).

In addition to phosphates, a local high concentration of nitrogen means animal or vegetable material at that soil level (Cornwall, 1966). "People have the same effect as other animals, concentrating nitrogen and phosphatic residues around their settlements and in their burial ground" (Limbrey, 1975:121). Animals concentrate nitrogenous, phosphatic and calcium materials more than plants, but calcium is a less valuable indicator, as many soils are naturally high in calcium. The worst soils for detecting chemical composition differences are sandy, acidic soil with good drainage. In such conditions, the chemicals tend to wash out of the soil more rapidly.

Grave soils, especially at the level where the body remains are found, will demonstrate a darker soil color. Bethell and Carver (1987) have examined this darker brown loam and the phenomenon of "pseudomorphs," three-dimensional shadows of a decomposed body. The pseudomorphs still show the human bone form and have also been called soil silhouettes. A chemical analysis of these silhouettes shows higher concentrations of phosphorous, copper, and manganese within the stained soils as opposed to the surrounding soil. The manganese levels are even higher than fresh bone, suggesting that manganese may be withdrawn from the surrounding soil during the decay process and become concentrated in the silhouette. Bethell and Carver believe that the darker color of the silhouette is caused by the manganese concentration. The maximum concentration of chemicals are found where the body actually lay in the grave. Bethell and Carver's study indicated that copper is lost from the bone during decomposition but is retained in the silhouette at levels higher than adjacent soils.

Another possible use of soil analysis is the comparison of soils from the search area with trace remnants found on the suspect's shoes, tools, vehicle fender wells, etc. Such a comparison may narrow down search areas and, on rare occasions, may conclusively connect the suspect to the burial site. Trace materials should be collected from the suspect's digging implements, vehicle trunk or truck bed, clothing, etc., for later comparison with grave site samples.

HEAVY EQUIPMENT

Some grave site searches may require the use of heavy equipment. The decision to use heavy equipment invariably means the destruction of surface and subsurface evidence. If all other methods have failed, heavy equipment might be used for a search effort but *never* for an actual excavation of the body itself.

Numerous authors recommend an elevated scraper as the machinery of choice. The scraper itself is pulled from the front by a tractor-cab. A cutter bar shaves soil from the surface and leaves behind only rubber tire marks. The advantages of such a piece of equipment are that it can shave off only a few inches at a time, collects rather than just pushes aside the overburden, and leaves a smooth working surface behind (Bass, 1963; Bass & Birkby, 1978; Ubelaker, 1984). A bulldozer pushes and mixes the topsoil and causes greater damage with its metal tracks.

Properly used, the scraper is economical when searching large areas and will cause minimal damage to a skeleton if the grave pit is found before the body level is reached. Ubelaker believed that the use of the scraper can be justified when investigators have no information about the location of a grave site or the burials are very old, as in archaeological settings, with a sterile topsoil cover. A scraper is best suited to flat terrain with minimum vegetation and in soil types that are expected to show the contrast between the grave and the surrounding soil clearly. The scraper should be stopped as soon as a possible grave site is located so that all available evidence can be recovered from the scraper bed. Bass (1963) recommended that the scraper blade be 9-feet wide and that each pass of the scraper remove only 2″ to 3″ of soil. Bass reported the successful discovery of 322 Indian burial sites by the use of a scraper. In those recoveries, there was no significant damage done to any of the skeletons by the equipment.

Bass and Birkby (1978) recommended a backhoe equipped with a toothless bucket in situations where a scraper was too large or unavailable for the job. The bucket will also leave a smooth surface so that differences in soil texture, color, and moisture content can be seen. A bucket without teeth may have to be fabricated by a welder. A backhoe, because of its limited mobility, will take much longer to search a given area than an elevated scraper. It can, however, operate in a much smaller or restricted area. An experienced operator should be able to remove only thin layers of soil at a time.

Bass (1963) recommended that at least two people serve as inspectors who will halt the machinery if any indication of a grave is found. The observers are watching for any disturbance in the soil. Bass and Birkby (1978) noted that color change is another indication of a grave site. The darker topsoil used to backfill the grave will contrast with the matrix. It will also appear darker because moisture sinks deeper into the grave soil and darkens it. If visual observation is not sufficient, the freshly scraped area can be tested with a probe until the outlines of a softer area are clearly defined.

Schiffer et al. (1977), in considering methods of doing archaeological surveys, recognized the value of equipment to penetrate the surface layers. For searches through leaf litter, pine duff, or other cover up to 20 cm deep, he recommended the systematic use of garden rakes or shovels. For searches into the soil 20 cm to 1 meter deep, he recommended the systematic use of power augers or coring tools. Below 1 meter in depth, he advocated heavy equipment to remove the overburden.

The attractions of heavy construction equipment are numerous. Their use is rapid, relatively inexpensive in view of the area searched, and places the burden of work upon the equipment operator rather than the investigator. The drawback to heavy equipment is, of course, the damage it does to potential evidence. Additionally, if the heavy equipment search fails, there is no going back to the less destructive methods. It may also be the responsibility of the law enforcement agency to repair all the damage done to the land by search efforts.

Chapter 5

PASSIVE GEOPHYSICAL PROSPECTING METHODS

"Under the wide and starry sky,
Dig the grave and let me lie.
Glad did I live and gladly die,
             And I laid me down with a will.
This be the verse you grave for me:
Here he lies where he longed to be;
Home is the sailor, home from the sea,
             And the hunter home from the hill."

Underwoods XXI *Requiem*
by Robert Louis Stevenson

Geology and geophysics are among the "earth sciences." Geology has been defined as the "science pertaining to the history and development of the earth as deduced from a study of rocks" (Beck, 1981:1). Geology usually involves direct observation of rocks, surface features, or bore-hole drillings. It is primarily qualitative and descriptive. Thus, "the detection and evaluation of ground surface disturbance is principally a geologic problem, as it involves directly observable phenomenon." In comparison, "the detection of buried objects is largely a geophysical problem, using interpretations based on indirectly observable phenomenon" (Davenport et al., 1986:2).

Physics is the science of the properties of matter and energy. Geophysics is the study of the physical properties of the earth and earth materials (Beck, 1981). Geophysics has also been defined as "a science based on the application of physical principles to the study of the earth" (Davenport et al., 1986:2). Geophysics is physics applies to the study of "solid earth" (Sharma, 1976). Geophysics can be considered a blend of physics and geology, as it is a study of the behavior of matter and energy in the earth (physics) and then the interpretation of that behavior to describe subsurface features and conditions (geology) (Loker, 1980). There are no sharp discipline boundaries, though geophysics tends to be more quantitative and based on instrument data as opposed to the qualitative visual descriptive field of geology.

Geophysics can be subdivided into two fields. The first is pure, or theoretical geophysics, based on the premise that the solid earth is an object with uniform physical properties. Theoretical geophysics is largely a laboratory and academic pursuit. Applied geophysics, or exploration geophysics, is concerned with anomalies in the earth and is traditionally linked with the practical business of locating economic resources such as minerals or energy. In recent years, applied geophysics has been routinely used in civil engineering projects to detect subsurface features before the construction of large buildings, dams, tunnels, and nuclear power facilities. It is exploration geophysics, or geophysical prospecting, which also lends itself to forensic applications.

As with archaeology, the search for a grave is a search for a buried object whose surface traces may have been obliterated. The search for remains is similar to the historical progression of methods to locate ore deposits (Dobrin, 1976). At first the search was confined to directly observable surface deposits. Later prospectors made a downward exploration of formations based upon surface geologic information. Lastly and most recently, physical measurements made at the surface yield information on the structure and composition of the earth's interior. Likewise, the search for a body generally begins with a search for obvious surface clues. If found, those surface signs stimulate a direct below-ground search. In the absence of surface evidence, geophysical search methods may reveal the burial site.

Geophysical surveys have been routine in mineral and petroleum exploration for the past 50 years. All the geophysical techniques used are based on contrasting properties, either physical or chemical, in the earth's materials. The fundamental limitation of all the techniques is that there may be an insufficient contrast between the target of interest, a buried body, and the surrounding formation. Though each geophysical technique has special capabilities and limitations, the universal rule is that no contrast means no detection. The contrast between the target and its medium may be one of acoustical velocity, electrical conductivity, material density, magnetic susceptibility, water content, or chemical composition.

There are two basic types of geophysical prospecting methods. Both methods involve the measurement of signals, either induced or natural. Passive methods measure natural signals generated by the earth which are inherent physical properties of the ground. Active methods use man-made (induced) signals transmitted into the ground, followed by a measurement of return signals by a receiver. Passive geophysical prospecting techniques are covered in this chapter and active ones in Chapter 6. The passive methods described are:

1. Gravity surveying
2. Magnetic surveying
3. Electrical self-potential surveying (SP)

Gravity surveying is based upon the detection of contrasts in the earth's gravity which are related to ground density. Magnetic surveying measures variations in the earth's magnetic fields. Self-potential surveying detects changes in naturally existing electrical currents in the ground. The active geophysical methods described are:

4. Electrical resistivity surveying
5. Electromagnetic surveying (EM)
6. Metal detectors
7. Seismic refraction
8. Ground-penetrating radar (GPR)

Electrical resistivity uses the induction of electrical current into the soil and the subsequent measurement of contrasts in the ground's resistance to the passage of that current. Electromagnetic surveying uses an induced magnetic field to measure differences in the ground's electrical conductivity. Metal detectors also use induced magnetic fields to detect buried metal objects. Seismic refraction measures the velocities of shock waves moving through the earth. Ground-penetrating radar uses reflected electromagnetic waves to detect density and electrical contrasts in the soil.

The success of all geophysical prospecting techniques is based upon the detection of anomalies. Those anomalies may be either positive or negative differences in measured data. There may be many causes for an anomaly, one of which may be disturbed soil as the result of a body burial. All the geophysical techniques are just aids to grave detection. Several different techniques may be used for corroboration before the decision to dig is made. Geophysical techniques are time consuming, but the time and effort is negligible compared to test digging.

As mentioned earlier, all geophysical methods involve the measurement of signals—induced or natural. All other detected, unwanted signals are "noise." Noise is always detrimental to geophysical surveying, as it can mask the sought-after signal. Noise can be natural, such as solar flares which disrupt magnetic surveys or wind vibrations which can complicate seismic work. Noise can also be cultural or man-made, such as traffic vibrations, power lines, or unwanted metal objects (trash) in the search area. To some degree, data manipulation can minimize noise, but all manipulations involve the loss of real signal data.

All geophysical techniques involve the interpretation of data. Siegel (1987) attributed 90 percent of the success of a geophysical search to interpretation of data by a geophysicist and only 10 percent upon the performance of the technicians in the field. The failure to detect a grave may be due to the instrument lacking sufficient sensitivity or it may be the result of ambiguous data which is not interpreted as an anomaly. Other sources of error include erratic performance of the instrument which is not readily detected as a malfunction, operator error due to inadequate training or practice, and false anomalies. False anomalies are geological features, natural or man-made, which mimic a grave site but are not actually the target of interest.

Some targets are not readily detectable by some geophysical techniques. Perhaps the target is too close to a false target, for instance, a body buried next to a pipeline. The ability of a technique to differentiate between objects close together is known as its resolution ability. Resolution varies with method, depth, and earth conditions. Perhaps the target is undetectable because of insufficient contrast with the host material, e.g. a body buried within a landfill. A target may simply be too small or be lying at an inappropriate depth for the technique used, either too deep or too shallow. There is a reciprocal relationship between the size of an object and the depth at which it can be sensed. In general, the deeper an object is buried, the larger it must be to be detected. As with other search techniques, the decision to use a particular geophysical method must be based upon the totality of conditions in the search area.

I have concentrated on those geophysical methods which can detect shallow anomalies, i.e. disturbances less than three meters below the surface. Other deep-seeking geophysical techniques, such as seismic reflection, may well miss shallow features. Many of the geophysical prospecting techniques presented are direction contingent. The techniques should be run both ways in a grid search pattern so that all possible orientations of the target are covered.

GRAVITY SURVEYING

The law of universal gravitation, discovered by Isaac Newton, states that "all bodies are attracted to each other with a force that is proportional to their masses and inversely proportional to the square of the distance between them" (Sazhina & Grushinsky, 1971). This law applies to the motion of the planets around the sun and to the mutual attraction of all objects on the earth. Gravity surveying measures the attraction force from the earth, one that is neither generated by the observer nor influenced by anything he does. This technique is passive, based on the measurement of a naturally occurring phenomenon.

The attraction force of gravity is measured in gals, named after Galileo who first attempted to measure the force of gravity. One gal is equal to an acceleration measure of a centimeter per second squared, acceleration being the force acting upon a unit of mass. In gravity surveying, the instruments are designed to measure differences in gravity from one point on the earth's surface to another rather than the actual magnitude of gravity itself. Since the change in gravity is small, the variation is usually measured in milligals which are one one-thousandth of a gal. Anomalies of interest to the exploratory geophysicists have a maximum value of approximately one milligal (Dobrin, 1976). Micro-gravity surveys used by archaeologists record variations of 0.01 milligals, a degree of sensitivity and precision available from modern gravimeters. Gravity surveying is commonly used in petroleum exploration, water basin mapping and for mineral prospecting.

If the earth were a perfect sphere of uniform density, gravity would be equal everywhere and would be measured as a single constant value. In fact, the earth is not spherical but has non-uniform density and is rotating. Thus, the force of gravity varies across the earth's surface. The variations caused by differing densities of subsurface rocks are important to exploratory geology. In a gravity survey, one measures minute variations in the pull of gravity caused by the rocks lying in the first few miles of the earth's crust.

The worldwide average for the force of gravity is approximately 980 gals. It varies from the equator to the pole by approximately 5 gals, being less at the equator. The objects of interest for the geophysicist are gravity anomalies which are not due to predictable variations. The distribution of gravity anomalies is a direct result of differences in the density of the earth's materials. One of the factors in bulk density is porosity, or the compaction of near-surface soils.

An important consideration in the use of gravity surveying is the spacing of the search grid. Most gravity surveying is carried out in a rectangular grid (Figure 5.1a). The measurement stations are an equal distance apart. The spacing pattern must be sufficiently dense to detail the feature that the survey is designed to locate. For oil exploration, the measuring stations may be a mile or more apart. For ore prospecting, 20 meters apart and for archaeological survey, 1 meter apart (Dobrin 1976). Such a simple box-like grid pattern is used in many geophysical prospecting methods. When the grid spacing is somewhat larger, additional coverage can be gained by staggering alternate search rows (Figure 5.1b).

The anomalies detected may be either positive (higher) or negative (lower) variations in the existing field. By adjusting the size of the grid, attempts are made to identify and specifically locate the anomaly by plotting its size, shape, and sharpness of the anomaly boundaries. A localized gravity anomaly due to subsurface conditions can be referred to as "source gravity disturbance" (Sharma, 1976).

All modern gravimeters are precise, portable and reasonably fast to operate with a typical sensitivity of 0.01 milligals. They are ruggedly constructed, since they must house sensitive measuring components. There are different types of gravimeters identified by their mechanical designs. The three basic measurement techniques are a pendulum, measuring velocity of a freely falling body, or weighing by means of a "spring balance." The "spring" may be a gas, thread or some other elastic material. Most modern instruments are of the spring balance type, determining the variation in the vertical component of gravity by measuring the change in the weight of a mass.

All gravimeters are sensitive to temperature changes, so they have either a constant temperature environment controlled by a thermostat or are well acclimated to the survey area and insulated from temperature change. The internal temperature of the instrument should not vary from the ambient environment by more than 2° C to 4° C (Sazhina & Grushinsky, 1971). Gravimeters are also sensitive to changes in atmospheric pressures, so they are either contained within a constant pressure chamber or have some other pressure-compensation system.

All gravimeters are subject to "drift" or variation in the readings caused by material fatigue. The elasticity of materials in the balance

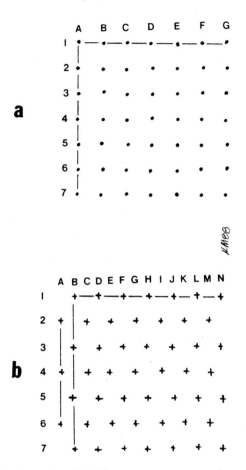

Figure 5.1. A standard search grid (a) has measurement stations an equal distance apart. Additional coverage of an area can be obtained by using a staggered-row pattern (b) of stations.

changes with time and use, requiring periodic calibration. The variation over short time periods is relatively predictable, can be measured and corrected for. The normal survey procedure is to first establish a base station within the search area. The instrument is then returned to this base station for additional readings every couple of hours. These readings provide a measure of drift during the course of the survey.

At each station in the survey grid, the instrument must be carefully leveled and, once set, must not be bumped or disturbed until the reading is completed (Figure 5.2). The instrument takes time to settle before an accurate measurement can be made, so readings are generally not recorded until one minute after the instrument has been set into position. The precise geographical position and elevation of the search area must be known and recorded. The necessary accuracy in elevation is one-tenth of a foot, since even a one-foot error in elevation can result in a 0.07 milligal change in the gravity reading (Dobrin, 1976).

Figure 5.2. A gravimeter must be carefully leveled before readings are taken. The instrument is moved about a grid to measure variations in the force of gravity. (Photography courtesy of GISCO.)

After all field data have been collected, corrections in the data must be made. A geophysicist should make these corrections and subsequently interpret the data. The first correction is a tide correction which compensates for the gravitational effects of the sun and moon. The next one is the latitude correction which compensates for the centrifugal force of the earth's rotation and for the equatorial bulge. Both of these corrections are made from published tables. The third correction is for instrument drift based upon the repetitious base station measurements. All values obtained during the survey are plotted against time. The next two corrections compensate for elevation differences. The first is the free-air correction which reduces all readings to a common elevation datum, such as sea level or the lowest elevation within the search grid. Then the Bouguer correction is made which compensates for the earth's mass between the actual measurement elevation and the sea level datum.

Lastly, corrections are made for topography in the search area. Both hills and valleys decrease the apparent force of gravity. Hills decrease the measured gravity because the mass of earth materials above the measurement point exert an upward pull on the instrument. Nearby valleys, on the other hand, decrease the measured gravity because less earth mass pulls from below the measurement point. Since topography is so difficult to quantify, topographic corrections are only approximations. The possible error is so large that gravity surveys are normally accurate only in flat terrain.

The final product of all these corrections and calculations is a contour map which shows the variations in gravity over the search area. This is known as a "Bouguer anomaly map." The anomalies displayed on the Bouguer map show the pattern of gravity variation due to horizontal changes in subsurface density. These may be attributed to either deep or shallow features. Deep regional effects can be removed by the smoothing or filtering of data, leaving only local effects. An experienced geophysicist will then interpret the map and, based upon the size, shape, and strength of anomalies, make recommendations on where to dig or conduct further tests.

MAGNETIC SURVEYING

Magnetic surveying is perhaps the oldest method of geophysical exploration. It is based on the fact, known for centuries, that the earth is a hugh, imperfect bar magnet. The core of that bar magnet is oriented close to the axis of the earth's rotation (Figure 5.3).

"At any point on the earth's surface a magnetic needle, if free to move about its center of gravity, will orient itself in a position determined by the direction of the geomagnetic field at that point" (Sharma, 1976:178).

The earth is surrounded by a magnetic field which is represented, by convention, as a magnetic dipole oriented with a positive end to the north and the negative end to the south. If the earth were of uniform material, the magnetic lines of force would be evenly distributed between the poles. The various materials in the earth have different magnetic

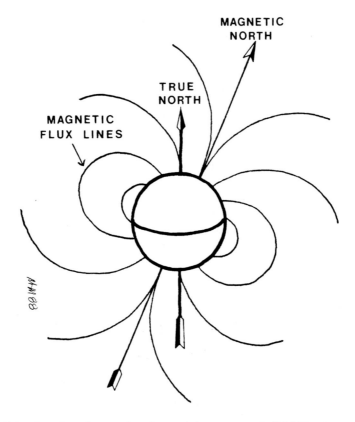

Figure 5.3. It has long been known that the earth has a magnetic field like that produced by a bar magnet, oriented close to the geographic axis of the planet.

susceptibilities however, so the magnetic lines of force are distorted. These distorted regional magnetic patterns are related to deep geologic structures (Davenport et al., 1986).

The conventional unit of intensity of the earth's magnetism is the oersted. This unit of measurement is too large, however, for geophysical prospecting, since anomalies may vary less than one one-thousandth of an oersted. A gamma is therefore used in geophysical fieldwork and is equal to .0001 oersteds. The total magnetic field of the earth is normally one-half oersted or 50,000 gammas, though it varies between 35,000 and 65,000 gammas. Anomalies of interest may be only a few gammas in contrast (GISCO, undated).

The irregularities of the earth's magnetic field can be seen on standard isomagnetic charts used in navigation. The changes in magnetic intensity vary principally with latitude. The magnetic field is less intense at the equator, where it can be as low as 30,000 gammas. The northern temperate latitudes have magnetic fields in the range of 40,000 to 50,000 gammas and it approaches 70,000 gammas in intensity near the poles.

A compass needle or bar magnet will naturally orient itself parallel to the invisible lines of magnetic force called flux lines. Magnetic force at any point has two characteristics, direction and intensity. Direction is further subdivided into the vertical component of the field which is the magnetic pull toward the earth and the horizontal component of the field which is its pull toward the magnetic North Pole. The field's declination is the angle between the horizontal component and the geographical or true North. Measuring magnetism is more complex than gravity surveying, since gravity only requires a measurement of the pull of attraction. Magnetic measurements not only include magnitude and direction but also involve attraction and repulsion. Magnetic results, unlike gravity, can also be greatly affected by small traces of powerful minerals (Dobrin, 1976).

Most geophysical instruments for measuring magnetism quantify the "total field" and do not break down the magnetic field into its components. They are designed to measure the intensity of the magnetic field at specific points on the earth's surface. Like gravity surveying, this technique passively measures the naturally existing force field. The intensity of the total field is influenced by the geographical location, atmospheric magnetic field fluctuations, geologic materials beneath the surface, and human activity. Fluctuations caused by human activity are of interest to archaeologists and criminalists. Magnetic prospecting has been successfully applied to archaeological work, and techniques have been developed to separate man-made anomalies from natural effects (Loker, 1980).

Total magnetic field direction and intensity also change with time. Long-term variations in the magnetic field are rarely significant in geophysical studies and are so minute that the technology does not currently exist to measure them (Sazhina & Grushinsky, 1971). There are also short-term variations in the magnetic field. There is a daily solar variation which is rhythmic over a 24-hour period and varies by approximately 30 gammas. There is also a lunar variation over the 25-hour lunar day. It is only about one-fifteenth of the solar variation, so it has little consequence in most magnetic prospecting efforts. There are also transient, erratic, and unpredictable disturbances from magnetic storms which are sunspot related and cause variations of as much as 1,000 gammas. These storms occur at approximately 27-day intervals (Dobrin, 1976). The solar wind distorts the magnetosphere, or external magnetic field of the earth, to such a degree that magnetic surveying must be discontinued during the few days that the storm lasts.

The magnetic field also changes with the subsurface physical properties of the earth and this is the basis for prospecting. The intensity of the field is a direct function of the underground materials' magnetic susceptibility. This is the degree to which a material can be magnetized and its response to an induced magnetic field. Susceptibility, explained another way, expresses the level of magnetization that can be created in a material when it is placed in a strong magnetic field (Aitken, 1970). The magnetic field measured may be that of the earth alone or the field associated with a buried object which is superimposed upon that of the earth. For instance, granite, gravel, and sedimentary rock have a low magnetic susceptibility, whereas iron (ferrous) objects and igneous rocks have high magnetic susceptibility. The magnetic character of rock depends upon its mineral content and its history of formation. Most important is the amount of ferromagnetic minerals, principally magnetite, present. Magnetite is part of virtually all rocks and soil.

The detection of near-surface anomalies by magnetic surveying is based largely on the LeBorgne Effect. LeBorgne discovered that soils near the surface had greater magnetic content than soils taken from deeper layers. Magnetic anomalies result when the layers are disturbed by excavation (Stanley & Green, 1976). A pit, ditch or grave can be detected by the greater susceptibility of the filling material over the adjacent earth into which the pit was dug. The less sterile the filling, the stronger the magnetic discontinuity. "Dirty" fill has higher magnetic susceptibility which is related to the concentration of organic material in the soil (Aitken, 1970).

As with other geophysical prospecting techniques, the detection of a magnetic anomaly depends upon the contrast between the target and the surrounding material. As an archaeological example, a limestone wall will have a weak or low magnetic susceptibility which can be detected in a topsoil with a strong susceptibility. Thus, the wall is detected by the absence of topsoil, not by the presence of the limestone wall itself. Differences in soil compaction may also be detected, leading to the discovery of such features as ancient roads or pathways (Weymoth & Huggins, 1985). Anomalies can, of course, be natural as a result of non-cultural processes. The shape, strength and orientation of the anomaly may give a clue to its source, but perhaps only excavation can identify the cause of the anomaly with certainty.

Anomalies represent a local change in the magnetization profile and the contrast may be either positive or negative. Anomalies may also express themselves as a dipole or an a monopole type. A dipole anomaly will show an adjacent high/low magnetic reading, whereas a monopole will be seen as a isolated high or low reading. A piece of ferrous metal is an object of high susceptibility and will show itself as a dipole anomaly. The anomaly from a surface or buried metal object may be so strong that other more subtle anomalies will be masked.

Magnetometer Types

There are several types of magnetometers which can measure variations in the earth's magnetosphere. Flux-gate magnetometers are commonly used in airborne and ground magnetic surveying. The instrument contains two magnetically susceptible materials powered to produce opposite fields. Any magnetism detected will reinforce one field and oppose the other. The advantages of the flux-gate magnetometer are that it is lightweight, requires no precise leveling, and is quick to use. It has sensitivity to a few gammas, often as good as one gamma (Sharma, 1976). The flux-gate instrument can be used to measure selected components of the magnetic field but is most commonly used to measure the vertical component.

Nuclear precession-type magnetometers, such as proton magnetometers, are based on the reaction of hydrogen atoms exposed to a magnetic field. A proton magnetometer has, at its core, a bottle of liquid. Within the liquid, the normal spin of protons is randomly oriented. An electric current is sent around the bottle and that creates an artificial magnetic field. When the field is applied, all the atoms align themselves within it. When the induced field is removed, the spinning protons "precess" for a short time in the direction of the earth's ambient magnetic field. The hydrogen atoms can be viewed as small gyroscopes as they rotate about their axes. The precessions, or gyrations, are at a frequency exactly proportional to the magnetic intensity of the earth's field. The precessions produce a small electrical charge which can be calibrated as a measure of the gravitational field.

The proton magnetometer has a greater sensitivity than the flux gate magnetometer (less than 1 gamma). Since it measures the total field, it is free from orientation errors. It has no moving parts and is usually equipped with a digital readout. It is fast to operate and can give readings at one- to three-second intervals (Stanley & Green, 1976). Some have memory capacity to store a sequence of readings for later processing.

Optical pumping magnetometers, also called alkali vapor magnetometers, use cesium or rubidium vapors which have been excited by light. The frequency of the electromagnetic energy given off by the vapor electrons depends upon the intensity of the magnetic field in the vicinity of the sensor. The instrument converts the measured energy frequency into a reading of magnetic intensity. The advantage of alkali vapor magnetometers is not only their increased sensitivity, 0.01 to .1 gamma, but their speed. They can make measurements at 10-millisecond intervals, thus giving near-continuous readings for mapping. The instruments can be mounted and used on moving vehicles. Like proton magnetometers, the instruments give direct digital readings of gamma intensity and some have memory capability.

Under comparable conditions, cesium magnetometers can detect features to a 5-meter depth compared to the 3-meter depth of proton magnetometers (Loker, 1980). In field tests, rubidium magnetometers were found inferior to cesium magnetometers because they needed more careful alignment which slowed the survey time by 20 percent. They are both insensitive to temperature variation and can be used in field conditions with ambient temperatures over 90° F. (Ralph et al., 1968). Since the magnetic field of the earth does not change with weather, all magnetometers can be used at any time of the year.

In a forensic case the magnitude of anomalies may be less than that found in archaeological situations. The additional sensitivity of alkali vapor magnetometers may be justified, despite the increased expense of the instrument. The alkali vapor magnetometer is also faster to use in the field (Figure 5.4). Scollar (1972) found that, using a proton magnetometer, two people could produce approximately 5,000 readings per day. At one-meter grid intervals, that was a coverage of one-half hectare (1.24 acres) per day. A hectare is a metric unit of land measurement equal to 10,000 square meters or approximately 2.471 acres. Stanley and Green (1976), using an alkali vapor magnetometer, found that two people using the same grid size could survey 15 hectares of open ground per day.

All magnetometer surveys require background information on changes in the ambient magnetic field. This is commonly accomplished by some system that incorporates a differential magnetometer survey. One magne-

Figure 5.4. An alkali vapor magnetometer is accurate, sensitive and fast in field use. (Photograph courtesy of GISCO.)

tometer is left in a fixed position and another is moved about the search grid in exploration. The stationary instrument is measuring simultaneously and records atmospheric, secular, and diurnal variations. This later enables the data processing to accentuate relevant anomalies while suppressing temporal disturbances in the earth's magnetic field. An alternate technique, using one magnetometer, is for the device to be periodically returned to a base station to check readings. This is similar to the procedure used in gravity drift corrections.

A magnetic survey requires two technicians: one to handle the moving sensor and another to record data. The stationary magnetometer is usually set up just outside the search grid area and, once established, is not moved or disturbed. The moving sensor operator must be "magnetically clean" and the sensor must be held still during each reading (Breternitz, 1983). Magnetically clean means that the holder must not have any quantity of metal on his person. Even small amounts can alter instrument readings. Possible sources of metal contamination include eyeglass frames or hinges, clothing zippers or buttons, clipboard metal, metal boot shanks, pen or pencils, etc.

The most commonly used proton magnetometer has a sensor carried on an 8-foot staff. The height of the sensor above the ground is varied, depending upon surface contamination. The higher the sensor is carried, the more it is removed from the influence of surface litter, operator clothing, etc. (Figure 5.5). The height of the sensor above the ground also influences the sensitivity. A sensor close to the surface, one to five feet, will detect small objects at a shallow depth. If surface noise to too great, the sensor must be raised but at a risk of missing small anomalies. Another method of reducing ground trash noise is to make the survey with a gradiometer. A gradiometer is a magnetometer with two sensor heads. One sensor is mounted on a staff and the other on a backpack so they are two or three feet apart. The gradiometer measures the difference between the two sensors, effectively eliminating most noise.

Magnetometer readings are affected by compass orientation, so the sensor operator faces the same way at each measured point. Normally, traverses are run in a north to south direction. This is done because at any given latitude, a north-south orientation will give a greater anomaly effect, enhancing the chances of finding a dipole (high/low) anomaly.

As with all geophysical prospecting methods, the first step in a survey is to establish a grid or search pattern. In an archaeological context, measurements are conventionally taken at one-meter intervals (Scollar, 1972; Breternitz, 1983). Breternitz (1984) reduced the grid size to 50 centimeters in the vicinity of an anomaly to enhance its definition. Grids should be marked out with wooden stakes and string or other techniques which do not involve the use of any ferrous metal stakes, nails, etc. The grid size should be related to the anticipated size of the target. Anticipated size is the likelihood of a magnetic contrast based upon the depth of burial, shape of excavation, and likely difference between the target and its matrix.

A magnetometer with a sensitivity of at least one gamma is commonly recommended. It should also have a precision, the ability to make repeated readings at the same point, of plus or minus one gamma. A sensitivity to one gamma is necessary to detect features of geological origin (Breternitz, 1983). Breternitz used instruments with a sensitivity of .25 gamma in his archaeological fieldwork.

As with gravity surveying, magnetic surveys require skilled interpretation of data. The processing of digital information is time consuming and expensive and now normally handled by computer. A number of information processing methods are available which can smooth and filter original data. Such processing may be useful to highlight anomalies.

Figure 5.5. The length of the staff on a proton magnetometer can be adjusted to compensate for surface metal litter. (Photograph courtesy of GISCO.)

The end product of data processing is a contoured magnetic intensity map (Figure 5.6). The identification of an anomaly is then based upon shape, border sharpness, size, intensity of contrast, and other features. As always, the detection of a feature depends upon its size, depth, and the degree of magnetic alteration, i.e. the contrast between the target and its matrix. During fieldwork, anomalies may be detected while the survey is still underway. In those cases, a hunt to pinpoint the location of the anomaly can be conducted immediately. Weymouth (1976) found that "the maximum value of an anomaly occurs to the south of the feature at a distance equal to about 1/3 of the depth of the feature." So if the target (metal object, etc.) is buried one meter deep, the maximum magnetic anomaly will be located approximately one foot to the south of it.

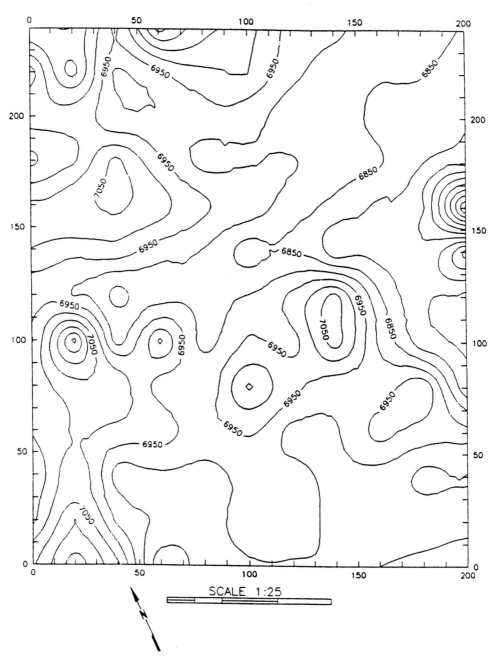

Figure 5.6. The end product of a magnetic survey is a contoured magnetic intensity map. The map will identify areas of magnetic anomalies. (Map courtesy of G. Clark Davenport.)

The contrast between a target and its matrix may or may not be related to the target size. A small, powerful magnet could show an anomaly equal to that of a buried automobile. Detectability also depends upon natural or cultural background noise. In order to be recognized, an anomaly must be several times larger than the resolution ability of the magnetometer and larger than the effective noise level in the search area. For example, if the instrument has a sensitivity of .25 gamma, the target must produce an anomaly at least one gamma or more at the surface to be detected (Breiner, 1973). The most important single factor affecting detectability is the distance between the magnetometer and the target. Targets closer to the surface are easier to find. A five-inch screwdriver buried at five feet produces a 5 to 10 gamma maximum anomaly, whereas buried at 10 feet, it produces only a 0.5 to 1 gamma anomaly which might not be detected (Davenport et al., 1986).

Most archaeological and forensic targets will show as a positive anomaly. They will be more magnetic than the surrounding or covering soil. It is possible, however, that they could show as a negative anomaly because undisturbed surface soil obtains a "viscous" magnetization. This is a form of remanent magnetization attained slowly over tens of thousands of years. If this soil is disturbed by digging a grave, the disruption of the soil's integrity creates a local negative anomaly.

If an anomaly is detected during the primary search pattern, its position should be marked on the ground. The search grid should still be completed for fear of losing complete coverage of the search area. It may later be found that the anomaly is not the target sought and the distraction caused by digging may keep searchers from thoroughly covering the area. Once the grid is completely covered, searchers can return to obtain a sharper definition of the anomaly. Figure 5.7 illustrates a method for pinpointing an anomaly source. During the primary traverse, the maximum point of change in magnetic intensity is noted on the ground. A second search pattern is then executed, oriented perpendicular to that of the first search traverse. Again, the maximum point of change is noted. Ever smaller grid sizes are used, continually alternating approach direction until the anomaly is pinpointed. The target object will be near the center of the high-low dipole. Sheer probability indicates that the target object is not likely to be under the primary traverse but is probably to one side or the other. Digging without further defining the anomaly will likely miss the target and waste time. Time spent in narrowing down the location of the anomaly will ultimately save excavation work.

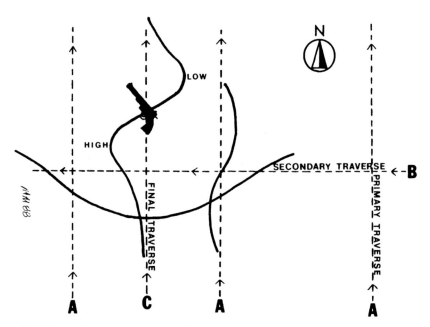

Figure 5.7. Alternating perpendicular traverses are used to pinpoint the location of a target anomaly. The middle primary traverse (A) detects a dipole anomaly. The secondary traverse (B) narrows the location by detecting a monopole anomaly, and the final traverse (C) fixes the approximate target location. (Adapted from Breiner, 1973.)

The advantages of magnetic survey technique are that it is quickly done, is sensitive to man-made features, and can be conducted over uneven terrain. It is unaffected by ground water, so it can be used where electrical resistivity or ground-penetrating radar might fail. The main drawback is that magnetic surveying is sensitive to interference. Results can be damaged by nearby metal or electrical currents, so it cannot be used around electrical power lines, radio transmission stations, or other power sources. It shouldn't be used near bridges, road culverts, or buildings. It cannot be used indoors because of electrical and metal interference. It may be inappropriate for areas containing lots of igneous rock, such as basalt, where the rocks have picked up strong magnetism from their volcanic creation. The technique cannot be used during magnetic storms. Interference can also come from metal litter in or on the ground or from buried water pipes or gas lines. It should not be used within 125 yards of railroad tracks, within 30 yards of automobiles, or within 35 yards of wire fencing, especially if they run in a north-south direction. The need to avoid sources of interference limits the technique to rural application.

SELF–POTENTIAL SURVEYING

A number of geophysical prospecting methods measure, either directly or indirectly, electrical conductivity or other electrically related properties of the earth. The first, self-potential surveying, is a passive system which measures the natural electrical charge that exists within the soil. Self-potential, or spontaneous polarization surveying, "involves the measurement at the surface of electrical potential developed in the earth by electro-chemical actions between minerals and the solutions with which they are in contact" (Dobrin, 1976:572). Minerals and soil solutions are involved in chemical reactions. Those reactions create a slight electric current flow in the ground which is measured by the self-potential instrument. Self-potential readings are a measure of both natural subsurface electrochemical action and man-made electrical fields that are perpetuated underground.

Self-potential, like gravity surveying, measures gross variations in the properties of the earth. It is suitable for identifying geologic features but is not normally useful for detecting man-made features which are smaller and more complex than geological features (Loker, 1980). Self-potential surveying is commonly used for detecting migrating water, especially for locating water seepage in dams, and for geothermal exploration. The technique works best in acidic soils between pH 2 and 5. It does not work below the water table, in permafrost or in very arid conditions. Spurious readings can result from changes in elevation, ground dampness, atmospheric conditions, or in areas of rapidly changing rock types. Likewise, it does not work well in areas where the soils are very electrically resistive (Reedman, 1979).

Self-potentials are measured between two electrodes, usually located one meter apart in the ground. Voltage will invariably be registered between any two electrodes in contact with the earth. In self-potential surveying, the two-electrode apparatus is moved about a grid. Between the two electrodes is a "sensitive high impedance direct current volt meter" (Beck, 1981). In an alternate technique, one electrode is kept stationary and is known as the base electrode and the other, known as the rover electrode, is moved about the grid. A combination of the two techniques can be used in which the electrodes leapfrog over each other as an entire search grid is covered. The end product of the survey is the contour map showing the natural potential, in millivolts, with measurements recorded midway between electrode positions. A reference electrode is often used to detect periodic changes in subsurface electrical conditions so that results can be plotted against time and drift corrections made. The reference electrode will detect changes in telluric currents, which are minute electrical currents travelling widely across the earth's surface (Davenport et al., 1986).

The electrodes used in self-potential surveying are a special type. If they were simply metal rods driven into the earth, the electrical interaction of the metal rods and the soil would overwhelm the self-potential measurements and interfere with natural potentials. The special electrode is a copper rod bathed in a metal salt solution, such as copper sulfate. It is contained within a porcelain or other porous material pot (Dohr, 1974). The electrode is place in the soil to establish a good electrical contact (Figure 5.8). Significant geological anomalies may be hundreds of millivolts in magnitude, with natural drift being only several millivolts. Most self-potential meters are sensitive to less than one millivolt and can be as sensitive as 0.21 millivolts (GISCO, undated).

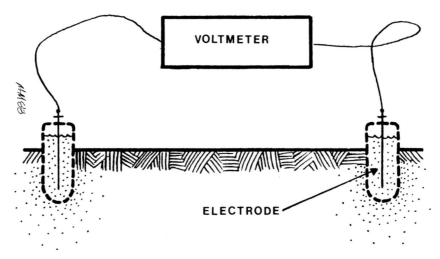

Figure 5.8. A self-potential survey system consists of a pair of insulated electrodes connected to a sensitive voltmeter.

As with other geophysical methods discussed thus far, the results from a self-potential survey require qualitative interpretation. The first step in interpretation is to establish a baseline of self-potential noise. Anomalies may then be positive, above the noise level, or negative, below the noise level. Anomalies may be caused by changes in soil moisture content, grain size, or mineral composition. The variations due to natural changes in the soil are usually greater than changes caused by man-placed material. Gradual changes reflect differences in composition or mineralization of the soils, whereas sharp, narrow anomalies are likely due to water content changes.

Self-potential surveys are rapid, inexpensive, and easy to perform. Unfortunately, they are not likely to detect human remains in a forensic situation unless the burial is accompanied by materials which will drastically alter the chemical composition of the grave site. Without such contrast between the grave fill and the surrounding matrix, the site is not likely to be detected by a self-potential survey.

Chapter 6

ACTIVE GEOPHYSICAL PROSPECTING METHODS

"Man, that is born of a woman, hath but a short time to live, and is full of misery. He cometh up, and is cut down, like a flower; he fleeth as it were a shadow, and never continueth in one stay. In the midst of life we are in death . . . we commend the soul of our brother departed, and we commit his body to the ground, earth to earth, ashes to ashes, dust to dust . . .

> The Order for the Burial of the Dead from *The Book of Common Prayer* (according to the Use of the Protestant Episcopal Church in the United States of America), 1888.

The previous Chapter Five concerned passive geophysical prospecting techniques which could be applied to the search for human remains. This chapter continues with a discussion of the active geophysical techniques, those that rely upon man-made signals sent into the earth.

RESISTIVITY SURVEYING

Electrical resistivity surveying is a geophysical technique for locating and mapping underground structural or chemical anomalies. Unlike self-potential surveys, during resistivity surveying, currents are artificially sent into the earth before measurements are taken. Resistivity is used to detect ore deposits, stratigraphic variations, and aquifers. It is also used for shallow exploration mineral prospecting and civil engineering. It was first used in archaeology by R.J. Atkinson in 1946 to locate neolithic ditches in England (Carr, 1982). Since that time it has been used to detect mine shafts, wells, masonry walls, roads, tombs, ditches, soil-filled pits, etc.

Resistivity surveys measure the potential of a given area of the earth to conduct electricity. Resistivity is the opposition of a given material to the passage of electricity. It is measured in ohm meters. The opposite of resistivity is conductivity, measured in mho meters (ohm spelled backwards). Conductivity is the ability of a material to transmit electricity through it (Loker, 1980). The basic assumption is that resistivity and conductivity are fundamental characteristics of all substances. The measurement of resistivity and the detection of any changes permit a tentative identification of subsurface physical conditions.

Resistivity surveying is based upon predictable electrical behavior in a solid medium of uniform resistivity. In such a theoretical situation, introduced current distributes itself both horizontally and vertically. In a homogeneous situation, lines representing equipotential values can be visualized as concentric spheres radiating from the current electrodes (Figure 6.1). The equipotential lines are gradients where the potential to conduct electricity is constant. The distribution of lines is dependent upon the relative separation of the current electrodes. If the spread between electrodes is known and the subsurface material is homogeneous, then the flow of current is predictable. Deviations from that prediction are due to variations in the conducting medium that distort the current flow. Since the area between the electrodes is set, it is possible to approximate the location of a subsurface discontinuity. Resistivity surveys measure these distortions and enable the experienced investigator to predict the type of anomaly encountered and its likely depth (Loker, 1980).

Anomalies of interest differ from their surroundings in properties that effect their capacity to conduct electric current. The ability of the soil to conduct electricity depends upon a number of factors. The porosity of the soil and chemical content of the water filling those pore spaces are the most important elements governing resistivity. They have more influence than the conductivity of the mineral grains of which the soil is composed. Soil porosity depends upon compactness and the geometric shapes of the water holding pores (Carr, 1982; Clark, 1970). The conductance of the soil is also dependent upon the total moisture content of the earth. The salinity of the pore space interstitial water is the critical factor in determining conductance (Dobrin, 1976). Pore space water contains salts dissolved from the soil materials and humics of biological origin. The quantity and solubility of those salts and acids determine the concentrations of ions in the soil. Most mineral grains are electrical insulators, so hard dry rocks are poor conductors of electricity. Electricity will instead travel through the fissures and cracks. In porous sedimentary rock, electricity will travel through the interstitial water. The resistivity of rock is thus related to its type, geologic age and formation process, all which influence its water-storage capacity.

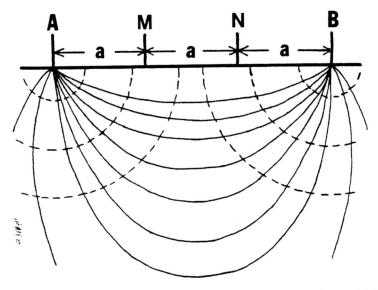

Figure 6.1. If the earth were a homogenous material, the paths of current flow (solid lines) and equipotential lines (dashed lines) would be predictable. They would radiate outward in all directions from the current electrodes (A and B). (Adapted from Loker, 1980.)

The range of resistivities of the earth's soils is enormous, from .0001 (10 E−5) to 10,000,000,000,000,000 (10 E+15) ohm meters. The category of good conductors includes those with resistivities between 10 E−5 to 1 ohm meters. Intermediate conductors are those between 1 and 10 E+5 ohm meters, and poor conductors are those with resistivity readings between 10 E+5 and 10 E+15 ohm meters (Dobrin, 1976). The median resistivity of rocks within 500 feet of the earth's surface is 150 ohm meters, in the intermediate range. In high rainfall areas, over 100 inches per year, salts are leached from the near-surface soils so that resistivity is very high and may be in the range of several thousand ohm meters. Resistivity becomes progressively lower until it reaches a minimum in semi-arid conditions receiving only 5 to 10 inches of rainfall per year (GISCO, undated).

The four-electrode array commonly used in resistivity surveys is shown in Figure 6.2. Current (I) is induced into the ground through two electrodes known as the current electrodes (identified as A and B). Positive ions dissolved in the groundwater will migrate to the negative electrode and negative ions will migrate toward the positive electrode. The electrical current used is direct current (DC) or low-frequency alternating current (AC). The voltage drop caused by soil resistivity is measured across the two inner electrodes known as potential electrodes (identified as M and N). The potential electrodes are connected to a sensitive volt meter (V). The voltage drop varies with the volume of material through which the current is passing, so the spacing of electrodes is always uniform. As a general rule, the depth of current penetration is nearly equivalent to the distance between adjoining electrodes (Loker, 1980).

INSTRUMENTATION

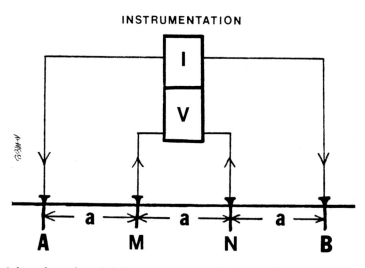

Figure 6.2. A four-electrode resistivity array is commonly deployed in a Wenner configuration. Electricity is induced into the ground from the outer current electrodes (A and B) and the voltage drop is measured by the potential electrodes (M and N). The electrodes are evenly spaced apart (a). (Adapted from Loker, 1980.)

The type of investigation underway determines the arrangement of the four electrodes. Resistivity surveying attempts to delineate resistivity boundaries, both horizontally and vertically. Measuring lateral changes is known as resistivity profiling, trenching, or surveying. Determining depth is known as resistivity sounding or drilling (Sharma, 1976). In studying lateral variations of resistivity, the electrode spread moves across the search area along traverse lines. The spacing between electrodes is kept constant. This is known as continuous profiling and is used for detecting shallow anomalies. If the center of the electrode spread remains fixed but the separation between electrodes is gradually increased, greater depth measurements can be made. This is the basic procedure in vertical electrical (VES) sounding.

There are three basic types of electrode configurations. The most common, employing equal spacing between electrodes, is known as a

Wenner arrangement (Figures 6.2 and 6.3). The Wenner arrangement is used principally for horizontal profiling, since it is the most sensitive to near-surface changes in resistivity. The Schlumberger arrangement has electrodes spaced unevenly. The distance between potential electrodes remains constant, but the outer current electrodes are moved farther and farther apart for vertical sounding. The spread is kept symmetrical so that the distance between the inner two electrodes is always less than one-fifth the distance between the outer two current electrodes. A Schlumberger arrangement requires a crew of three technicians, whereas a Wenner arrangement requires only two. Either the Wenner or Schlumberger arrangements can be used for continuous profiling or vertical electrical sounding. The third configuration is known as the dipole arrangement. The two current electrodes are kept together and the two potential electrodes are kept together, while the distance between the two pairs of electrodes is varied. The interpretation of data from a dipole arrangement is more complex. It is principally used in mining exploration. All other electrode arrangements are variations on these basic three designs.

In all arrangements, steel or cooper-clad steel electrodes are driven into the ground. The penetration is only deep enough to make good electrical contact. In dry conditions the soil around the current electrodes may have to be moistened. The sensitivity of the resistivity equipment is a function of both the power of the current source and the sensitivity of the current measuring device. The capability of the system may be improved by increasing the performance of either component.

The result of a resistivity survey is *apparent* resistivity and may not be the *true* resistivity because one layer in the area may dominate the measurements. Apparent resistivity is calculated from the distance between potential electrodes, the voltage drop and the standard amperage of the current used. This reading does not reflect the resistivity at one point but is rather a summary of the conditions of the soil through which the current is flowing, i.e. the entire area encompassed by the electrode spacing. The area between the potential electrodes contributes more to the results than the larger volume between the current electrodes (Figure 6.4). The most influential of all is the shallow area directly between the potential electrodes. If the spacing of electrodes is small and the target object deep, it will exert minimum influence on the distribution of equipotential lines and may go undetected. Likewise, if the spacing of electrodes is too wide, small features near the surface may go undetected

Figure 6.3. The Wenner arrangement of electrodes is principally used for horizontal profiling since it is sensitive to near-surface changes in electrical resistivity. (Photograph courtesy of GISCO.)

because the equipotential lines are so far apart that the insignificant distortion caused by a small object will not show up. If the currents are spread out over a large volume of soil, the results are averaged by the instrument without target detection (Loker, 1980).

Using a Wenner electrode arrangement, the distance between electrodes is commonly referred to as "a." For a detailed investigation using horizontal resistivity survey techniques, the electrode spread "a" should be equal to the likely target depth. If one assumes that a grave should not be any more than one to two meters deep, then maximum likelihood of detection will result from an electrode spread of one meter as well.

Resistivity surveys are generally conducted in a series of parallel line traverses. The outer current electrode on a line may be separated from the adjacent outer electrode by the distance "a" (normal electrode spacing). For a more detailed survey, the adjacent lines may be overlapped for more complete coverage (Figure 6.5) (Clark, 1970). As with other geophysical prospecting techniques, the survey values are plotted on a scale diagram of the search area. Regardless of the type of electrode arrangement used, the resistivity readings are plotted at the center of the

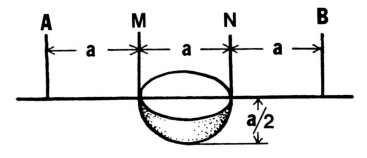

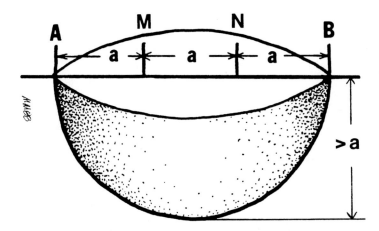

Figure 6.4. The area closest to the center of the electrode spread (between M and N) contributes the most to the resistivity measurement. The larger area, shown in the lower drawing (between A and B), contributes less to the overall reading. (Adapted from Carr, 1982 and Loker, 1980.)

electrode spread. Contour lines are then drawn between points of equal resistance. The end product should show anomaly areas of low or high resistivity, corresponding to better or poorer conducting areas.

As discussed before, a grave containing a body can be described as an organically enriched area of disturbed soils. The contrast between that area and natural soils should produce a difference in electrical resistivity. The grave area should have a higher moisture content and a higher organic matter component. The digging will increase the porosity of the soil. These changes have different effects upon soil resistivity. Adding organic matter should lower resistivity, as should the disturbance caused by soil mixing. Pure water has a high electrical resistivity (low conductivity), but the resistivity of soil water is dependent upon its chemistry and

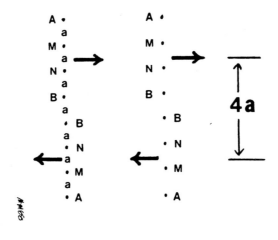

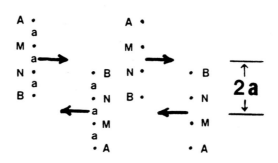

Figure 6.5. Resistivity surveys are normally conducted along parallel traverse lines with the outer electrodes separated by a uniform distance (a) (upper diagram). More detailed coverage can be obtained by overlapping traverses (lower diagram) which reduces the distance between center points from 4(a) to 2(a). (Adapted from Clark, 1970.)

temperature. Increasing pure water content raises resistivity, but partially saline soil water lowers resistance.

Overall, disturbed sites should show lowered electrical resistivity, and the best differentiation should be seen when soil moisture is high or low and soil temperatures are high (Carr, 1982). Neither very wet or very dry conditions are conducive to soil resistivity survey. The sensitivity of all instruments is reduced by very dry conditions, so a little natural or artificial moistening of the soil before the survey may help (Clark, 1970). Survey results are often unpredictable because of changing soil moisture conditions. Water content can vary with area as well as with time. Fluctuations in soil moisture may be seasonal and even daily, depending upon weather. Thus, it is not possible to obtain absolute quantifications of soil resistivity but only relative difference between points at the time of surveying. The resistivity survey will establish background or normal ranges of resistivity values and then spots with large deviations can be followed up with excavation.

Underground electric currents will seek the path of least resistance. Areas of high resistance will deflect current, while areas of low resistance will channel current into that zone (Figure 6.6). A highly resistive buried object (i.e. masonry wall) crowds current lines toward the surface and results in a higher surface resistivity reading. A buried low resistivity area, such as a grave, will pull current downward into the soil resulting in a surface measurement which reflects the overall lower resistivity.

There are a number of limitations on the use of electrical resistivity surveying. The most profound is that anomalies of interest may have a low contrast with surrounding materials. Soils naturally show great variability in physical and chemical factors, and man-made disturbances may be in the range of natural variation. The resistivity signature of a grave may be only insignificantly different from its matrix. Additionally, even if an anomaly is detected, there is no way to know from the surface whether it is natural or man-made. In all resistivity surveying there is a high noise factor compared to the target signal. Noise is introduced because the target may be covered by highly variable soils. Other local variations include drainage pattern, plant growth, temperature and man-made earth working. The situation is especially difficult in cultivated land which is repeatedly worked and subjected to fertilizing practices (Carr, 1982).

Considering the range of possible archaeological targets, a grave is a relatively small anomaly of interest. It may be so small that it cannot be detected within economical limits. Likewise, rounded features like graves are harder to detect than linear or square features such as building ruins. Vertical disturbances like pits are less distinct than continuous or horizontal features such as trenches.

Resistivity surveys also show a decreasing accuracy with depth because of the increased volume of soil within the survey area. In a forensic situation, this is not a problem since graves begin at the surface and have a relatively shallow total depth. Rough terrain may hurt the accuracy of resistivity readings, so notes should be made of topographic changes for consideration by the data interpreter. Changes in terrain can either focus

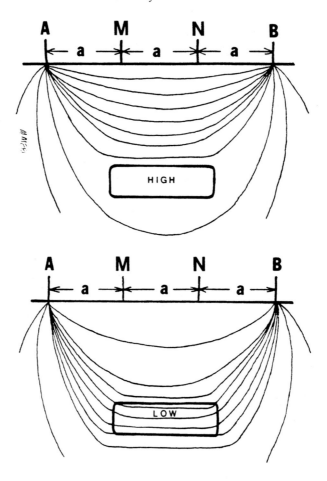

Figure 6.6. A layer of high resistivity will cause an increased resistivity reading at the surface (upper diagram). A layer of low resistivity (lower diagram) will draw current down and result in a lower surface resistivity reading. (Adapted from Loker, 1980.)

current or dissipate it. In addition, known anomalies such as irrigation ditches should be avoided while conducting a survey. Such features should be kept at least 2 "a" away from the electrode spread. These nearby structures will affect the resistivity results because the current spreads sideways in the soil as well as downward. The resistivity measurements will be an average of *all* nearby conditions (Clark, 1970).

There may also be a problem with spurious data caused by chemical reactions between electrodes and the electrolytes in the soil. There are a number of physical and electronic methods to prevent this problem, including the use of insulating electrodes as discussed in the electric self-potential method section. Electrical resistivity traverse lines must avoid metal fences, railroad tracks, power lines, buried cables, etc. No electrode should be closer to any such object than the total distance between the current (outer) electrodes (3 "a"). If the search must be done closer, then the electrodes should be arranged perpendicular to any source of interference.

Despite the limitations, there are a number of advantages to electric resistivity survey search technique. It is relatively inexpensive, easy to do, and based on well-known physical principles. It is certainly cheaper in time, labor and cost than test excavations. A four-electrode resistivity array can be mounted on a vehicle for continuous readings. Such a system uses adjustable, sliding electrodes equipped with salt water jets to cut into the soil and make good electrical contacts (Hesse et al., 1986). Additionally, unless an electrode strikes a piece of evidence, a survey will not damage the subsurface crime scene area.

Electric resistivity surveying, when used systematically, certainly has the potential to locate a grave site that would otherwise be invisible from the surface. It may be an especially powerful tool when used in conjunction with a magnetometer survey. Since the two techniques depend upon different physical properties, they are complimentary and any anomaly detected by both techniques is unlikely to be false. Like a magnetic survey, resistivity survey results can be initially interpreted in the field. The immediate feedback can shorten the time necessary to reach a decision on where to dig.

Another benefit of resistivity survey is that both it and ground-penetrating radar are influenced by soil moisture which affects ground conductivity. Both radar and resistivity survey work best in soils with low conductivity. Therefore, resistivity can be used to test the soil for the applicability of the more expensive and hard to obtain radar apparatus.

ELECTROMAGNETIC SURVEYING

Electromagnetic search methods are based on the principle that electromagnetic waves create electric currents in conductors. These induced currents are themselves the source of new electromagnetic waves which can be detected by suitable instruments. Electromagnetic waves sent into the ground can be a potent probe of the subsurface layers. Electromagnetic instruments can measure the electrical conductivity of the ground from the surface and this parameter can be plotted on a map. They can also be used to pinpoint the location of a small buried conductor such as a piece of metal (Wait, 1982). Metal detectors are a type of electromagnetic instrument specifically designed to detect and locate small metal targets laying near the surface. Electromagnetic profiling (surveying) is used for geological survey, engineering and groundwater studies. In that context, it is particularly useful for locating underground pipes, cables, and hazardous waste. In military application, it is used for detecting mines, other underground objects and caches. In archaeology, it has been used to detect large earth features such as refilled ditches, mounds, and underground chambers (Bevan, 1983). Ubelaker (1984) reported that electromagnetic surveys have been used to define cemetery limits which were detected by slight variations in soil conductivity.

Electromagnetic surveying is another of the active or induction methods of geophysical prospecting. The propagation of electromagnetic waves through the soil depends upon the magnetic permeability of the soil, its electrical conductivity and the dielectric constant of the soil materials. The dielectric constant is the physical property which governs the propagation of electromagnetic waves. It reflects the response of a material to an impressed electrical field (Loker, 1980). Ground conductivity is the ease with which electrical current can flow. The results should parallel electrical resistivity studies, though each technique has its own advantages. Electromagnetic surveys are faster than resistivity because there is no contact between the instrument and the earth. A technician simply walks along the search pattern and notes instrument readings. Surveys can be done in brushy areas or anywhere that the technician is able to walk. It is particularly suitable for areas where the surface soil is dry, hard, rocky, or the vegetation is so dense as to preclude resistivity surveys. An electromagnetic search can be done by one person, not the two or more needed for resistivity equipment. Since there is no contact with the ground except for the searcher's footsteps, there is less damage to the crime scene. Both systems require expertise for the qualitative interpretation of field data.

A generic electromagnetic surveying system is composed of three principal parts. The first is a transmitting coil (Tx) which is energized to produce a powerful electromagnetic field called the primary field (Figure 6.7). These oscillating magnetic waves pass into the ground and induce alternating electric (eddy) currents in conductive materials. These currents are the source of new electromagnetic waves which are sent out from the ground. This secondary field is picked up by the receiver coil (Rx). The secondary field will differ from the primary field in intensity, phase, and direction (Parasnis, 1979). The secondary field combines and interferes with the primary or transmitted field. The resultant field is received and compared to the primary field by the instrument. For these discrimination and comparison tasks, the instrumentation must be more sophisticated than that required for simple resistivity measurements. The ratio of the induced (secondary) field to the primary field is approximately proportional to the conductivity of the ground.

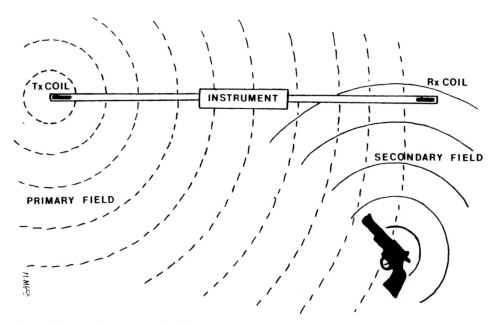

Figure 6.7. An electromagnetic (slingram) survey instrument produces a primary field which enters the ground. There, a secondary field is produced by a conducting object. The instrument then analyzes and measures the resultant field. (Adapted from Bevan, 1983.)

There are a variety of techniques and instruments available for making electromagnetic surveys. They can be divided into two broad categories based on whether the primary field source moves with the receiver or is stationary. In mobile systems, the transmitting coil and receiving (search) coil move together but remain a fixed distance apart. They are carried in line along a survey traverse. This system is used for shallow but rapid reconnaissance work. In the stationary technique, the Tx coil remains fixed within the search area and the Rx coil is moved about. This system is used for lateral profiling or for depth sounding. Instruments may measure various components of the magnetic field (horizontal, vertical, etc.) and many instruments are adjustable for different frequencies and power levels. Higher frequencies create more underground eddy currents and proportionately greater secondary fields. The higher frequencies, however, may stimulate unwanted currents in moderate conductors and thus mask the detection of true targets. The depth of penetration is also a function of frequency. Most commercial models are equipped with at least two frequencies separated by a factor of four, e.g. 400 Hz and 1600 Hz. The general rule is that the greatest depth of search for an electromagnetic instrument is less than half the distance between the transmitting and receiving coils. Therefore, a four-meter separation between the coils should be adequate for searching for a grave two meters deep (Beck, 1981).

The system most applicable to forensic and archaeological work is known as the horizontal loop, loop frame, co-planer loop, or slingram method. It consists of a single instrument which can be carried by one person (Figure 6.8). It contains a long antenna rod with a transmitting coil at one end and a receiving coil at the other. The device is usually carried at a height of one meter above the ground and care must be taken to keep the rod level. This leveling factor makes electromagnetic survey-ing easiest in flat country. If slight hills are encountered, the loop should be kept parallel to the slope of the hill. Under such conditions, sensitiv-ity of the instrument is decreased. Terrain effects are usually minimal, but topographic changes should be recorded to assist data interpretation. The maximum depth of detection is six meters (highest sensitivity is for features in the top one meter of the soil), but, like resistivity, EM surveying averages subsurface conditions. A slingram instrument is best at detecting large, deep earth features and buried metal near the surface.

Electromagnetic surveying measures only apparent, not true conduc-tivity of the ground. Conductivity is commonly reported in units of millimhos per meter. The newer unit name is millisiemens per meter, abbreviated mS/m, which is numerically equivalent to millimhos per meter. Since resistivity is the arithmetic reciprocal of conductivity, milli-siemens per meter can be converted into ohm meters by dividing the millisiemens per meter into 1000. This enables a direct comparison of the results of electromagnetic and resistivity surveying. Higher millisie-mens per meter means the soil beneath the instrument is a better conductor. The instrument provides nearly continuous readings and the data can be entered as a function of location. A single traverse produces a profile graph of subsurface conductivity. An entire grid search of an area pro-

Figure 6.8. A slingram electromagnetic instrument can be carried and operated by one person. Maximum sensitivity is obtained when the device is kept parallel to the ground surface. (Photograph courtesy of GISCO.)

duces an isoconductivity contour map such as that shown in Figure 6.9. Keller and Frischknecht (1966) recommended that measurements be taken at stations separated by approximately one-half the distance between the transmitting and receiving loops. So, using a four-meter bar, reading should be taken every two meters along the traverse line. Measurements can be made closer together when a buried conductor is indicated. For archaeological surveying, Bevan (1983) recommended halting for a measurement every meter. The readings are recorded on a map at the midpoint of the instrument, i.e. where the operator is standing. Bevan reported that this procedure was adequate to detect anomalies at least one to two meters wide in one dimension. He noted that instruments are available that can detect larger and deeper anomalies and still other systems that can find smaller and shallower targets. As a general rule, targets can be detected to a maximum depth equal to their largest dimension. Bevan reported that he was able to obtain an average of a thousand measurements per day.

There are certain limitations to the use of electromagnetic surveying. At low ground conductivity levels, it is difficult for all but a very powerful device to magnetically induce an underground current. At

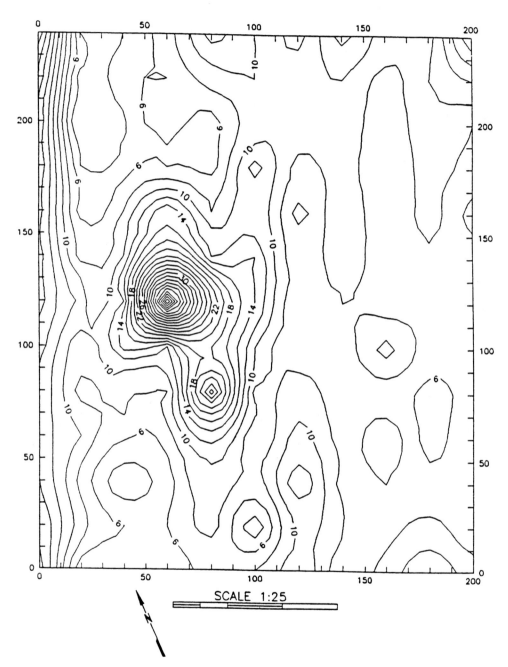

Figure 6.9. The end product of an electromagnetic survey is a contour map which reveals electromagnetic anomalies beneath the surface. (Map courtesy of G. Clark Davenport.)

high terrain conductivity levels, the secondary field is no longer proportional to the ground conductivity, so the instrument is less reliable. Thirdly, electromagnetic instruments are severely affected by cultural and natural features of a conducting nature. Electrical storms, for instance, even at a distance, can produce spurious readings and mask subsurface anomalies (Davenport et al., 1986). The devices are so affected by metal that they should not be used within 10 meters of a fence and cannot be used in the vicinity of pipes, power lines, etc. This limits their use in urban areas because of the many possible sources of interference.

Electromagnetic surveying methods can be used in wooded areas so long as the four-meter bar can be maneuvered and kept in line. The instruments can make errors of approximately 5 percent, depending upon elevation. Conductivity readings tend to go up if the operator is in a depression and down if the operator is on a hilltop. A large amount of rock in the soil may decrease conductivity readings, whereas organic matter raises them. Bevan (1983) suggested that an instrument sensitive to between 0.5 to 500 millisiemens per meter is adequate for terrain conditions where there is no metal or other interference. The great advantage in using electromagnetic surveying is that the appropriate equipment simultaneously detects metal objects and measures apparent soil conductivity/resistivity.

METAL DETECTORS

Metal detectors are electromagnetic devices that will detect conductive metals and some minerals whenever these substances come within the instrument's search area. They work on the same principle as electromagnetic surveying equipment. The basic instrument consists of an adjustable stem holding, at one end, an antenna with transmitting and receiving coils and, at the other end, a console or control box. In operation, a small current is sent to the transmitter coil (winding). The winding generates an electromagnetic field which is transmitted into the air and ground in the immediate vicinity of the search head. The field enters the conducting objects and creates tiny circulating eddy currents. The power for the eddy currents comes from the electromagnetic field. The resulting power loss, used up in the generation of the eddy currents, is sensed by the detector. Additionally, eddy currents generate a second electromagnetic field, a portion of which returns to the instrument and strikes the search coil. The strength of the secondary field is dependent upon the conduc-

tion ability of the object detected (Garrett, 1985). The secondary field
and or power loss are measured by the instrument and displayed on a
meter or as an audio signal. Modern metal detectors are sensitive,
lightweight, reliable, and are able to detect targets several feet into the
ground (Figure 6.10). The principles used in ground-searching detectors
are the same as those used in weapon detectors. Both security metal
detectors and ground search units have gone through an evolution of
techniques and instrumentation (Wallach & Ricci, 1977).

Figure 6.10. Modern discriminating metal detectors are sensitive, lightweight and reliable.
(Photograph courtesy of G. Clark Davenport.)

Metal Detector Types

Pulsed induction (PI) metal detectors send a one-half millisecond
electromagnetic pulse into the ground. During the transmission, the
receiving coil is off. The eddy currents induced in a conductive object
persist even after the transmission stops. The rate of decay of the induced
magnetic field is sensed by the receiver. PI detectors are suitable for all
metals and all terrain. They may also be used underwater, including salt
water. They have good depth penetration but are not accurate at pin-

pointing small target locations. They also suffer from high power consumption. PI detectors are light in weight and have a sensitivity approximately equal to that of very low frequency (VLF) detectors. They are not able to distinguish between metals and mineral deposits. They are super sensitive to iron and its derivatives which make them popular for security purposes. PI detectors are principally used in underwater operations.

The oldest style metal detectors still in common use are beat frequency oscillators (BFO). They have been the "workhorse" of the metal detector field for a long time, only recently being replaced in popularity by the VLF detectors. BFO detectors are suitable for general use under virtually all conditions. They are now primarily used for mineral prospecting rather than metal detection. The BFO detector contains two frequency oscillators. One is in the control box set at a fixed reference frequency which is crystal controlled and cannot change. The other oscillator is located in the search head. It changes frequency in response to the secondary electromagnetic field. When the detector is passed over metal, the variable oscillator increases its frequency, raising an audible tone (Fischer, 1980). The BFO detector is low cost and simple to use. Because it operates on a high frequency, however, it can only penetrate to a limited depth. An advantage of the BFO detector is that it can discriminate between metal objects and mineral deposits. It is not as sensitive to iron as other detectors, so it is the tool of choice when the search area contains ferrous litter which would distract the more sensitive VLF detectors. Some experts recommend that both a BFO and a VLF detector be available for a search. Field conditions then dictate which detector should be used (Garrett, 1985).

Transmitter-receiver (TR), also called induction balance (IB) detectors, are the rarest detectors in use. The search head of the instrument contains both transmitting and receiving coils. The coils are physically arranged and powered so that a balance is set up between them (Figure 6.11). When there is no metal present, the fields remain in balance. When a metal object is near, however, power is used up by the secondary field, causing an imbalance which is detected and reported by the instrument. TR detectors are sensitive to small objects and have good depth penetration. They excel at pinpointing small objects and have great sensitivity to non-ferrous metals. Different coil patterns are available so that they can be used in a wide scan or pinpoint mode. The drawback to the conventional TR detectors is that they are ineffective over mineralized ground, being unable to discriminate between minerals and metals. The most common use for TR detectors is coin hunting. The devices work best over flat ground and erratic results may occur if the search head is moved in a jerky fashion. They cannot be used in water or other wet conditions (Lagal, 1982).

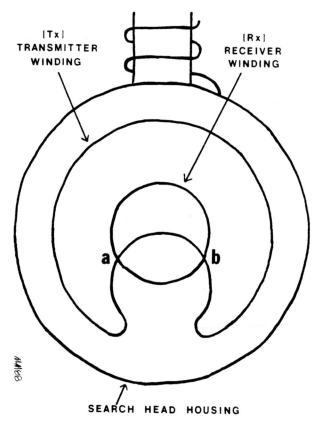

Figure 6.11. Transmitter-receiver (TR) detectors are designed so that the Tx and Rx windings are in balance at points (a) and (b). A target coming into range upsets the electronic balance which is sensed and reported by the instrument. (Adapted from Garrett, 1985.)

Very low frequency (VLF) detectors are a type of TR detectors. They are nearly identical in operating principle except for two things. First, they operate at a very low frequency which gives them greater penetration. They also have additional circuitry which enables them to discriminate between metals and minerals, eliminating soil mineral noise. This gives them increased sensitivity to metal objects. They are currently the most popular metal detector. VLF–TR detectors are sold under a variety of trade names. They can be identified by their ability to "zero out" the effect of mineralized soils or rocks. VLF detectors may be too sensitive to ferrous objects, making it impossible to search an area littered with trash. Because they operate at low frequency, they may be affected by power lines, electric lights, or other forms of electrical interference. They are more complex, so more time and practice is needed to master the instruments. The operator must learn to tune the instrument to enhance the target signals while lessening noise. Discrimination circuitry can theoretically be added to any detector type but has reached its maximum development when applied to TR-type detectors. VLF–TR discriminating detectors are factory calibrated for universal application to metal and mineral prospecting. The ground-cancelling adjustment is necessary because iron minerals are common in soils of many search areas (Garrett et al., 1980).

Next to the type of instrument chosen, the major variable in search capabilities is the search head of the instrument. Most good modern detectors have interchangeable search heads. Search head sizes vary from a ³⁄₄-inch probe to 24-inch "deep seekers." In general, large heads can penetrate deeper but are only able to locate big pieces of metal. They eliminate signals from small items, treating them as noise. The smaller search heads are better for detecting small objects at shallow depths. In forensic situations, Garrett (1985) recommended a 7- to 8-inch search head, which is adequate for locating coins and jewelry. This is the size most commonly provided on sophisticated detectors.

Search heads may have their transmitter and receiver windings in a co-planer or co-axial configuration. The co-planer configuration is shown in Figure 6.11. The co-planer design is thinner, lighter, and the most common. In a co-axial loop arrangement, the windings are stacked on top of each other, resulting in a thicker and heavier search head. They are less sensitive to electrical interference than co-planer configurations. Regardless of the search head type, the coils should be held level, parallel to the ground and moved slowly and methodically during the search operation.

All search heads have a target center which is the most sensitive area. It should be identified and marked before search efforts begin. In co-axial loops, it lies in the dead center of the search head. In co-planer loop arrangements, it lies in the forward center of the search head in the area called the toe. The location of the target center is important because it is used to pinpoint the underground location of small objects. Garrett (1985) contained directions for locating the target center of a search head.

The obvious advantage to metal detectors is that they can seek out tiny metal objects through soil, concrete, asphalt, plaster, foliage, and water. They can be used to locate hidden metal even if it's is behind walls or under pavement or stone. They can detect iron, brass, copper, nickel, aluminum, steel, tin, lead, gold, silver, and bronze. They can detect metal fragments as small as .05 centimeters square in size and can also detect air cavities within compact soil. In testing it was found that the devices could find a single coin at the following depths: BFO detector— 10–20 centimeters; TR/IB and PI detectors—20–30 centimeters; and VLF detectors—30–40 centimeters (Fischer, 1980).

Metal detectors have limitations, as do all geophysical prospecting instruments. In trying to locate a body, the victim must be associated with metal. Dental fillings, metal buttons, and jewelry are large enough to be found, presuming they are within the detection range of the instrument. The second limitation is that metal detectors have a limited depth range. Fischer (1980) found that, in archaeological situations, the device was adequate for surface finds and depths to 10 centimeters so long as the metal objects were not very corroded. The depth to which an object can be detected depends upon the strength of the electromagnetic field, the target size, and the surface area of the target. In theory, an electromagnetic field is emitted from the search head and goes to infinity. In practice, the strength of the fields drop quickly so that it has several thousand times less detection capability at six feet than it did at one foot.

Target size is an obvious consideration, in that larger targets are easier to find and can be detected deeper in the ground. Target size, however, pertains principally to surface area, not mass or volume. The detector senses the surface area where the eddy currents are set up. For example, a coin oriented on its edge may not be detected until it is four inches from the search head. If it is lying face up, it may be detected at eight inches.

The detection area for an instrument is strongest in a cone-shaped area directly under the search head (Figure 6.12). Surrounding that is a fringe area in which objects may be detected, but the signal is so weak that it may be overlooked by the operator. Garrett (1985) said that detecting weak signals from the fringe area is the main reason for using earphones which enable the operator to hear more subtle audio signals. The ability to recognize signals from the fringe area improves with

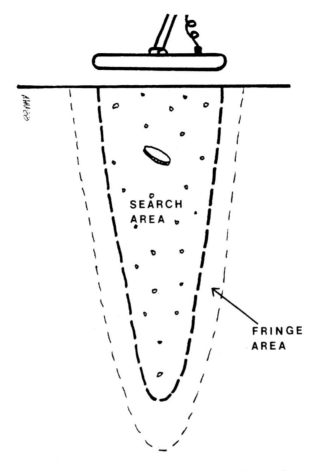

SEARCH
AREA

FRINGE
AREA

Figure 6.12. The primary search area of a metal detector is an inverted cone directly beneath the search head. Weak signals may also be received from the adjacent fringe area, but they may not be detected by the instrument operator. (Adapted from Garrett, 1985.)

practice and experience. Under most favorable conditions, a single coin might be detected at a maximum depth of two feet (Garrett, 1985). For forensic archaeology purposes, Morse (1983) recommended that a metal detector should be able to detect a .22-caliber bullet at least two inches deep. Morse felt that metal detectors should be used as an aid to excavation rather than as a means for locating a buried body. The advantage of using a metal detector before digging is that evidence can be located in situ. This provides accurate position mapping rather than waiting for the evidence to be found during the dirt screening process. He therefore recommended that a metal detector be used before digging and then repeatedly at every 2–4 inches of excavation.

Another drawback of metal detectors is that all metals located need to be excavated. The device is not specific to a possible buried body, as opposed to a methane vapor detector which should only give a signal over decomposing remains (McLaughlin, 1974). Metal detectors exhibit variable performance depending upon the earth's magnetic field, humidity, soil density, and soil consistency. They work best in areas with dry, compact soils and small amounts of metal litter (Fischer, 1980). The metal detector cannot be used to find a metal object concealed behind or within other metal, and a small target may be swamped by a nearby larger metal object. This limits the usefulness of metal detector searches near underground pipes, light poles, or any other metal objects which penetrate into the ground. In such cases, the detector should be used in a search pattern that runs parallel to the pre-existing metal structure. Metal detectors may also be disrupted by magnetite (black magnetic sand) which gives the strongest signal of all naturally occurring minerals. Despite attempts to increase the discrimination ability of instruments, they can still only indicate probabilities. The ultimate answer, to whether a detected object is the target sought or noise, is to dig it up.

Over the years there has been no appreciable increase in the depth range of metal detectors. The improvements have been a reduction in size, weight, and current drain of instruments. There has also been increased sensitivity resulting from better signal-to-noise discrimination. The problem remains that for any object to be detected, it must be within the three-dimensional search area of the device. The ground over which a metal detector scans is referred to as the search matrix. The soil penetrated by the electromagnetic field is said to be illuminated by the instrument. A metal detector's response, at any given moment, is caused by all the objects within the illuminated region. The response will be weighted toward objects that are more highly conductive, such as aluminum, or have a larger surface area.

Garrett et al. (1980) and Garrett (1985) contained recommendations for conducting searches using a metal detector. Garrett suggested that grid lines be established, approximately 3 to 6 feet apart. The search is then conducted in accordance with the grid search pattern, with traverses being run first one way and then in a perpendicular direction. This maximizes the chance of finding an object, since a different orientation to the search head may enhance the object's detectability. He next suggested that the metal detector (VLF/TR type) be set to the VLF mode and adjusted to the surrounding ground level of mineralization. The hunt then begins with the searcher scanning a wide path in front of him as he walks forward. It is recommended that the searcher walk ahead and move the search head back and forth in a straight line in front of himself, not in swinging arcs to the side (Figure 6.13). The search head scan lines should overlap one-third to one-half to minimize the underground area that is not covered by the detection field of the instrument (Figure 6.14).

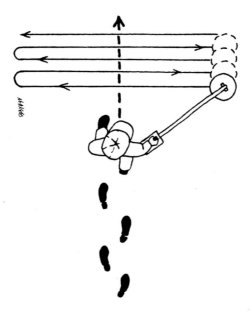

Figure 6.13. The metal detector search head should be swept back and forth in front of the searcher. Each straight line sweep should overlap the previous sweep so that the search area is uniformly illuminated by the instrument. (Adapted from Garrett, 1985.)

If the instrument gives any indication of metal, it should be positioned over the target to see if the increased response level continues. The signal could indeed be a target, an instrument malfunction, or an operator error. If the signal remains, then the instrument should be backed to the pre-target area to see if the signal decreases to the previous level. During this procedure the tuning of the device should not be altered. If the signal does decrease, then the spot should be marked and the search continued. Once the search head goes past the target area, the signal level should either drop down again or get stronger if the center of the target is still being approached. If the operator is convinced a target has been located, then the device should be switched into the TR discrimination mode to see if the object is predominantly an iron (ferrous) or

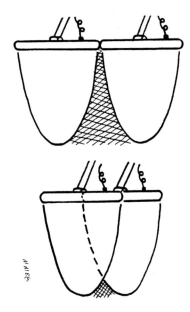

Figure 6.14. Since the search area beneath a metal detector is cone shaped, some of the ground is not thoroughly scanned (crosshatched area). Overlapping sweep lines (lower diagram) will minimize the area that is missed. (Adapted from Garrett, 1985.)

non-ferrous material. If the instrument still indicates a target of interest, the digging may begin or the target may simply be marked and the search continued.

Garrett recommended that the search head should be suspended one to two inches above the surface of dry soil. Over a stream or water, it should be held four inches to a foot high. If the device is equipped with a submersible search head, it can be held directly in the water. The operating height of a metal detector is determined by the amount of mineralization present in the soil. A greater search head standoff will minimize interference from small objects.

Authors uniformly recommend VLF/TR metal detectors as most suitable for archaeological and forensic use. Fischer (1980), after testing all four types in the field, found that the VLF was the best choice. It gave faster indications of targets, greater sensitivity to small objects, more precise fixes on the targets, had lower power consumption, and was able to discriminate metal types. Its only drawback was greater complexity than other detector types, requiring more training and practice to achieve operator proficiency. Garrett concurred with Fischer's recommendation but went further to present the various advantages and applications of different search head types and sizes. Garrett (1985) also devoted an entire chapter in his book to law enforcement applications for metal detectors. He also discussed the desirable and undesirable characteristics of various detector designs as they apply to instrument selection. His comments and recommendations covered such things as instrument balance, detection depth, sensitivity, variation or drift, scanning width, etc.

SEISMIC METHODS

Seismology began as the science of earthquakes but now includes various types of earth movement. The field is often divided into natural seismology which remains concerned with earthquakes, volcanos and other natural occurrences and explosion seismology which studies man-made shocks, including seismic prospecting. Seismic prospecting is used in a variety of ways, including mining, civil and soil engineering. It is broken down into two related but different prospecting methods: reflection and refraction. Seismic reflection prospecting is the most common geophysical technique is use today, widely used for petroleum exploration. Most of the literature on seismic prospecting concerns reflection methods. Seismic refraction was important in earlier oil exploration efforts but is now principally used for geological reconnaissance and engineering site investigations, particularly in determining the distances through overburden to bedrock. The basic procedure in seismic surveying is to generate seismic waves at the surface and then record the resulting waves which return to the surface through different paths. Analysis of the wave travel times assists in the identification of subsurface features.

The first step in a seismic survey is to introduce an impact to the earth (Figure 6.15). This shock may be from an explosive, a mechanical vibrator, a compressed gas or weight-dropping "thumper" or a captive chamber gas explosion. For small area searches, sufficient shock can be initiated by striking a metal plate on the ground with a sledge hammer.

The return shock waves are detected and recorded by a geophone, also called a seismometer. The geophone is in direct contact with the earth, usually spiked into the soil. Its function is to convert the motion of the earth into electrical signals. At the moment the shock is delivered to the earth, timers begin. As the "first arrival" shock wave reaches each geophone, a timer is stopped. The geophone senses all of the earth waves, but only the first one is customarily recorded in refraction prospecting. Depending

Figure 6.15. During a seismic survey, a shock is introduced into the ground (background) and the return shock waves are detected by geophones and recorded (foreground). (Photograph courtesy of GISCO.)

upon the type of soil and background noise, geophones can detect the small shock waves from a person of average weight walking at a distance of 30–50 yards. This capability is the basis of seismic intrusion detection systems (Murray & Tedrow, 1975).

Both reflection and refraction seismic methods depend upon elastic wave theory. Earth shocks are elastic waves because they cause deformation of the material through which they pass. An elastic solid is capable of recovering its original shape after a deformation. The stress supplied by a shock wave causes a temporary deformation known as a strain. When the stress is removed, the material returns to its previous unstrained position. Seismic waves pass through the ground according to this principle and their speed depends upon the elastic properties of the soil materials.

There are two types of waves that travel through elastic solids: compression waves (p-waves) and shear waves (s-waves). Both are defined by their effect on the particles of material as they move through a solid. P-waves cause particles to move in the same direction as the wave's propagation. S-waves cause particles to move perpendicular to the direction of wave propagation. The motions of p-waves cause particles to move alternately closer together (condensation) and then farther apart (rarefaction) during each wave passage (Figure 6.16).

Seismic waves can be pictured in motion as concentric spheres radiat-

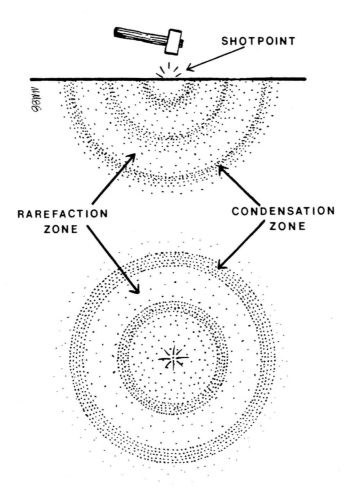

Figure 6.16. Alternating high and low pressure shock waves radiate out from the shock point. Waves of high pressure are known as condensation or compression zones and low pressure waves are called rarefaction or dilation zones. (Adapted from Dobrin, 1976.)

ing out from the shock point. Away from the shock point, the wave becomes sufficiently large that it can be mathematically treated as a flat plane known as the wave front. This simplifies the geometry involved in subsequent calculations. One could draw an imaginary line between any particular point on an advancing wave front back to the shock point. This "ray" would be perpendicular to the movement of the wave front. The ray describes the path and the direction of the wave travel. Each ray can be considered parallel to the others. As the wave front strikes the boundary between two materials, a portion of the energy is reflected away and a portion of it is transmitted into the new material but at a slightly changed trajectory known as refraction. The proportion of the wave that is reflected or refracted depends upon the density contrast between the two layers (Figure 6.17). It also depends upon the angle of incidence of the energy striking the interface. The energy reflected back from the interface is detected at the surface by geophones. Seismic reflection prospecting attempts to record and interpret as many of these reflected waves as possible, thus mapping below-ground structures. The refracted shock waves continue down, striking more layers and at each layer the reflection/refraction phenomena is repeated.

Reflection prospecting records the return pulses from *many* layers, whereas refraction surveying records refracted energy to determine the depth of a *particular* layer. Reflection prospecting gives more information on deep subsurface features, but the interpretation of data is complex because there are so many signals which must be examined. Refraction is used for shallow prospecting and the data treatment is simpler because there are fewer signals of interest. Shallow refraction seismic exploration has been used in archaeology, but most technical information and current developments in seismic work are from the geo-exploration field.

The basic seismic exploration system has only three functional components. The first is the source of the wave or the shock point apparatus. The second component of the system is the array of surface receivers, the geophones, which detect the shock waves. The third component is the instrumentation which amplifies and records the signals from the geophones (Figure 6.18a). The geophone signals are generally recorded in chart form.

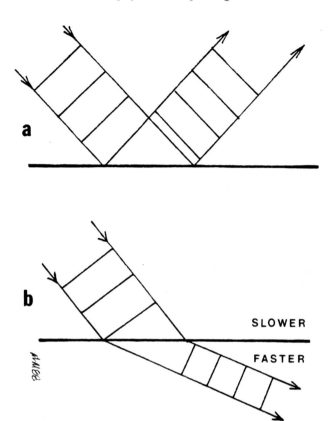

Figure 6.17. When a shock wave front strikes the interface between layers of different densities, part of the seismic energy is reflected (a) and part of it is refracted (b). (Adapted from Dobrin, 1976 and Loker, 1980.)

SEISMIC REFRACTION TECHNIQUE

From basic physics, we know that the angle of shock incidence equals the angle of reflection. In seismic work this is known as the "normal angle." If an advancing shock wave passes from a faster to a slower medium, the angle of refraction is toward the normal angle. If the wave passes from a slower to faster medium, the angle of refraction is away from normal. Eventually, depending upon the contrast between layers, the angle of incidence of energy reaches the "critical angle." At that point, the wave doesn't penetrate but is carried (refracted) along the interface. As it travels the boundary, it creates motion in the particles on its path. Each particle disturbance becomes the center of new waves

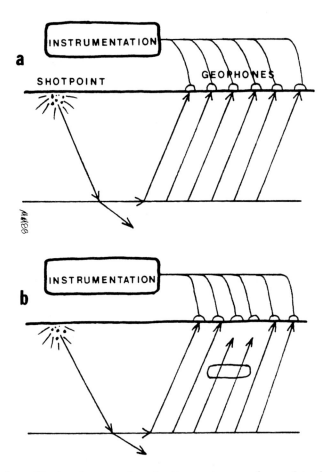

Figure 6.18. A profile-shooting seismic refraction system can be used to detect subsurface anomalies. In homogenous conditions (a), refracted return waves will be separated in time only by the distance of the geophone from the shot point. The disturbed soil of a grave will retard the speed of the return waves, making it detectable as an anomaly (b). (Adapted from Sharma, 1976.)

which travel up to the surface where they can be recorded by geophones. This is the basis of the seismic refraction method.

The normal earth situation is for the slower soil materials to lie in a bed above the faster materials. This is related to the normal compaction of earth materials with time and depth. If there were a transposition so that a slower layer were beneath a faster, the refracted shock waves would go down and be lost. In such an unusual situation, refraction surveying could not be used. Refraction technique is most successful over a known shallow interface between the topsoil and compacted under bed. If the soil is deep and relatively homogeneous in density, anomalies are not likely to be detected. Before seismic survey techniques are considered, the underground structure in the area should be examined, either by drilling or by referring to local geological maps.

Under ideal circumstances, a grave should be detected as a low-speed anomaly. Loose, dry soil has a wave velocity between 800 to 1700 feet per second, whereas compacted soil has an average velocity of 2300 to 2500 feet per second. Water is even faster at 4600 to 5000 feet per second, so the higher water content of a grave site may partially mask its seismic signature (Sharma, 1976).

The spacing and pattern of geophone arrangement depends upon the type of feature sought. The distance between geophones should be less than the size of the target. Again, a spacing of one meter is a good starting spread. The distance between the shock point and the geophones also varies with test conditions. Four different types of geophone arrangements are shown in Figure 6.19. Profile shooting is the arrangement best suited to archaeological and forensic use. The shot points are at each end of a linear geophone spread. Normally, 12 or 24 geophones are used, all recorded simultaneously by the instrument. One advantage of profile shooting is that the data results are easier to interpret. The geophone signals are recorded end to end to provide a profile of the material through which the shock wave passes. Generally, shock waves have arrival times ranging from only .01 to .1 seconds (10 to 100 milliseconds), so the timing accuracy is the most critical component of the system. When mapping the subsurface profile, the first arrival times are plotted against the distance to the geophones from the shock point (Figure 6.20). If the subsurface conditions are homogeneous, the arrival times should appear as a straight line. A buried anomaly may either speed up or slow down the wave propagation and should be detected by waves that arrive either earlier or later than the adjacent waves. Since digging and refilling makes the soil less compact, graves should appear as slow-velocity anomalies (Figure 6.18b).

The main limitation to seismic prospecting is the likelihood that a grave will not be sufficiently different from the surrounding soil to be detected. Seismic refraction is intended for highlighting large geologic features, not man-made alterations to the topsoil. In trying to apply seismic refraction to archaeological prospecting, Loker (1980) found the techniques were time consuming and the results ambiguous. Interpretation was too subjective and difficult because anomalies only showed

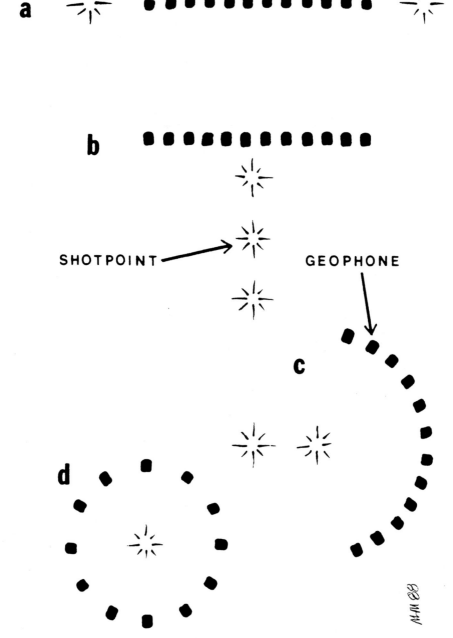

Figure 6.19. The geometric arrangement and spacing of geophones in seismic refraction surveys vary with test conditions. Four common patterns are profile shooting (a), broadside shooting (b), fan shooting (c), and circle shooting (d).

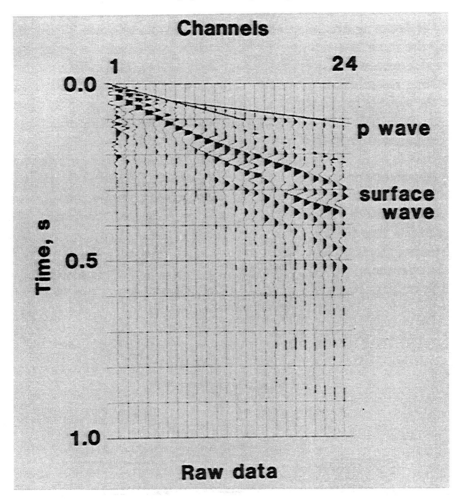

Figure 6.20. During a seismic survey, shock wave arrival times are plotted against distance from the shock point to the geophones. In this case, twenty-four geophones equally spaced in a line have been used. (Chart courtesy of G. Clark Davenport.)

millisecond variances in first arrival times. Many conditions could cause such tiny variances. His review of other seismic survey work in archaeology found only modest successes. His conclusion was that seismic refraction resolution is insufficient to detect near-surface man-made features.

GROUND–PENETRATING RADAR

Ground-penetrating radar (GPR) is also known as subsurface interface radar (SIR). It is perhaps the newest of the geophysical prospecting techniques. It was first developed during the 1960s by the military as a way of detecting non-metallic buried mines and explosives (Cook, 1974). Impulse radar that can provide continuous profiles of subsurface conditions have been available since about 1970 (Morey, 1974). This system has a strong resemblance to shallow reflection seismic systems and is based on the same principles as atmospheric radar to be discussed in Chapter 7. In both cases a pulse is transmitted and the echo of that pulse is received as it reflects off objects in its path (Figure 6.21). The end product is a graphic record of subsurface features. The instrumentation of the system correlates the composition and configuration of subsurface materials and the behavior of the radar waves introduced into the earth. The principal difference between earth-probing radar and other radar systems is that GPR is designed to probe and explore opaque solids instead of the transparent atmosphere.

In operation, the radar apparatus is moved over the ground, all the while emitting repetitive, short-duration electromagnetic pulses into the

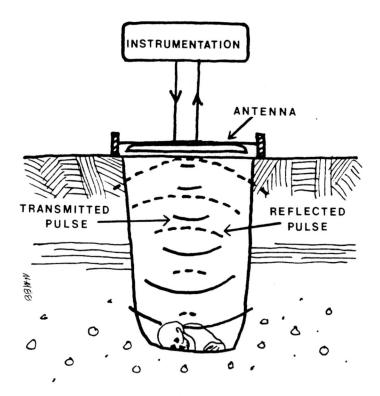

Figure 6.21. Ground-penetrating radar (GPR) operates on the same principle as airborne radar systems. An electromagnetic pulse enters the earth and a portion of that energy bounces back from underground targets.

earth. The pulses from the transmitting antenna travel at speeds proportional to the characteristics of the material through which it passes. When the material changes, the pulse speed changes and some of the energy is reflected back to the receiving antenna. The travel time of the reflected pulse is proportional to the depth of the interface. Materials vary in their ability to propagate very high frequency waves. To some degree, all materials slow down or absorb radio waves (signal attenuation).

The ability of the earth to propagate radio waves depends upon several factors, including soil conductivity, water content, soil density and porosity, temperature, the physical structure of the soil, the frequency of the electromagnetic wave, and the amount of salt in the ground solution. The most important factor is the electrical conductivity of the soil which determines the speed of wave propagation and the depth of penetration.

The speed of wave travel is a terrain property expressed as the material's relative dielectric constant (Fischer et al., 1980). The dielectric constant is expressed in electrostatic units (ESU). Radio waves travel fastest in air which has a dielectric constant of one and slowest in sea water which has a dielectric constant of 81. All earth materials lie somewhere in between. Most hard rock has a dielectric constant of 6–16 ESU, dry soils 10–15 ESU, saturated soils 20–30 ESU, and wet clays 40–50 ESU (Morey, 1974; Loker, 1980). The transparency of the soil to radar regulates its useful probing distance. For instance, dry sands are very transparent, fresh water wet sands have medium transparency, and salt water wet sands are the least transparent. The typical usable depth penetration of a radar system, operating at 200 mHz (millions of cycles per second), is one to four meters (Vickers et al., 1977). Morey (1974) estimated that in wet sand, radar could penetrate 75 feet but only 5 feet in wet clay and less than one foot in seawater. The limited penetration ability of radar is not a handicap to most forensic applications.

The resolution ability of GPR makes it a powerful tool. Active radar interrogation of the subsurface can detect a one-inch diameter plastic pipe, buried horizontally, under 2.5 feet of soil. It can identify the depth of that object to within four or five inches and locate its horizontal location with the same degree of accuracy. Its detection ability is even better with metal objects. Radar can detect larger plastic objects, metal pipes or electrical conduits at depths to 10 feet. It can also locate air voids beneath the surface and disturbed soils, such as areas that have been excavated and refilled (Moffatt, 1974). It has even been used to map the contents of subterranean chambers (Marbach, 1987). GPR can penetrate asphalt pavement, flooring, concrete, soil layers, fresh water, ice, and stone slabs.

Radar penetration can be reduced by layers with high dielectric constants such as clay, silt, or salt water. GPR can be defeated by sheet metal or metal reinforcing mesh with grid size smaller than 4 inches. The general rule is that near-surface materials with resistivities of 30 ohm meters or less (good conductors) will attenuate radar pulses so much that underlying layers cannot be illuminated (Davenport et al. 1986). This is the reason that pretesting should be done to determine if ground conditions are suitable for radar.

Other factors govern the ability of radar to detect a target, such as the shape of the target and its orientation with respect to the antenna. The radar signal can be altered to help resolve an underground anomaly. Changes can be made in the pulse time, frequency, antenna orientation, and polarization of the radar signal. Normally, a radar pulse has a duration of only a few nanoseconds (billionths of a second). Earth-penetrating radars usually operate at frequencies from 5 mHz to 5,000 mHz. The corresponding radar wavelengths are from 40 meters to 2 centimeters (Cook, 1974). The resolution ability of a system is roughly equal to a sphere with a diameter of one-half the wave length. There must be a balance between depth of penetration and resolution ability. High frequency means shallow penetration but high resolution ability. Of the antenna systems available, the most common range is between 80 and 900 mHz (Davenport et al., 1986). A 400-mHz antenna used by Fischer et al. (1980) gave adequate penetration of one to two meters, which should be enough for forensic work.

Virtually any man-made change in the ground will change the physical parameters of density and water content so that they can be detected by radar. As the radar instrument passes over an area disturbed by excavation, anomalous reflections will be recorded on the strip chart. Normally, the transducer cart is pulled along traverse lines at a slow walking pace (Figure 6.22). For rapid reconnaissance, the antenna could be mounted on a vehicle and moved at up to five miles per hour. For a detailed search, it should be moved at one mile per hour or less. Flat ground is the most suitable for radar, since the antenna works best if it is flush with the surface. The radar cart is usually equipped with wheels or runners, but it is not very maneuverable. In rough terrain, two people could carry the instrument, so long as they can maintain a constant elevation above the ground's surface.

Figure 6.22. Commonly, the radar system is housed on a cart or sled so that it can be pulled over the ground. Radar works best over flat terrain where the antenna can be kept flush with the surface. (Photograph courtesy of GISCO.)

Prior to the initiation of a radar search, a soil sample from a depth of at least one foot should be taken from the search area. This soil sample should be wrapped in a watertight container and tested by a soil laboratory for electrical properties. The results will determine whether the site is conducive to a radar search. As a second confirmation step, Vickers et al. (1977) recommended that an electric resistivity survey be conducted in the search area. This is intended to confirm the soil laboratory results and predict the usefulness and performance of radar. The results of both tests will also help in choosing the best radar frequency to use.

In setting up traverse lines for radar, there is a trade-off between the probability of detecting a target and the rate at which ground can be covered. Fischer et al. (1980) recommended a two-meter spacing between traverse lines in an archaeological context. He felt that that spread gave complete coverage to a depth of two meters so that even minor metal artifacts would be detected. A more thorough search would require a tighter spacing, perhaps one meter between search lines. The next step is to prepare search lines. It may be necessary to clear brush or other obstructions so that the antenna is as close to the surface as possible. The necessity for a smooth ground surface may limit the practical applications of ground-penetrating radar to pavement, lawns or areas leveled by heavy machinery. The search area should be mapped for trees, boulders, or other features which may influence or hinder the completion of the search pattern.

Normally, antenna frequencies are tested before the search gets underway. The frequency is selected for optimum performance based upon the soil type, resolution needed (target expected), and the depth of penetration required. The interpretation of data is more site specific with ground-penetrating radar than with other geophysical techniques. Test runs should be conducted and results compared with the known geologic features of the area to be sure that the radar system is accurate under local conditions. Often, test pits or other experiments must be conducted to obtain depth calibrations, sample anomaly signatures, etc.

The use of ground-penetrating radar allows for completely non-destructive data collection. The results are printed in real time so the graphic representation of subsurface features is available to searchers in the field (Figure 6.23). As with most other geophysical tools, the continuous strip charts can be digitized and enhanced by computer. The profiles will record and display differences in horizontal and vertical dimensions, but these results must be correlated to surface location and keyed to the search pattern used. Fischer et al. (1980) suggested that anomalies detected be marked directly on the ground as soon as they are discovered. In the field, gross anomalies can be seen on the charts without going back and having to match digitized data with the grid system. "It will never be easier to find the spot (of the anomaly) than it is when you have just passed it" (Fischer et al., 1980:51). This will speed up the search because there is no need to wait for the production of contour maps. Some other geophysical prospecting instruments, such as magnetometers, can also be equipped to produce continuous strip charts, but the additional instrumentation is often bulky and heavy or requires special handling.

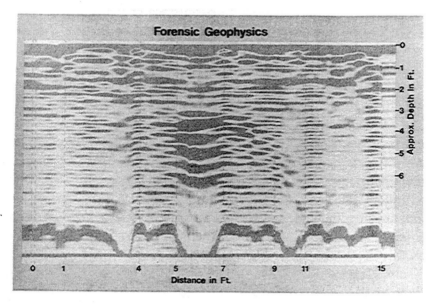

Figure 6.23. The ground-penetrating radar instrument can print out the results in the form of a strip chart which is immediately available to searchers. (Chart courtesy of G. Clark Davenport.)

Ground-penetrating radar systems can provide detailed location information and rapid coverage of large search areas. Loker's (1980) field results pointed out the clear division of labor between the physically related seismic refraction and radar profiling. Seismic refraction showed gross features at depth and radar profiling showed fine shallow features. The radar unit moves slowly over the ground, yet rapidly sends and receives pulses, so it has "the finest resolution of any current geophysical prospecting technique" (Loker 1980:52). Loker reviewed four archaeological site reports where radar was used, both in the United States and Central America. He found that radar was most useful in favorable conditions of an arid area with sandy soils. Vaughn (1986) verified that radar could distinguish bone from surrounding peat and soil in 400- to 500-year-old grave sites in Red Bay, Labrador. He found that ground-penetrating radar, though expensive, was easy to use, fast, non-intrusive and non-destructive and could even be used over frozen or snow-covered ground.

CONCLUSION/RECOMMENDATIONS

A principal advantage of all geophysical prospecting techniques is that they are non-destructive to the subsurface crime scene. This they share with non-intrusive foot search methods, remote sensing, and aerial photography. Geophysical prospecting methods can be used as the principal means of search or as a way of refining and corroborating the results of other non-destructive searches. Geophysical methods have long been used to obtain confirmation of archaeological features detected on aerial photographs.

The advantage of gravity surveying is that it requires minimal manpower, only one technician in the field and another to do the interpretation. Modern gravimeters are very sensitive and accurate and they are not depth limited. The drawback is that they are slow to use and the error in instrument setup may be larger than the anomaly produced by a grave site. They give no field indications of anomalies and would have to be located directly over a grave on a very small search grid to make detection likely. Gravity surveying is not likely to be the most successful technique to use.

Magnetic surveying requires a high sensitivity to detect the subtle changes in the earth's magnetic field. Though available instruments are sensitive to one-tenth of a gamma, the disturbance from a typical unconsolidated grave site is tiny. Unless the grave contained a substantial quantity of metal, insufficient contrast might exist for detection. Magnetic surveys are also affected by external conditions and can only be used when atmospheric conditions are stable.

Self-potential surveying measures the background voltages naturally occurring in the soil. There is no information available about the amount of electrical variation caused by a single grave. Self-potential is the techniques of choice only for measuring the underground movement of water, such as detecting leaks in dams. A grave site is unlikely to produce an anomaly sufficient to be detected with currently available instrumentation.

Electrical resistivity surveying may well detect a burial. A recent grave is an area of uncompacted loose soil which would be more resistant to electrical current travel than the surrounding ground. Resistivity surveys have found underground walls, wells, and other shallow anomalies. With current instrumentation, resistivity studies can be done concurrently with self-potential measurements.

Electromagnetic surveying senses change in ground conductance. It may detect small anomalies such as areas of high soil compaction. In all cases, however, there may be alternate causes for an anomaly besides a grave. Electromagnetic surveying can be confounded by nearby electrical interference which limits its usefulness in cities.

Metal detectors can be used to locate ferrous or non-ferrous metals, but the depth of detection is very limited. A four-inch search coil is only capable of detecting small metal objects to a depth of three to four inches, though an eight-inch coil may detect large objects down as far as four to five feet. To be found by a metal detector, a grave would have to contain a metal object, since the device is not sensitive to any other subsurface characteristic.

The best application of seismic refraction is in engineering, not forensic prospecting. A small system, based on the shock from a hand-held hammer, could be used. Loose soil, such as that found in a grave, should show resistance to shock wave transmission. Burials may be so small, however, that they could only be detected in areas of otherwise very homogeneous conditions. Seismic refraction is also time-consuming and may be too slow for the complete and thorough coverage of a search area.

Ground-penetrating radar is an excellent technique for detecting density variations in the soil down to 20 feet. In alluvial soil, a grave might not show up at all because the normal matrix is already loose. A radar system requires adjustment of frequencies to conditions and may need considerable field fine-tuning. The units are expensive and complex but have fine resolution ability and can detect metal at depths below that which could be illuminated by conventional metal detectors.

The difficulty in recommending geophysical prospecting techniques for forensic use is that no one has identified the geophysical properties of a grave. A big-budget operation could use (1) ground-penetrating radar, (2) electrical resistivity surveying, (3) magnetometers, and (4) electromagnetic surveying. A low-budget search operation could be accomplished using only (1) electrical resistivity and (2) metal detectors. There is no single method which is the best for all field conditions.

Chapter 7

REMOTE SENSING

"Hamlet: How long will a man lie i' the earth ere he rot?

First clown: I' faith, if a' be not rotten before a' die — as we have many pocky corses now-a-days, that will scarce hold the laying in — a' will last you some eight year or nine year: a tanner will last you nine year.

Hamlet: Why he more than another?

First clown: Why, sir, his hide is so tanned with his trade that a' will keep out water a great while; and your water is a sore decayer of your whoreson dead body. Here's a skull now: this skull has lain in the earth three and twenty years."

Hamlet, Act V, Scene I
by William Shakespeare

ELECTROMAGNETIC RADIATION

All matter, at temperatures above absolute zero (0 degrees Kelvin), emits electromagnetic radiation (EMR) due to atomic and molecular vibrations. As temperature increases, EMR levels increase. All this radiation falls somewhere along the electromagnetic spectrum (Figure 7.1). The wavelength of this radiation varies from very short, high frequency, such as gamma rays, to very long, low frequency, as in radio waves. Only a small portion of this spectrum is detectable by humans. Much of the world around us is beyond the reach of the sensors we are born with. Unaided, we are limited to the contact senses of touch and taste and the proximal senses of hearing, sight, and smell.

Electromagnetic radiation must reach the sensors by passing through the atmosphere. Some wavelengths pass through easily and some not at all. Electromagnetic radiation passing through the atmosphere may be subject to atmospheric scattering. This is the unpredictable diffusion of radiation by interaction with atmospheric constituents. For instance, atmospheric scattering causes the apparent blueness of the sky due to increased scattering of radiation in the blue portion of the visible spectrum.

135

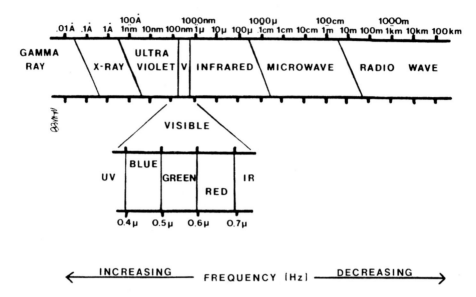

Figure 7.1. Atomic and molecular motion radiates electromagnetic waves from matter. All the various wavelengths of energy fall somewhere along the electromagnetic spectrum. (Adapted from Nunnally, 1973 and Lillesand & Kiefer, 1987.)

Radiation may also be absorbed by atmospheric components, such as water vapor, carbon dioxide, ozone and dust (Lillesand & Kiefer, 1979). Some EMR may be blocked by other electromagnetic energy and by physical barriers, such as vegetation.

Just as some wavelengths of the electromagnetic spectrum are interrupted by the atmosphere, other wavelengths pass through "atmospheric windows." Visible light, for instance, travels well through an unobstructed atmosphere to reach our eyes. The atmospheric windows are contrasted to "atmospheric walls" which interrupt transmitted energy. Some of these atmospheric windows are quite narrow. For instance, in the infrared portion of the spectrum, the energy passes only in the 3 to 5 micrometer or 8 to 14 micrometer wavelength regions. Sensors designed to measure this emitted thermal radiation must operate within the atmospheric windows (Morain & Budge, 1978).

Most scientific attention has been given to those portions of the electromagnetic spectrum that can be detected by sensors with sufficient resolution to identify objects or targets of interest. The challenge of remote sensing instrumentation is to design devices which can detect and measure electromagnetic energy and convert the resulting signal into images which can be perceived by human senses (Lintz & Simonett,

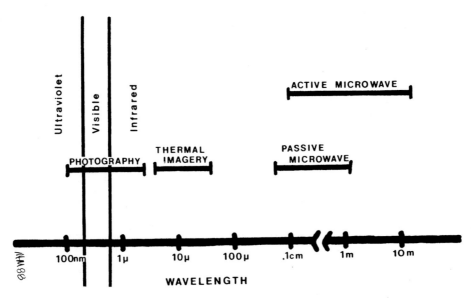

Figure 7.2. Various portions of the electromagnetic spectrum, beyond normal human senses, can be detected by electronic instruments. The signals can then be converted into images which can be seen, stored and manipulated. (Adapted from Lyons & Avery, 1977.)

1976). Figure 7.2 depicts the remote sensing technique to be discussed and the approximate portions of the electromagnetic spectrum in which they operate.

THE MULTI-CONCEPT

In previous chapters, techniques of contact sensing, such as soil sampling, have been discussed as they might be applied to the search for buried bodies. Walking ground searches can be considered a type of proximal sensing in which the sensor, human eyes, are in close proximity to, but not touching, the search area (Figure 7.3). Also within the category of proximal sensing would be scanning the ground, by eyesight or instrumentation, from a "cherry picker" or other slightly elevated platform. The next highest observation platform might be a low-altitude hovering helicopter or low-flying airplane. The acquisition of the physical attributes of an object, without contacting or touching it, as from aircraft, would be considered remote sensing. Remote sensing has also been called "simply the monitoring, inspection or recording of data from a remote vantage point" (Ebert & Hitchcock, 1977:192). Remote sensing is traditionally understood to be instrumentation carried aloft by aircraft or satellites.

Only low-altitude remote sensing techniques extract sufficiently detailed information to be applicable to the problem of finding bodies or grave sites. The low-altitude remote-sensing techniques to be covered in this chapter include passive microwave detection, active microwave (radar), and thermal imagery. Aerial photography, another remote-sensing technique, will be considered in subsequent Chapter 8.

Figure 7.3. Remote sensing is different from contact or proximity sensing because the instrumentation no longer touches the search area. Remote-sensing techniques normally encompass all altitudes from low-flying aircraft to satellites in orbit. (Adapted from Lillesand & Kiefer, 1987.)

Satellites, aircraft, and helicopters are all platforms from which remote sensing can be performed. A multi-stage inspection of a given area might make use of several of these. As with other search techniques, the objective is to detect anomalies on the ground surface. The use of multiple search techniques increases the chances of detecting those anomalies. Just as multi-stages can be employed, multi-spectral or multi-band instruments can be used. This means searching the target areas with a variety of sensing devices which sample different parts of the electromagnetic spectrum. Likewise, multi-directional searching is viewing the area from different directions, altitudes, and angles. Multi-time sensing is repeated scanning at different times of the day and multi-date searching means different days or seasons. Various image-enhancement techniques can take sensor data and electronically alter them to increase the possibility of spotting anomalies.

The multi-concept (Simonett et al. 1983), then, is the multiple searching of an area, by a variety of techniques, to increase the chance of detecting the target sought. The target, in the case of a grave site, may be a ground disturbance no larger than one meter wide by two meters long. No single remote-sensing technique can invariably locate such a small anomaly, and all require subsequent field verification or "ground truthing."

Remote sensing has several advantages over ground searches. The first is the improved vantage point of height, in essence a "bird's-eye view." The second advantage is the speed with which a large area can be searched. Once the images have been obtained, time and action have essentially been stopped. The photographs or images may be examined and analyzed at length without degradation of the information. The information can be obtained before darkness, snowfall or other search obstacles arrive. The imagery also becomes a permanent record which can later be re-examined or used as evidence in court proceedings. Lastly, remote sensors can "see" beyond the human senses. They have a broadened spectral sensitivity and can derive information about the environment not otherwise available.

TARGET DISCRIMINATION

Remote sensing is concerned with two categories of EMR from the earth's surface: that which falls on it and is reflected and that which is emitted from the surface. Disturbances in the soil which mark a grave site can be detected by remote sensors because they emit or reflect electromagnetic energy differently from the undisturbed soil around them. For instance, radiation reflection depends upon moisture content, soil texture (proportions of sand, silt and clay), surface roughness, organic matter content, etc. These factors are complex, variable and interrelated.

For a grave site to be located by remote sensing, the target image must pass through three levels of discrimination. First, the anomaly must be detected. The suspicious object or area is somehow differentiated from its surroundings. Then the anomaly must show some traits of a grave, such as a ground depression or area of retarded plant growth. Then, lastly, the anomaly must be fully analyzed to see if its size, shape and location are consistent with a grave site. Each level of discrimination requires progressively better image resolution (Lintz & Simonett, 1976).

Resolution is equated with fineness of detail. It measures how well the sensor can record objects distinctively. There is a perpetual trade-off between resolution and area coverage. If the image is to be large scale with good resolution, then only a small geographic area can be covered on each image. Trying to cover a large area in fine detail can result in an unmanageably large number of images which need to be examined and analyzed. The resolution depends upon sensor type, image processing, atmospheric conditions, and any uncompensated aircraft motion. In aerial photography, for instance, resolution depends principally upon the camera and lens used, film type and processing technique.

Scale is related to resolution in a commonsense way. Scale is a mathematical relationship between the size of objects as represented on the remotely sensed image and the actual size of the objects themselves. The resolution is fixed once the image is obtained, whereas scale may be changed by enlargement or reduction. Scale can also be adjusted in aerial photography by changing the magnifying power of the lens or changing the altitude of the aircraft's flight.

Large-scale images are most likely to show small anomalies. For instance, an air photo scale of 1:3000 has been used by wildlife managers to survey deer, sheep, and antelope in a rangeland setting (Carneggie et al., 1983). A scale of 1:2000 has enabled foresters to identify tree species (Heller & Ulliman, 1983). Small features are best detected on large-scale aerial photography, between 1:500 to 1:2000. Such photographs can be taken from a plane flying at altitudes of 100 to 200 meters.

A common problem with all remote-sensing imagery is correlating the images with the actual ground features. An anomaly may be plainly visible on the imagery but invisible from the ground. Each image from the sensor must contain some reference point which can be tied to the ground. Bearings can then be taken from the reference points to the anomaly. In an urban or suburban area, sufficient references may be provided by buildings, streets and other identifiable features. In a rural area, however, landmarks may be too scattered or indistinguishable to serve as unique reference points. In those areas, colored ground panels or other objects will have to be placed throughout the search area. The markers used must be large and distinctive enough to be recorded on the image and specific enough to unambiguously identify the ground area covered by the image.

The selection of a remote sensor or sensors is not easy. One solution is to bring all available sensors to bear on the target area. This would certainly yield the most information. Realistically, the use of all sensors is too expensive. There will always be a compromise between the amount of information desired and the cost and time available for the search. Prime considerations are the size and nature of the search area. Such factors as topography and ground cover determine which, if any, remote-sensing methods are feasible. Climate also plays an important role in decision making. Searching in fair weather is far different from searching through heavy snowpack in midwinter. A final consideration is the availability of equipment and expertise in a given region. Aerial photography services are widely available, but thermal and microwave imagery are not. Current information about remote sensor availability can be obtained from the American Society of Photogrammetry, 210 Little Falls Street, Falls Church, Virginia 22046. Publications of the society, including the comprehensive *Manual of Remote Sensing*, contain additional information about remote-sensing services.

PASSIVE MICROWAVE

Passive microwave sensing employs a radiometer to measure the intensity of the microwave radiation which emanates from all objects in the natural environment. The radiometer measures this naturally emitted energy in the same electromagnetic spectral region as some radar systems, generally in the 1 mm to 1 m wavelength region (Morain & Budge, 1976). These microwaves are short compared to radio or television waves, but long compared to visible light. The atmospheric constituents, especially water vapor, absorb some of these wavelengths, so radiometers must be designed to measure microwaves within the atmospheric windows.

There are three properties that determine the character of an object's microwave signature (Figure 7.4). Emittance is the radiation from the object itself. The second property is transmittance, i.e. the radiation transmitted through the object from subsoil, rocks and other under-

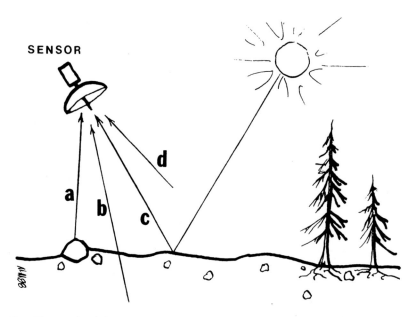

Figure 7.4. The passive microwave signature of an object is determined by its emittance (a), transmittance (b), and reflectance from the surface (c). The sensor will also detect and record microwaves emitted by the atmosphere (d). (Adapted from Lillesand & Kiefer, 1987 and Holter, 1973.)

ground objects. The third property is reflectance or the amount of reflected radiation which comes from the sky, clouds, sun, etc. An object's emittance, transmittance and reflectance are, in turn, functions of its temperature, shape, surface type, angle to detector, and other factors (Holter, 1973).

Any radiometer, whether it measures microwave or thermal radiation, has a relatively narrow field of view (Figure 7.5). The radiometer measures the radiant energy that emanates from objects within that instantaneous field of view and within its designated wavelength range. In practice, the field of view mechanically swings side to side so that the device becomes a scanning radiometer. In this manner, wider sections of the ground can be scanned along and beneath the flight path of the aircraft (Figure 7.6). The measurements from the radiometer are recorded, amplified, and converted to an image which can then be examined. An image is simply a pictorial representation of sensor data. A photograph is only one type of image, being an image which is detected and recorded directly on film.

The advantage to passive microwave sensing is that the transmitted portion of the energy is coming from underlying sources, not just the surface. This penetration through the overburden makes it useful in

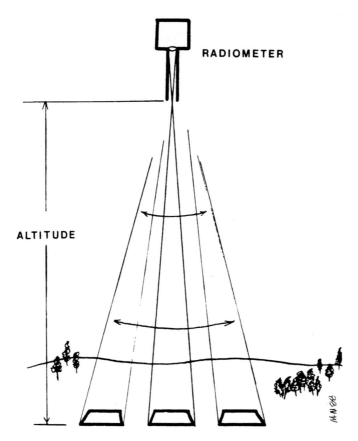

Figure 7.5. A scanning radiometer sweeps side to side and measures radiation from each instantaneous field of view. (Adapted from Lillesand & Kiefer, 1987.)

studying such things as soils and polar ice. Passive microwave is most commonly used in meteorological and oceanographic studies. The problem with passive microwave sensing is that, compared with thermal imagery or active radar systems, it has lower sensitivity and poorer resolution. The coarse images from airborne scanning microwave radiometers, even at low altitude, have a spatial resolution of only one to two meters (Ulaby & Carver, 1983). Objects smaller than that are probably undetectable with currently available systems.

Passive microwave resolution is related to antenna beam width. A large beam width is needed to collect enough radiation for recording. The length of antenna is obviously limited to the size of the aircraft fuselage. Resolution is better if short-wavelength microwaves are col-

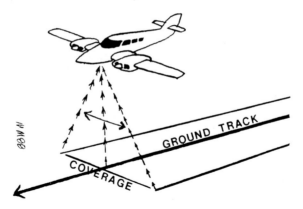

Figure 7.6. The coverage pattern of a scanning radiometer is beneath the aircraft as it follows its flight path. This is contrasted with the coverage pattern of side-looking airborne radar shown in Figure 7.8. (Adapted from Thackrey, 1973.)

lected. Other factors include the mechanical performance of the receiver and prevailing atmospheric transmission factors. Even under the best conditions, passive microwave is most suitable for identifying large terrain features such as roadways, buildings, water/land boundaries, etc.

ACTIVE MICROWAVE (RADAR)

Whereas passive microwave sensors simply collect and measure ambient microwave signals, active microwave systems send out (emit) waves. The pulses move through space, strike objects and are reflected back to the radar receiver as much weaker pulses (Figure 7.7). The word radar was originally abbreviated from the words *ra*dio *d*etection *a*nd *r*anging.

Most radar systems operate at short wavelengths between 0.86 and 3.3 centimeters (Innes, 1973). These radio wave pulses are emitted for only microseconds. Modern pulsed radars use the same antenna to transmit and receive. The transmitter is switched on and off thousands of time each second so that the instrument can distinguish between the powerful transmitted pulses and the returning weak pulses.

Radar operates on wavelengths midway between far infrared and longer VHF radio waves. Fittingly, it has some of the imaging capability of visible light with some of the atmospheric-penetrating capability of radio. It is useful because it has relatively good resolution ability and excellent penetration of haze, smoke, rain, and other adverse weather conditions. It can "see" through a complete cloud cover and be used at night. It has the ability to penetrate to the ground surface through snow

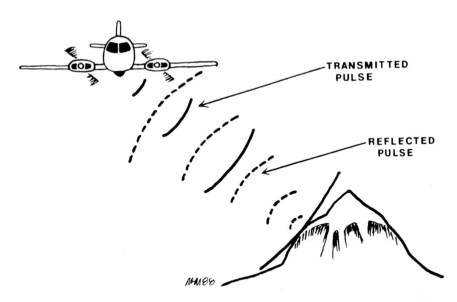

Figure 7.7. Side-looking airborne radar (SLAR) is an active remote-sensing technique. Brief electromagnetic pulses are transmitted and the reflected echoes are received, analyzed and recorded.

and light vegetation cover. It can also penetrate through some shallow topsoils. Passive microwave detection is limited to the small amounts of natural radiation, but pulse radars can generate powerful man-made signals. Ground images can be enhanced because the radar signal's timing, strength, phase, and polarization can be changed. The principal drawbacks of radar are its high cost and limited availability.

The returning radar waves are received, amplified, and then displayed as an image similar in appearance to a black-and-white photograph. The radar system is actually measuring three attributes of the returning signal from a stationary object: its strength, direction, and distance. The reflection characteristics of the target depend upon the wavelength of radar used. Radar can be directed on various bands, such as K, X, C, etc. K (0.75–2.40 centimeters) and X (2.40–3.75 centimeters) are the most commonly used in ground-imaging systems (Sabins, 1976).

Reflectance characteristics also depend upon the polarization of the radar signal. As with polarized light waves, radar waves can be sent oriented horizontally or vertically, making four combinations possible: horizontal transmit-horizontal receive (HH), horizontal transmit-vertical receive (HV), vertical transmit-vertical receive (VV), and vertical transmit-horizontal receive (VH). The radar system can be like-polarized, cross-polarized or not polarized at all, also called multiple-polarized. The detection of cultural features such as roads, building, etc., seems to be enhanced with the HV operation mode (Lewis, 1973).

Terrain characteristics also affect the image quality, such as the geometric shape of the target, its size, and surface roughness. Smooth surfaces, like calm salt water or a concrete slab are spectacular reflectors of radar signals. Rough surfaces cause more random backscattering of the radar pulses, resulting in a weaker signal back to the receiver. Vegetation, depending upon structure and moisture, does not reflect radar signals as well as bare ground. Reflected signal strength also depends upon the electrical characteristics of the target. Reflected radar signal strength increases with the electrical conductivity of the material. Therefore, metallic objects appear conspicuously bright in the imagery. Wetter soils are more prominent than dry soils because of their higher electrical conductivity.

The side-looking airborne radar (SLAR) is the most common type of ground-imaging radar. It produces pictures of the illuminated terrain beneath and to one side of the aircraft's flight path (Figure 7.8). The antenna is mounted along the fuselage of the plane. The pulses are transmitted at right angles to the aircraft flight direction. SLAR emits a narrow fan-shaped beam. A portion of the energy (backscatter) is returned and digitally recorded or converted to light energy recorded on a photographic film. The film advances in proportion to the aircraft's speed so that a continuous radar image is produced. The strength of the return signal is recorded as the degree of brightness on the photograph.

Side-looking airborne radar has a point of view similar to that of oblique aerial photography. The angle (called look angle) from the sensor to the target is neither directly horizontal nor directly vertical, resulting in a distortion of the image. This is the reason that SLAR is used primarily for terrain reconnaissance, not for accurate mapping. This viewpoint causes two other complications or limitations on SLAR's usefulness. The first, as previously mentioned, is that the angle of the target to the sensor partially determines the strength of the bounced signal. Slopes or hills which are perpendicular to the radio waves reflect strongly, but slopes which are nearly parallel to the beam are weakly registered. This phenomenon is called foreshortening and is illustrated in Figure 7.9. The figure also shows a companion problem of the oblique viewpoint. Objects behind hills, buildings, or other high points are in a

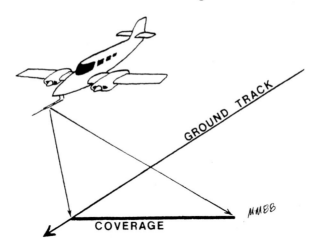

Figure 7.8. The ground coverage pattern of SLAR is beneath and to one side of the aircraft's flight path. This results in a distorted view of the ground and explains why radar is used principally for terrain reconnaissance and not precise mapping. (Adapted from Viksne et al., 1973.)

radar shadow and will not be seen on the imagery. Full coverage of an area, therefore, demands at least two and perhaps as many as four flight paths to be sure that the radar images fully bracket a target area. These phenomena make radar imagery more useful in a country rather than city setting. The city is full of flat concrete surfaces which reflect radar like mirrors. This means that a city radar image will be a mosaic of bright glints and deep shadows.

Another limitation on the use of side-looking airborne radar imagery is its resolution ability. It is generally coarser than air photos, though recent developments in synthetic aperture systems have made it nearly comparable. The ground resolution of SLAR is controlled by two independent variables. They are the pulse wavelength and the antenna beam width. Shorter wavelengths result in higher resolution ability, but they are defeated by light vegetation cover and only penetrate the immediate topsoil of the ground. Intermediate wavelengths can penetrate vegetation and are more sensitive to deeper soil moisture content. Long wavelengths can penetrate up to several meters of soil in some instances and can penetrate all but the most dense forest cover (Moore, 1976). Important factors in penetration include moisture content and geologic material characteristics. Radar penetration sharply decreases with higher soil moisture content.

Antenna length also affects resolution ability. There are two kinds of

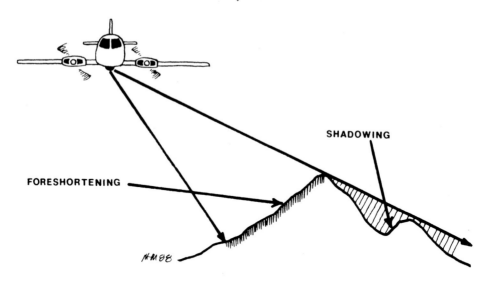

Figure 7.9. The oblique viewpoint of SLAR causes the problems of foreshortening and shadowing. These problems mean that at least two and perhaps as many as four flight paths must be flown to completely cover and bracket a search area. (Adapted from Viksne et al., 1973.)

side-looking airborne radar. One is real aperture radar (RAR) which means that the actual (real) antenna length (aperture) determines the resolution ability. The mechanical limitation on this system is the length of the aircraft fuselage onto which the antenna is mounted. The RAR system has the advantage of being less complicated and less expensive than the synthetic aperture radar (SAR).

Synthetic aperture radar, also known as focused radar, depends upon electronic processing of the radar signal to make it equivalent to a longer antenna. In flight, each successive pulse transmitted originates slightly farther along the flight path. The instrumentation sums the echoes from those successive pulses to synthesize a very long antenna array (Scott, 1987). This results in a higher resolution ability because the instrument is no longer restricted to the actual antenna size. Estimates of civilian (SAR) radar resolution vary from approximately 15 meters down to 7–8 meters at a range of less than 5 kilometers (Moore et al., 1983). Government and military radar resolution is much better. The interpretation of high-resolution, large-scale radar imagery is similar to the aerial photography interpretation principles presented in Chapter 8.

INFRARED SCANNER IMAGERY

The infrared portion of the electromagnetic spectrum is customarily divided into three regions. The near, or reflective, portion includes wavelengths between approximately 0.7 to 1.5 microns. The lower portion of this field can be recorded on infrared sensitive camera film. The middle range, between 1.5 and 5.5 microns, can be detected by scanners which record emitted and reflected infrared radiation. The far band of infrared radiation contains those with wavelengths between 5.5 and 1000 microns (Estes et al., 1983). The usable infrared range is from the upper limit of visible light to the lower limit of microwave radiation.

Within the infrared range, two atmospheric windows are commonly used by remote-sensing devices. A window between approximately 4.5 to 5.5 microns is used for the detection of small, hot objects and a larger window between 7.5 and 14.0 microns is used for terrain mapping (Lowe, 1976). The best window for aerial remote sensing is between 10.5 and 12.5 microns where molecular absorption in the atmosphere is at a minimum. This is also the range of maximum sensitivity for detecting graves and lost persons as body temperature emits IR radiation in the 10 micron range (Bucher, 1989).

Infrared scanner imagery is also known as electronic or aerial thermography, thermal imagery and by other names. Infrared scanners can detect slight differences in the thermal (heat) radiation emitted from objects on the ground. Like a passive microwave radiometer, the field of view of an infrared radiometer is swept across the ground in a path perpendicular to and beneath the flight line of the aircraft (Figure 7.6). The scanning rate is adjusted to the speed of the plane. The result is a photograph-like image of the ground's infrared radiance. This recorded data from non-visible wavelengths results in an image commonly called a thermogram, which can be subjected to interpretation and analysis. Objects can be identified by their shape, texture, size and tone. The tone of an object is a function of its surface temperature. The scanner detects only the surface temperature, seldom more than 50 microns deep. It does not, like passive microwave, give an indication of internal or bulk temperature.

The amount of thermal energy emitted by the ground or an object is determined by the physical properties of the object and the environmental conditions. The physical properties of the object include its absolute temperature, surface texture, color, composition and transmitting/

emissivity. Differences in emissivity means that objects with the same temperature will vary in their thermal output (Baker, 1975). Important environmental conditions include the time of day, air temperature, wind velocity, precipitation and geothermal heat flow.

The final product of infrared scanner imagery is a continuous thermal picture of the terrain along the aircraft track in which hot objects are light and cold objects are dark. The thermogram shows the contrast between objects and their environment. The images are generally in a black-and-white format, but they can be enhanced to show various temperature gradations by color.

Thermal imagery can be obtained either by day or night. By day, however, the energy recorded will be both reflected electromagnetic radiation from the sun and emitted infrared energy from the ground. Daytime thermal imagery in a sense duplicates infrared aerial photography. For most applications, night time imagery is preferable, since only emitted radiation reaches the sensors (Figure 7.10). Thermal imagery is best obtained on clear dry nights with minimum surface wind. The thermal signature of a grave will be more apparent in dry soil conditions. Wet ground tends toward a temperature and moisture equilibrium. The images can be confounded by uncompensated aircraft motion, so level, smooth flight is essential. Radio transmission can also distort the images, so radio silence is maintained during scanner runs. Thermal radiation can also be obscured by dust, fog, smoke, and heavy atmospheric water vapor. Local conditions vary with altitude, site, time, and weather. The infrared detector itself must be cooled to near absolute zero and insulated throughout the operation. As with microwave systems, aerial thermal imagery services are expensive and not widely available.

There are other lesser problems with infrared scanner imagery. High temperature "hot spots" on the ground will cause "blooming" which may obscure nearby less-warm objects. There is also distortion in the imagery because the image is nearly vertical beneath the flight path but approaches an oblique angle near the edges of the scan lines. This creates shadowing, as seen in active radar systems, which may hide targets of interest.

While the resolution of thermal imagery is not as good as photographs, recent developments have improved it to such an extent that it is second only to photography in showing ground detail (Jorde, 1977). The "instantaneous field of view" (IFOV) of a thermal radiometer can be adjusted. When it is small, there is good resolution ability. Such a small ground resolution cell, however, means that tiny temperature differences

DETECTOR

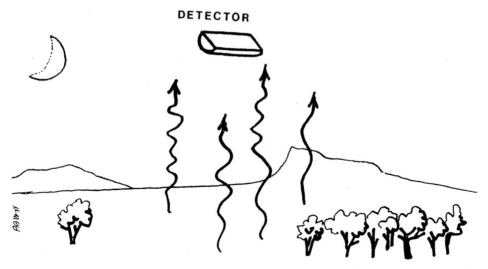

Figure 7.10. Most infrared scanner imagery is done at night so that reflected energy from the sun is not recorded. The best images are obtained on nights that are clear and dry with a minimum of surface wind. (Adapted from Leonardo, 1973.)

cannot be detected. On the other hand, large ground resolution cells allow a sensor to detect slight energy differences on the order of 0.1° C. At that setting, the resolution ability is approximately 2.5 meters (Lillesand & Kiefer, 1987). Most scanners with good resolution can detect temperature differences at least as slight as 1 degree Centigrade.

The potential value of thermal infrared imagery is its ability to detect minor differences in temperature at the ground's surface. This temperature difference can be an indication of the thermal properties of the soil or result from an internal heat generation source, such as body decomposition. As discussed in previous chapters, disturbances in the soil change the ground so that a grave site may appear thermally different from the surrounding surface. To some degree, surface temperature is an indicator of subsurface conditions.

It has been shown that bodies, during active decomposition, exhibit temperatures far above their surrounding soil. As reported by Rodriguez and Bass (1983), surface bodies may be so hot that they are uncomfortable to examine with bare hands. The heat is caused by anaerobic and aerobic bacterial action and the high metabolic rate of carrion insect larvae. The body is essentially a closed ecosystem, and the warming of the carcass by the activity of the maggot mass is relatively independent of the ambient temperature. Studies showed that at a burial depth of four feet, the body averaged 3.4° C warmer than the surrounding soil. The body/soil temperature differential increased with shallower burial depth. At two feet the temperature differential was approximately five degrees and at one-foot depth, the bodies were between 7 and 10 degrees warmer than the surrounding soil. These temperature differences are well within the range that can be detected by fine resolution thermal imagery. The decision to use infrared imagery is based on the premise that this heat and/or the soil changes caused by digging are sufficient to make the grave stand out as warmer than the surrounding matrix.

Thermal imagery can also detect live animals on the ground's surface. Thermal imagery studies have shown that deer and livestock can be detected and counted from an altitude of 500 to 1000 feet (Carneggie et al., 1983; Poulton, 1975). Success in detecting deer was enhanced when the deer were against a background of snow and in the open, not under trees. Night was found to be the best time for such work, but the low altitudes (below 2,000 feet) made flying dangerous in mountainous terrain. For safety, imagery can also be done in the dawn or pre-sunrise period or under a heavy, total cloud cover without rainfall. The differences between infrared scanner imagery and infrared aerial photography will be covered in Chapter 8.

Thermal imaging can also be done from the ground or from a slightly raised platform such as a "cherry picker." Infrared video cameras are able to generate real-time images from the IR radiation they pick up and process. The resulting picture is displayed on a television monitor and/or recorded with a video tape recorder. The resolution of the system depends upon the sensor, the type of optical lens being used and the signal processing within the camera system. Some thermal imaging systems or infrared cameras may require liquid gas or thermoelectrical cooling which makes them less portable. Others, such as pyro-electric vidicon (PEV) cameras, do not require any coolant for operation. They are battery powered, lightweight, instantly operational and the output signal is TV compatible (Bucher, 1989).

ULTRAVIOLET LASER FLUOROSENSOR

A new technique, presently being used to detect gas pipeline leaks, might be applicable to body searches. The same technique is also used by the U.S. Coast Guard to detect oil spills. The system employs a high-power laser operating in the near ultraviolet EMR range. The laser causes hydrocarbon gases to fluoresce. This fluorescence can be detected and recorded by an airborne scanner (Measures, 1984). Since decomposing bodies release hydrocarbon gases, they might be detectable with this active remote-sensing system. The gases present over a grave should be revealed as a bright spot anomaly (Heimmer, 1989).

Chapter 8

AERIAL PHOTOGRAPHY

"If you plan to dig another's grave, dig two."

Anonymous proverb

Aerial photography was the first remote-sensing technique and remains the workhorse of the airborne repertoire. The aerial photograph, particularly in the stereo (three-dimensional) form, contains more information per unit area than any other form of sensor image (Rinker, 1975). A camera was first hauled aloft in a balloon in France in 1856. Within decades, it was widely employed as a military observation device. It was first used in archaeology in 1906 when Lieutenant F.A. Sharpe of the Royal Air Force took aerial photographs of the Stonehenge ruins from a hot-air balloon (Cochran, 1986). Buried archaeological remains were first seen by the military pilots of World War I. O.G.S. Crawford, a British World War I aerial observer, encouraged the photography of archaeological sites. His work and later publications, especially as founder and editor of the British archaeological journal *Antiquity*, earned him the designation "the Father of Aerial Archaeology" (Ebert & Hitchcock, 1977). The first use of aerial photography in American archaeology was in 1921 when Lieutenants A.C. McKinley and H.P. Wells took photographs of the Cahokia site in Illinois. The archaeological use of photographs has been primarily to locate and evaluate sites for excavation. Recently, photographs have been used for analysis of land use patterns, not just site discovery.

The ability to detect buried sites from aerial photography is based upon the nature of the sites and the setting in which they occur. One relies upon the fact that the target differs from its background in some parameter such as color, brightness, texture, or shape. The hope is that some combination of film, filter, scale, camera, and lighting will make the target easier to see in the picture. The primary advantage of aerial photography is the elevated point of view. A plane or helicopter can be stationed anywhere above the target so that a panoramic view is not

155

limited to a nearby tall building or hill. With aircraft, a large area can be covered and recorded with a minimum of personnel. There is a high hourly cost, but it may be reasonable when compared with a huge ground search effort. Aerial photographs have the best resolution of any remote-sensing technique. Photographed objects are easily identified because the camera principally records the same wavelengths as the human eye. Colors, shapes, brightness, etc., are therefore familiar and recognizable.

As with other forms of remote sensing, aerial photography depends upon the fact that all matter reflects, absorbs, transmits and emits electromagnetic energy. The extent of each depends upon the electrical properties of the material, its temperature, and the frequency or wavelength of the electromagnetic energy involved. In conventional photography, the film records reflected sunlight in the visible portion of the electromagnetic spectrum (Figure 8.1). The emphasis in this chapter will be on low-level photography which shows the most ground detail.

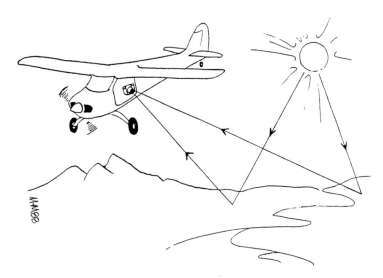

Figure 8.1. Conventional light photography, in this case high oblique angle aerial photography, records sunlight reflected off the ground. (Adapted from Leonardo, 1973.)

Before embarking on an aerial photography effort, several questions must be considered and answered (Eastman Kodak, 1985), especially the size of the target. A reasonable target size for an isolated grave site is approximately one meter by two meters. Based on that target size, other questions are: What level of detail resolution is necessary? How much area needs to be covered? What is the vegetation ground cover in that area? What format will the imagery take, transparencies or prints? What are the expected prevailing atmospheric conditions? When and how will the weather change? When must the photography be done? Can it be postponed until the best conditions are available? What resources are available in the local area and how much money can be spent? The answers to these questions will determine which form of aerial photography (or other remote-sensing technique) should be used.

The scale of the photographs is one of the decisions to be made. Scale is the ratio of the size of the object in the photograph to its actual size on the ground. In a vertical aerial photograph, it is determined by the focal length of the lens and the altitude from which the photograph is taken. The calculations become more complex in oblique photography, which is photography from an angle rather than from directly overhead. A large scale has an advantage in spatial resolution. Spatial resolution is the distance that must separate two objects in order for them to appear separately on the image. If two objects are separated by less than the resolution distance, they will appear as one object in the picture. Resolution ability depends upon the scale of the photograph and the film grain size.

Most archaeological aerial surveys are done on a scale of 1:5000 or the smaller 1:10,000 (Cochran, 1986). A scale of 1:12,000 means that one inch of the photograph equals 1,000 feet on the ground. In other words, a scale of 1:12,000 indicates that the ground distance is 12,000 times longer than the photograph distance. Target objects appear larger in the large-scale photograph. The trade-off, as with other forms of remote-sensing imagery, is that the larger the scale, the less terrain is covered in each photograph. Complex or large archaeological sites are easy to discern, but small sites are naturally more difficult to see and require a larger-scale photograph. An isolated grave is a very small target and requires the largest scale practically available.

Another factor governing the quality of aerial photographs is the direction of the sun in relation to the camera. The sun position in turn determines the type of shadowing on the ground. The smallest shadows are near noontime. Shadows may be desirable for revealing elevation contrast. With the sun behind the camera, there is virtually no shadowing, yielding low scene contrast. Photography towards the sun may show too much shadowing so that information in the shadowed area is lost. Side lighting is often preferred as a compromise.

Vibration of the camera during photography reduces image quality. Vibration can be reduced if there is no contact between the photographer's upper body, lens, or camera and the plane. A gyro stabilizer will assist in holding a camera still and is particularly helpful in motion picture, video camera, or slow shutter speed photography. A gyro stabilizer, however, makes it difficult to pan the camera or to change the point of aim quickly (Eastman Kodak, 1985).

Weather also obviously affects aerial photography success. Clouds can obstruct in two ways. In the air they form a block between the camera and the reflected light coming from the ground. Heavy clouds may also cast deep shadows which will appear as dark blotches on an otherwise properly exposed photograph. An overcast sky will reduce the contrast between ground objects, and even a light haze will cause some blueing of the film because blue wavelength light is more susceptible to scattering.

Another decision that must be made by the photographer is the form he wishes his final image to take. Static photographs may be either prints on paper or transparencies, sometimes called diapositives or positive transparencies. They are actually prints made on film or glass. Transparencies give finer detail and sharper definition than paper prints, but they must be viewed on a light table where the light is transmitted up through them instead of being reflected down from above. Transparencies are not convenient to carry and use in the field. Transparencies, of course, can be transformed into prints for fieldwork. Photographs can generally be enlarged two to four times and still maintain good pictorial quality (Spurr, 1973). The information obtained in an enlargement, however, is no more than can be seen by using a magnifying glass over the print or transparency.

The search supervisor must decide whether the photographs should be taken from a vertical or oblique perspective. Vertical photographs are those images taken at less than three degrees away from an imaginary line going downward vertically from the aircraft. More than three degrees deviation is considered to be an oblique photograph. A low-angle oblique photograph includes part of the horizon, whereas a high-angle oblique photograph does not. High- versus low-angle oblique has nothing to do with the elevation of the camera but with the way it is aimed (Figure 8.2).

Vertical photographs taken straight down at the ground show the most detail since all objects are revealed (Figure 8.3). They are also the least

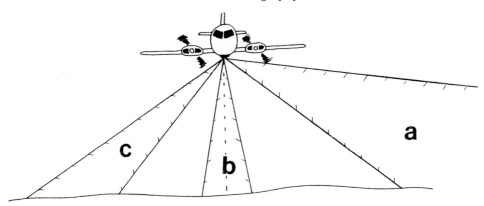

Figure 8.2. A low-angle oblique photograph (a) includes part of the horizon, whereas a high-angle oblique photograph (c) does not. A vertical photograph (b) is taken directly beneath the aircraft.

subject to distortion and are therefore used for mapping and measurement purposes. A special plane and camera are normally used for taking vertical photographs. The lens is designed to represent every object in its correct position, assuming that the land is flat. There is some distortion toward the periphery of each image frame because the ground slope does vary and wide-angle lenses are often used. Strips of 60 percent overlapping photographs are customarily used so that each object is covered by at least two photographs (Figure 8.4). When adjacent photographs are combined in a stereoscope, a three-dimensional picture is seen. The photographs are tied to ground control points so that accurate plans and measurements can be made. This is the core of the science of photogrammetry (Wilson, 1982).

A stereoscope is an image-splitting optical device that permits the illusion of three dimensions. It highlights differences in the vertical relief of ground features. It is one of the basic tools, along with the magnifying glass, of the photo interpreter. Methodically taken vertical photographs can be overlapped to create a complete mosaic of a search area. Because it is difficult for a fixed-wing aircraft to fly low and slow, rarely can vertical photographs be taken at a scale greater than 1:1,500. Larger scales can be obtained from a helicopter-mounted camera or from various enlargement and magnification processes (Wilson, 1975).

Oblique photographs (Figure 8.5) are a more natural and familiar point of view because they resemble the view from a tall building or mountain. Each oblique photograph frame covers a greater area than a large-scale vertical photograph. Oblique photographs do not require a

Figure 8.3. Vertical photographs show the most detail and are the least subject to distortion. A special camera and plane are normally used for taking vertical aerial photographs. (Photograph courtesy of Scharf and Associates, Inc.)

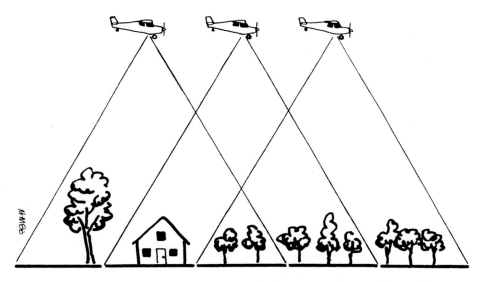

Figure 8.4. Vertical aerial photograph is normally shot in strips of overlapping frames so every object is covered at least twice. When the adjacent frames are viewed under a stereoscope, a three-dimensional image emerges. (Adapted from Spurr, 1973.)

special plane or camera. They can be easily taken from a small, propeller-driven plane with overhead wings. The plane must have a window that can be opened or removed so that photographs are not taken through the glass. The disadvantages of oblique photography are that they portray a distorted image of the ground, and, in hilly country, objects of interest can be hidden behind high points unless full circular coverage is obtained.

"Do-it-yourself" oblique photography is generally done from a height of several hundred meters. It is best to use a pilot experienced in aerial photography work and a plane that can maintain a slow airspeed of 100 to 200 knots (Harp, 1975). A 35-millimeter camera is adequate for the job and it can be aimed and released in a normal hand-held fashion. Lenses commonly used are wide-angle to low-power telephotos. Faster shutter speeds are preferable to minimize the blur resulting from aircraft motion and vibration. The camera focus is set to infinity and may be taped in position to prevent accidental modification. Speeds must be at least as fast as 1/250th of a second, with 1/500th of a second recommended by Ebert and Lyons (1983). Light meter readings may be taken on the ground, then again in the air, and a compromise setting made. Another rule of thumb is to set the camera down one *f*-stop below that which is suggested by a conventional light meter. As always, bracketing exposures is recommended. Ultraviolet or haze filters are commonly employed in

Figure 8.5. An oblique photograph is a more natural and familiar point of view because it resembles the view from a mountain. Oblique aerial photographs do not require a special plane or camera. (Photograph courtesy of Scharf and Associates, Inc.)

color photography and a yellow (minus blue) filter is used for panchromatic film. A lens hood is always in place to prevent the sun's rays from striking directly upon the lens.

Several authors recommended taking oblique photographs from all possible angles, since faint ground marks might be visible for only 15 degrees of a full circle (Wilson, 1975). Such variations will depend primarily upon the sun's position. A plane can circle the target area to obtain multiple ground contrast conditions (Figure 8.6). Precise positioning can be obtained by helicopters, but they are notorious for increased craft vibration.

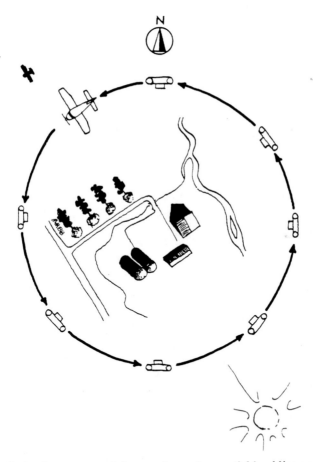

Figure 8.6. Full circular coverage of the search area is essential in oblique aerial photography so that targets are not hidden behind or beneath other features. Full coverage will also take advantage of different lighting conditions which may enhance target detection.

Stereo photographs can also be taken from an oblique angle. While the plane is in its circular path, a photograph is taken; then, after a pause of a few seconds, a second photograph is taken. Viewed together, these result in an exaggerated stereo effect. Eastman Kodak (1985) suggested a two-second pause between photographs taken from an altitude of 5,000 feet at a slow airspeed.

CAMERA TYPES

There are several types of camera designed specifically for aerial photography use. Most are vertical-angle cameras for professional photographers. The first type is the conventional aerial camera designed to be rigidly affixed to the floor of the aircraft. It has a large film magazine and, in its simplest form, is equipped for handling one type of film and filter combination at a time. Similar to the stationary camera is a panoramic camera which, rather than being mounted in a fixed position, moves or pans over the terrain during flight. Though a panoramic camera covers more area per flight line, its photographs are distorted and cannot be used for detailed mapping (Colwell, 1976).

Continuous strip photography involves a single fixed camera designed for low-altitude, high-speed, high-resolution photography. A strip camera exposes a long roll of film, over a narrow opening, at a rate synchronized to the forward speed of the plane. Depending upon the system, either stereo or mono photographs can be taken. With such a system, prints can be made on a scale as large as 1:72. Such a large scale has been used to study cracks in airport runways. Strip cameras have also been used for surveying highways or railroad lines, since, at a scale of 1:1,200, they can show 145 kilometers of ground distance on one unbroken picture strip (Estes, 1983).

Multi-spectral photography usually involves gang-mounted cameras which are aligned close to each other so that they record essentially the same ground area. Each is equipped with a different filter/film combination so that each image is slightly different. Later, image-enhancing devices can reconstruct the scene by superimposing the multiple images. Similarly, a multi-bank system splits a single lens image into several cameras so that several simultaneous photographs are taken of exactly the same area. Again, different film/filter combinations are used, increasing the variety of images which are recorded on any single flight. These simultaneous photographs in different bands of the electromagnetic spectrum usually cover portions from the near ultraviolet to the near infrared. Even conventional color photography can be thought of as a special type of multi-spectrum reconnaissance, since several bands of visible light are simultaneously recorded. Multi-spectral photography is usually taken during the summer to highlight vegetation color differences (Hampton, 1974). Multi-bank cameras, like other fixed vertical aerial cameras, yield good photographs only when insulated from aircraft vibration. They must also be synchronized to the speed of the flight. Compensating devices adjust to aircraft yaw, pitch, roll, or abrupt elevation changes. The ideal is photography as clear as could be obtained from a stationary platform.

Oblique photographs can be taken be any hand-held camera. A 70-millimeter format is considered better because of its larger transparency size, but a 35-millimeter format is adequate. Both systems have a variety of lenses available and can be adjusted for fast shutter speeds. Many film types are commercially available and both camera systems are easy to handle, aim and shoot. Oblique photography can also be done with hand-held videotape recorders or motion picture cameras. The advantage of videotape recording is that the scenes can be viewed on television, enhanced electronically like photographs, or be made into hard copies. Video tapes are especially good for detecting linear features on the ground, and one author, Loose (1977), claimed they were better for this purpose than either black-and-white or color still photography.

FILM TYPES

PANCHROMATIC. The first aerial photographs and most photographs on file in government repositories are black and white (panchromatic). Panchromatic film has a spectral sensitivity of between 0.36 to 0.72 microns, or approximately the same as the human eye (0.4 to 0.7 microns). Panchromatic is primarily used for mapping since it is inexpensive, easy to use and has excellent resolution. It is normally exposed through a minus blue (Wratten 12) or amber (Wratten 15) filter to reduce fogging by particles in the air. It depicts the scene in various tones of gray, depending upon the terrain's reflection and transmission of light. As with all films, there is a trade-off between the definition of detail and the speed at which the film can be exposed. The higher the film speed, the less light is needed. As film speed is increased, however, graininess also increases. Another advantage of black-and-white film is greater exposure latitude so that usable photographs can be taken in marginal lighting conditions such as dawn and dusk. Each photograph is an accurate rendition of the scene, since there is no concern for duplicating natural color balance. The natural appearance of objects means that panchromatic photographs are easy to interpret. Black-and-white aerial photography was called the most efficient remote sensor for the archaeologist by Gumerman and Lyons (1971).

VISIBLE COLOR. The advantage of color photography is that the human eye can discern only a few hundred shades of gray but thousands of color variations. The human eye can separate 100 times more color combinations than gray scale values (Estes, 1983). Black-and-white transparencies are limited to 30 or 40 shades of gray and even fewer in a print. Color transparencies, on the other hand, can portray up to 500 colors (Rinker, 1975). Thus, the eye can see minor details and note anomalies more easily in color images. Color film is sensitive to the three primary colors of blue (0.4 to 0.5 microns), green (0.5 to 0.6 microns), and red (0.6 to 0.7 microns). All other hues are combinations of the primary colors. Modern color films nearly equal the resolution abilities of black-and-white films. Color images are good for photo interpretation because of the natural appearance of objects. They are similar to the originals as seen in white light. Color films are particularly good for highlighting natural features such as vegetation and soil type, but they may be no better than panchromatic films for detecting "cultural features" such as roads, buildings, etc. (Gummerman & Lyons, 1971).

Color film can be shot in either print or transparency format. The 70-millimeter color transparencies are the best for detailed photo interpretation because they yield more tone and intensity variation than prints. All transparencies need special handling to avoid scratches, dust, and fingerprint damage. Black-and-white or color prints can be generated from transparencies for field use. Color aerial photography is more costly than panchromatic photography. Many authors recommended both color and panchromatic taken simultaneously, since contrasting and comparing the photographs will furnish complementary information.

INFRARED PANCHROMATIC. Black-and-white infrared film was formerly called camouflage detection film because of its first military usage. It is primarily sensitive to the blue violet spectrum in the visible range and the near infrared. Through proper filtering, radiation in the blue range is blocked out, resulting in photographs portraying the green, red and near-infrared parts of the color spectrum. If shot through a dark red filter (Wratten 89-B), only near-infrared light penetrates, screening out ultraviolet and visible light. In such a format there is loss of image sharpness. Black-and-white infrared film does not show the detail of visible black-and-white films. Photography through a yellow haze filter is commonly called "modified infrared" (Lyons & Avery, 1977). This format has good haze-cutting capability but poor shadow penetration. Objects can be seen within shadows on panchromatic visible light film but not on infrared film.

The advantages of infrared are its ability to penetrate haze and detect light reflected beyond the visible spectrum. In particular, plant health can be discerned. A symptom of plant injury is the loss of the plant's ability to reflect infrared light. Healthy plants appear bright and unhealthy plants appear darker. Foliage also shows a wider range of gray tones and assists the photo interpreter in differentiating plant species. As well as vegetation differences, soil moisture content is highlighted by infrared. Since reflected infrared light is used, most photography is taken during the midday period. All infrared films must be protected from high temperature and are normally stored frozen. Once thawed, they have a short shelf life.

Infrared film only detects actinic radiation, or that which falls into the region for which the film is sensitive. There is invisible electromagnetic radiation at both ends of the visible light portion, but only the nearest portion of the infrared bank is photographically actinic. Above the actinic band, thermal infrared imagery techniques begin (Eastman Kodak, 1972).

INFRARED COLOR. Color infrared, also called "false color" film, has an intentionally shifted color balance so that it has an unnatural appearance to the human eye. The three layers of the film are sensitive to green, red and near infrared. In contrast, regular color film is sensitive to blue, green and red. A yellow (minus blue) filter such as a Wratten 12, 15 or Kodak 96-B is used to block blue-range light waves. Since color infrared film reflects the differential reflection of infrared light, features are translated into false colors: green objects appear blue and red objects appear green. Healthy vegetation appears bright red because the higher water content of robust leaves reflects more infrared light (Jorde, 1977).

The advantages of color infrared are those of black-and-white infrared, better haze penetration and discernible vegetation differences. Color infrared film is particularly useful in seeing tonal contrasts which may appear the same in regular color but different in infrared. Its ability to detect plant variation makes it especially useful in forestry, botany, and agronomy. Since vegetation damage may show a grave site, it should assist in detecting such targets. A disadvantage of infrared film is the slow film speed which makes it harder to use near dawn or dusk which are the best times for shadow effects. Additionally, light meters are no longer reliable since some of the infrared light is beyond the light meter range. Gumerman and Kruckman (1977) suggested that for Kodak 2443 Color Infrared Film an ASA/ISO setting of 125–150 should be used with a starting exposure of 1/250th of a second shutter speed and an *f*-stop setting of 8.

Studies by Poulton (1975) showed that deer carcasses on the ground could be seen best on infrared color aerial photography. This was attributed to two effects. First, nutrients from decomposition fertilized the nearby plants which showed up as a vigorous red ring surrounding the carcass. These fertilized plants could be differentiated from the other plants beyond the reach of the fertilizer. Secondly, the normally yellow-brown deer carcass tended to blend in with the ground cover but showed up bright white on infrared color film. Overall, the deer carcasses stood out as miniature white/red bull's-eyes in the spring landscape.

ULTRAVIOLET. Ultraviolet light occurs adjacent and contiguous to the visible portion of the spectrum but on the opposite end from infrared. Ultraviolet light can be seen by honeybees and can be recorded photographically. Ultraviolet light is commonly divided into the near, far, and extreme ranges based upon the wavelengths. All the wavelengths are shorter than we can normally see, being located between visible light and x-rays. The sun is the primary source of ultraviolet energy. Ultraviolet energy is readily absorbed and scattered by atmospheric gases.

Ultraviolet light can be detected by scanner imagery or ultraviolet filtered cameras and films. Some surface types and objects show higher contrast in ultraviolet than visible light. Some of these are water (including snow), concrete slabs, asphalt, and metal. Ultraviolet-sensitive photography can give information about soil types, crop conditions and water resources. Various rocks have different reflectance factors which enable, for instance, limestone outcrops to be readily identified. Similar to active microwave (radar) sensing, metal surfaces, such as unpainted metal roofs, show high contrast in ultraviolet. This means that ultraviolet photography and radar might both be useful for locating vehicles, lost aircraft, or other large metallic objects (Cronin et al., 1973).

AERIAL PHOTOGRAPH INTERPRETATION

Each photo interpreter has his own procedure when approaching a photo interpretation task, but success can be enhanced by first considering human vision factors. The examiner should have excellent natural or corrected vision and normal color perception (not color blind). The best possible lighting conditions should be available to perceive the nuances of color, tone, texture and relief. Approximately 50 footcandles of light are needed at the photograph level, or enough light for the darkest part of the image to be clear. The light should shine on to the photograph but not reflect directly into the viewer's eyes. The light should be steady, even, and cool such as that available from an adjustable fluorescent lamp. The slightly pinkish-tone fluorescent light, designed to be cosmetically flattering, will enhance the capacity of the viewer to see red colors (Estes & Simonett, 1975).

Most interpreters will perform a "first scan review" which is a once-over of the picture to familiarize themselves with the general terrain features and assure photograph orientation to the ground. Photographs are normally arranged so that shadows fall towards the viewer. From the beginning of the first scan, any anomalies noted on the ground's surface should be marked. The best technique is to mark the anomaly with a pin prick and then identify the target by notation on the back of the photograph. Writing on the front of the photograph may obscure other clues. The interpreter then moves to a detailed, methodical search, generally along the flight line to take advantage of any photographic overlap. The photographs should previously have been arranged and numbered consecutively along the flight path.

The detailed search may be conducted three times: first with the naked eye and then with the two most basic photo interpretation aids, a magnifying glass and stereoscopic viewer. A magnifying glass of two power was recommended by Wilson (1982). A stereoscopic viewer (Figure 8.7) is used for overlapping vertical photographs or other stereo pairs. The photographs are laid side by side under the viewer and adjusted until the two images are fused into a three-dimensional representation. Magnification attachments are available to enlarge the image. The detailed examinations should be conducted both by the naked eye and under magnification so that the interpreter avoids being too preoccupied with minute detail.

The next step is to compare the photographs with references such as

Figure 8.7. Overlapping vertical aerial photographs are laid beneath a stereoscopic viewer (stereoscope) and the instrument is adjusted until the two images are fused into a three-dimensional image. (Photograph courtesy of GISCO.)

topographic or county maps and other available imagery (e.g. thermal, microwave). This is an attempt to resolve or identify some of the detected anomalies. The resolution of the image, of course, determines the ability of the interpreter to identify targets. There is always a practical limit on interpretation imposed by the photographic detail shown.

If available time and money allows, images can be subjected to various electronic alterations. Electronic processing of imagery is generally divided into two categories: image manipulation and image enhancement. Image manipulation is correcting the image for atmospheric or instrument degradations. It attempts, for instance, to correct for photographic distortions or uncompensated airplane motion. It may also attempt to restore features lost because of over or under photographic exposure. Image enhancement includes those processes which attempt to improve the image quality. Contrast enhancement stretches color or tone differences. Edge enhancement heightens the variations between brightness levels. Other sophisticated instruments can combine and compare photographs from multi-band cameras.

Densitometry is a form of contrast enhancement which begins with the measurement of the relative darknesses of the image. It measures the density of individual pixels (picture elements) which make up the image. The densities in a photograph are the chemically reproduced patterns of light and dark which correspond to lightness and darkness on the ground. After the density levels or "gray scales" (Jorde, 1977) are measured, colors are assigned to each density level. These artificial color contours underscore contrast, since it is easier for the eye to distinguish between colors than between grays.

Edge enhancement is another electronic process in which two images of a photograph, a positive and a negative, are electronically superimposed and then slightly offset. This procedure highlights the borders of features, especially linear shapes such as roads, field edges, etc. (Jorde, 1977). Regardless of any electronic processing done, the aerial photographs should always be re-examined by another person. The second interpreter should have a completely new set of photographs so that he will not be influenced by the notations of the first interpreter.

As a product of these examinations, a collection of anomalies will be noted. These need to be winnowed to the ones which must be investigated by "ground truthing." Ground truth checking, or field searches, assign meanings to the patterns or anomalies detected on the imagery. Ground investigations have four purposes (Dozier & Strahler, 1983). The first is to calibrate or correct for image distortion. The second is to correlate physical and radiative properties, such as matching image color and soil type. The third purpose is training and accumulating data which can simplify subsequent interpretation jobs. Lastly is verification, the actual investigation of image anomalies to see if they could be grave sites. As with any search technique, someone must eventually examine the site and decide whether or not it warrants an excavation.

There are six basic parameters used in air photo interpretation which, in combination, help identify objects or ground features (Cochran, 1986). The first is color or tone which is the relative amount of light reflected by objects. This is determined by the amount of illumination, atmospheric conditions, surface type, film properties, etc. The second basic parameter is apparent texture which is the visual impression of roughness or smoothness of the object. This is partially affected by the scale of the image and the property of the film, especially grain size. The third clue is pattern, the spatial arrangement of features or objects, particularly the repetition of features which assists identification. An example of pattern is the characteristic arrangement of headstones which identifies a cemetery. Shape is the geometric outline of the object, and size is the dimensions of the object under inspection. The sixth clue is shadows which are areas of minimal light reflection which often reveal shape and relief. The degree of shadowing may either help or hinder photo interpretation efforts. Relative heights or depths may be particularly important factors shown by shadows.

To these basic parameters, other authors added site and association (Estes, 1983). Site is the location in which the object or target appears. For instance, whether a particular object appears downtown or out in the country makes a difference. Likewise, its association with other features may identify the object or its purpose. As an example of site and association, a circular building in a suburban subdivision might be a water tower. A similar object next to a barn in the country is probably a grain silo.

Archaeologists using aerial photos are principally concerned with shadows, soil color variations and crop marks. Landscape shadows are caused by differences in height of the ground surface. These marks are best revealed in oblique photography, taken near sunrise or sunset, with the plane oriented so that the shadows face the camera. The shadows may reveal mounds, banks, ditches, or other features (St. Joseph, 1966). Shadows will be minimal at midday and then lengthen throughout the day. The smallest shadows occur and most commercial photography is taken between 10:00 A.M. and 2:00 P.M. Shadowing may be dramatic at one hour before sunset. Even minute surface irregularities might be displayed, though small variations may be lost in larger shadows. Shadows are affected by the direction and elevation of the sun. Photographs should be taken on several days and at different times of the day. This allows the photographer to benefit from all possible shadow situations. Maximum shadowing effect is seen with the photographer looking toward the sun and the least with the sun behind the photographer. Haze causes reduced shadowing because the light rays are scattered between the ground and the camera, reducing clarity and tonal contrast. Unfortunately, haze is common during early mornings and late afternoons. Shadowing is important, because the depression caused by the collapse or compacting of a grave site may last for five to ten years after burial (Bass & Birkby, 1978).

Soil marks are variations in the color of the soil, often caused by man-made disturbances. Soil variations may be especially prominent in newly plowed farm fields. Subsoils tend to be lighter in color than topsoils and show up on aerial photography as light spots on the ground. Dark soil spots may actually be "damp" marks caused by the collection or retention of water, another characteristic of graves (Grady, 1989). Soil differences may be important to archaeologists where human activities have transported soil to or away from its native source.

Crop marks are vegetation patterns caused by past human activities. Differential plant growth may be either positive or negative, i.e. the human activities may have favored plant growth or hindered it. Even such small archaeological features as post holes have been identified by crop mark differences (St. Joseph, 1966). Crop marks depend upon vegetation type, yearlong weather patterns, soil type, and other factors. They are seen well in the driest season of the growing year and best during droughts when plants are stressed. The maximum difference in plant growth is usually seen near harvest time. Long-rooted cereal crops, such as wheats, oats and barleys, show the marks best. The cereals are responsive to soil moisture, are sensitive to disturbance, and their close plant spacing shows detail well.

Root crops, such as sugar beets and potatoes, may also show crop marks, but the wide spacing of plants shows only large-scale disturbances. Hay and other grasses tend to conceal subsoil features. They show marks only during severe drought conditions and are conventionally harvested throughout the summer before crop marks have had an opportunity to show themselves. Many crop marks are invisible until just the right combination of crop stage and weather occur. Plowing will not prevent crop marks or interrupt features which are below the depth reached by the plowshare.

Positive crop marks are made by plants that are taller, darker, or thicker than the surrounding plants. Soil disturbances, such as graves, may be favorable to plant life in a number of ways. First, when the ground is water-logged in the spring, disturbed soil may have better drainage. In contrast, when the weather is dry, the disturbed soil may allows roots to grow deeper to reach water reservoirs. Depressions may collect runoff and remain damp. Additionally, decomposing flesh adds nutrients to the soil. Added nitrogen is especially important and may mean larger plant size, greater leaf area, more "greenness" and a longer growth period. Crop marks reflect soil acidity which in turn may be altered by the decomposition process. Excessively low PH (acidic) soils retard phosphorus availability so plant growth and color is poor. Lastly, a grave may benefit plants because disturbed soils are usually darker. They obtain more warmth from the sun so their seedlings are the first to sprout. Those warmer areas will display the first color in the spring and attain the greatest plant height.

Negative crop marks, also called crop stunting or parching (Grady, 1989), result from retarded plant growth. In poor areas, smaller plants appear later in the spring with less color and brightness. A crop may fail altogether and that portion of the field go to weeds. In a short season, marginal plants will be the first to turn yellow. Negative crop marks are caused by the reverse conditions of those which caused positive marks. At maximum stress, the distinction between positive and negative marks may be completely obliterated as the entire crop is lost.

As with shadowing, photography angle and direction may change the visibility of the crop marks. Crop height is best revealed by photographing towards the sun, but color is best detected by photographing away from the sun. The waving of a crop in the wind may confuse the scene. This effect may be minimized by photographing directly upwind or downwind (Jones & Evans, 1975). Wilson (1982) believed that single inhumation graves are probably too small and inconspicuous to be seen by crop marks alone unless there were other signs as well.

Aerial photography does not have to be abandoned in the wintertime. Light snow cover may display brilliant shadow clarity. Each change in slope may be signalled by a corresponding change in the color tone of the snow. A thin snow cover is particularly good for detecting differences in surface texture. For example, thin snow shows a smooth spot among brush or rough spots in a smooth field. With greater snow depth, elevation differences blur until they are completely obliterated. Light wind and snow combined may result in differential drifting. An area may be swept clear except for pockets or depressions which hold the snow. This may add to the compaction of a grave site, and the increased moisture may facilitate plant growth. During the spring melt, the snow will last longest in these hollows. The best photographic conditions for snow are bright sunlight with the sun less than 20 degrees above the horizon (Wilson, 1982).

The search supervisor will have to determine whether aerial photography is likely to assist in a search for human remains. Clearly, it is best for open lands, desert country and agricultural fields. It may be little help in forest land, swamps or commercial orchards. It should be used immediately after a disappearance and again after the search area has received a lot of water and will show maximum compaction (Morse & Stoutamire, 1983). High-altitude and satellite photography is not likely to be useful, so an investigator will have to depend upon recently taken low-altitude (less than 450 meters) photography. Oblique photography can be done immediately depending upon weather conditions, but vertical photography requires professional assistance. Arid climates such as the American Southwest are particularly suitable to aerial photography searches because soil and plant damage persists for a long time. Aerial photographs should be taken before a ground search is begun, since it may inadvertently create false anomalies and destroy real evidence, e.g. vehicle tracks. Air photo interpretation before the ground search may also eliminate the need for two trips to the area, the first time for general exploration and the second time to check out individual anomalies (Cockran, 1986).

If the investigator is going to depend primarily upon shadow marks, contrast is maximized by matching a red filter with black-and-white film or by using black-and-white infrared film. Soil color differences are shown best by color film and will be most prominent after a rainstorm. The vegetation contrast will be seen in plants when their root zones intercept subsoil disturbances. They will be most clearly evident in photographs taken by color infrared and color film. Tartaglia (1977) recommended, for archaeological and ecological studies, color infrared film with appropriate filters. He believed that it was superior to black-and-white infrared, color, or black and white. Hampton (1974) recommended a three-camera system. The first camera had Kodak Aerochrome #2443 color infrared film shot through a Wratten 12 yellow filter. The second camera was equipped with Kodak Plus X panchromatic film and the third camera with Kodak Ektachrome color film. Rinker's chapter in Wilson (1975) contained a chart showing the sensitivities of various film and filters. It also contained application recommendations. For small archaeological site detection, Rinker recommended Kodak Tri-X film unfiltered, Kodak Ektachrome color film and Kodak Ektachrome infrared film.

The Eastman Kodak (1985) publication on aerial photography also made specific film recommendations, though not all the films are available in 35-millimeter format. The Kodak publication also suggested trial exposures and appropriate filters for each film. Their recommendations are summarized in Figure 8.8 (Eastman Kodak, 1989).

There must be consultation between the pilot and the investigator before aerial photography work can begin. They will have to decide, using available information and maps, which areas are to be photographed,

FILM TYPE	*RECOMMENDED KODAK FILMS*
Black-and-White	PLUS–X AEROGRAPHIC 2402 (ESTAR Base)*
	Tri-X AEROGRAPHIC 2403 (ESTAR Base)*
	PLUS–X Pan
	PLUS–X Pan Professional
	TRI–X Pan
	T–MAX 100 Professional
	T–MAX 400 Professional
Black-and-White Infrared	Infrared AEROGRAPHIC 2424 (ESTAR Base)*
	High Speed Infrared
Color Print	AEROCOLOR Negative 2445 (ESTAR Base)*
	KODACOLOR GOLD 100
	KODACOLOR GOLD 200
	KODACOLOR GOLD 400
	VERICOLOR HC Professional
	EKTAPRESS GOLD 100 Professional
	EKTAPRESS GOLD 400 Professional
Color Transparency	AEROCHROME MS 2448 (ESTAR Base)*
	EKTACHROME 100 HC
	EKTACHROME 100 PLUS Professional
	EKTACHROME 200 (Daylight)
	EKTACHROME 200 Professional
	KODACHROME 200 (Daylight)
	KODACHROME 200 Professional
Color Infrared	AEROCHROME Infrared 2443 (ESTAR Base)*
	EKTACHROME Infrared

*Films for aerial cameras.

Figure 8.8. Eastman Kodak (1989) film recommendations for aerial photography. The films are listed in order of preference. Some of the listed films are for aerial cameras only (denoted by *), but the others are for conventional cameras.

on which dates and at which times. They should agree upon acceptable minimum weather conditions. The best weather for photography is clear (visibility of 15 miles or more), with wind no more than 10 to 15 miles per hour. They will also have to agree on a flight position, direction and altitude which is compatible with the mission purposes. The pilot will know current FAA restrictions which generally limit fixed-wing aircraft to an altitude of 1,000 feet in a congested area and 500 feet in open areas. Helicopters have no such restrictions (Eastman Kodak, 1985). If repeated low flights are anticipated, property owners or appropriate agencies should be notified, since observers may become concerned about a continually circling, low-flying plane. Time spent in the air is costly, so the investigator/photographer should have his cameras, film and filters ready to go. Wasted time can also be minimized by having a good communications system between the pilot and the photographer. The investigator should record flight information which may be needed for court or for the photo interpreter. He should note the flight speed, direction, drift, altitude and times of each flight path. Collaboration and cooperation are necessary between the pilot, photographer and photo interpreter if results are to be maximized and costs minimized.

Chapter 9

PARAPSYCHOLOGICAL METHODS

"Man is a museum of diseases, a home of impurities; he comes to-day
and is gone to-morrow; he begins as dirt and departs as stench. . . ."

> From *The Mysterious Stranger,* a short
> story by Mark Twain, Samuel Langhorne
> Clemens

T here are two basic parapsychological techniques for finding burial
sites, both of which involve the use of persons claiming to have
extraordinary sensory abilities. The first technique is the use of dowsers,
also known as "witchers" or "diviners." The second is the use of psychics
or "sensitives." Rarely are the use of these techniques initiated by law
enforcement agencies. Rather, their use is the result of pressure from the
victim's family or from desperation when more conventional search
techniques have failed.

Parapsychological techniques are in sharp contrast to those methods
contained in the previous chapters. The previously discussed search
techniques are based on sound scientific principles and have proven
successful in the field. Parapsychological methods are neither. Despite
the claims of their proponents, there is no scientific evidence that
parapsychological methods work. Nevertheless, it is important for investigators to understand the techniques so that they may objectively evaluate unsolicited tips from dowsers or psychics. Knowledge of the technique
is needed by the search director so that he may defend his decision to
reject parapsychological methods. An investigator must be prepared to
answer questions raised by the family and press about these methods. He
will need accurate information if he hopes to dissuade the family from
employing psychic practitioners. An investigator who understands the
theories and common practices of dowsers and psychics is better prepared to detect fraud and prevent victimization of the family. Should
parapsychological search methods be forced upon him, the investigator
must know how to control and manage them so that they are non-

179

destructive and will not detract from or impede conventional efforts. Lastly, an investigator must be prepared to penetrate the cover story of an informant who claims to have received information about a crime from a psychic source.

DOWSING

Dowsing is a very old practice, certainly dating back at least 400 years and perhaps thousands of years. A rock painting of a dowser appears in an African cave which has been dated by Carbon-14 analysis to 8000 years ago (MacLean, 1976). Georgius Agricola described, in *De re metallica* (1556), the use of a forked twig by German miners to locate minerals beneath the surface (Wyman, 1977). Numerous authors cite the exploits of Jacques Aymar, who, in France (1692), used a divining rod to lead police to a fugitive murderer. The defendant's confession later confirmed the trail divined by Aymar (Baum, 1974). Dowsing has remained popular in Europe, where most of the more than 700 books about dowsing have been published (Wyman, 1977).

American interest in dowsing increased in the 1950s after the publication of three books by Kenneth Roberts. The books, *Henry Gross and His Dowsing Rod* (1951), *The Seventh Sense* (1953) and *Water Unlimited* (1957), presented the exploits and successful cases of dowser Henry Gross (Willey, 1984). In 1961 the American Society of Dowsers, Inc. was founded. The American Society of Dowsers, Danville, Vermont 05828 is still active and publishes its quarterly digest, *The American Dowser.* Dowsing continues to inspire private and public interest. Dowsers were used by the military in World Wars I and II and even by the Marines in Vietnam to find buried weapons caches and booby traps (Wolkomir, 1985).

Dowsing includes a number of different techniques and tools. It has been used, in one form or another, to search for minerals, oil, buried bodies, lost objects, missing persons, archaeological sites, sewers and pipes, underground tanks, water, downed aircraft, shipwrecks, lost animals, pipeline leaks, and even for medical diagnosis (Graves, 1976). Willey (1984) recommended the reader think of dowsing as a "searching tool" which can be used to ferret out locations, objects, and information. Most dowsers specialize in just a few fields and use individual techniques, equipment and procedures to suit the search.

Tools

There are four principal categories of dowsing tools. They are: (1) the forked stick or y-rod, (2) the pendulum, (3) angle rods, and (4) the flexible wand or "bobber." Some dowsers have created elaborate dowsing gadgets, while others use only a bare hand and no physical tools at all. Most advocates claim that the dowser senses the object of the search and "the dowsing instruments are mechanical amplifiers of small neuromuscular reflexes, the most commonly used reflexes being those of hands" (Graves, 1976:31). That is, the tool is allegedly amplifying the body's reaction to some perceived stimulus.

The y-rod, forked stick, or spring rod is the most well-known dowsing device. The pliable forked branch, often made of willow, maple, witch hazel or fruit tree wood, was formerly the preferred tool, specially for divining water. Diviners claim that they cannot only detect the presence of water but determine its quality, depth, quantity, and direction of travel. The wooden rods are about 18 inches long and have the approximate diameter of a pencil. Y-rods are now made out of metal wire, nylon strands, fiberglass, or other plastics (Figure 9.1). Man-made materials are now preferred because the rods can be used indefinitely, allowing the user to become accustomed to the rod's "feel." Tree branches had to be freshly cut to assure flexibility. In use, the y-rod is held in both hands, palms up, generally at about waist level. The action of the rod tip conveys information to the user. Each rod and target may have a different language, with variables being such things as rod tip movement direction, strength, speed, etc. (Figure 9.2.)

The pendulum is merely a weight suspended by a flexible link and is the most popular dowsing tool in Europe (Baum, 1974). Pendulums show enormous variability (Figure 9.3). They are usually a wood or metal tube or box suspended by a chain, string or wire. The pendulum body is often hollow so that a specimen of the object sought can be placed inside. Such a system is frequently used in dowsing for oil or minerals. Pendulums vary in weight, size, color and shape. The chain may be lengthened or shortened and each dowser holds it in his own particular fashion (Figure 9.4). It is the movements of the pendulum which conveys information to the dowser. The pendulum may swing fore and aft, sideways, or diagonally. It may spin clockwise or counterclockwise. Its path of travel may scribe out a perfect circle or an ellipse. All these motions must be translated by the dowser into the answer for the question being asked of the tool (Howell, 1979).

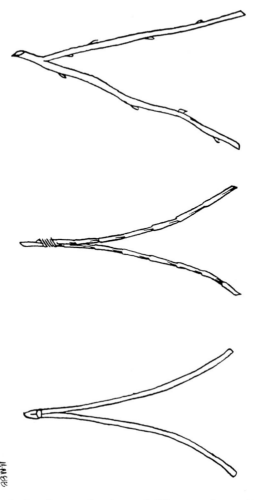

Figure 9.1. Y-rods are the best known dowsing tool. They may be made out of wood, metal, plastic or other flexible material. (Adapted from Willey, 1984.)

Angle rods are L-shaped rods used in pairs. They are commonly made of welder's brazing rod, coat hangers, or other small-diameter metal rods. Again, individual preference will determine the dimensions of the tool (Figure 9.5). One of the angle rods will be held in each hand at waist or chest level. As the search pattern is executed, the rod tips move and supposedly convey information to the dowser. The tips may remain parallel, diverge, or converge in any given instance, again requiring the dowser to interpret the tool's actions (Figure 9.6).

The bobber or wand is simply a flexible, long, straight pointer made of wood, metal, or plastic (Figure 9.7). In use, the tip of the wand moves

Figure 9.2. The Y-rod is normally held palms up at about waist level. Rod tip movement conveys information to the dowser. (Photograph by the author.)

and, like the pendulum, its various oscillations must be observed, analyzed, and translated into information. Like the y-rod, the bobber may also yield information from the strength of its reactions as well as from the direction and type of motion (Figure 9.8).

Search Techniques

Field dowsing is the well-known dowsing technique. It is employed when the dowser has been called upon to locate an object in a limited area, such as searching for water near a proposed homesite. In this technique, the dowser walks the land, attempting to locate a subterranean target. The dowser, or his associate, will mark the points of strongest

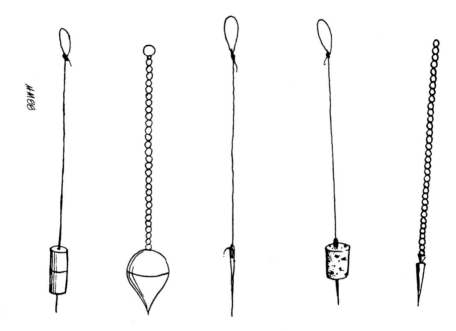

Figure 9.3. Pendulums are simply weights suspended by flexible lines or chains. They are often hollow so that samples of the target, e.g. mineral ore, can be placed inside them. They vary in weight, size, color and shape. (Adapted from Willey, 1984.)

target indications. The area will be worked systematically and repeatedly until a clustering of indicators is obtained (Figure 9.9). Drilling or excavation will then begin in the center of the "hottest" area.

In remote dowsing, the dowser stands still rather than walking the land. He will attempt to detect the target from a distance. It is a process of narrowing down the target area for subsequent search. The dowser may, for instance, stand at the edge or corner of a property and take a direction bearing toward the target. The procedure is then repeated from another corner until the object is located by triangulation (Figure 9.10). Similarly, the dowser may walk a property line and note any reactions from his tool. He will then walk a perpendicular property line, again noting target indicators. Further searches can then be made of those areas where indicator lines intersect (Figure 9.11). Once remote dowsing has narrowed the search area, field walking is usually undertaken. Remote dowsing has also been called "scanning" or "casting" (MacLean, 1976) and can be used where it is not possible to actually walk the search area, e.g. thick jungle or shallow swamp.

Information dowsing is another technique in which specific questions

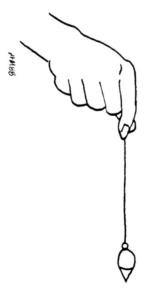

Figure 9.4. Each dowser has his own technique for holding the pendulum. The movements and swing of the weight are translated by the operator into answers to the questions asked by the searcher. (Adapted from Graves, 1976.)

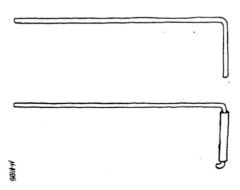

Figure 9.5. Angle rods are dowsing tools used in pairs. They are normally made out of thin metal rods but vary in material and dimensions depending upon the preferences of the dowser. (Adapted from Willey, 1984.)

are asked, a la Ouija board. These are similar to the questions which might be asked of a psychic, except that the motion of the divining tool gives the answer. The use of a tool for information gathering is based on the assumption that divining is a mental, not physical, process. Proponents of this technique emphasize that answers are based upon conditions existing at the time of questioning, so the technique cannot foretell

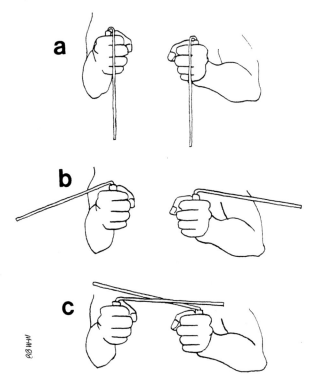

Figure 9.6. Dowsers derive information from the movements of the angle rod tips. The tips may remain parallel (a), diverge (b), or converge (c). (Adapted from Howells, 1979.)

the future (Willey, 1984). As in all dowsing, the searcher must "mentally define exactly what you want to find (or know)" (MacLean, 1976:26). The dowser tries not to let his mind wander. MacLean described "monkey thoughts" as drifting ideas that destroy concentration and confound results.

Map dowsing may be done using a map, aerial photograph or even a sketch. It is a form of simulated field or remote dowsing. Proponents argue that it can be done at any distance from the actual search area, even cross-country or across the globe. They claim it can even be done by telephone without maps if topographic descriptions are sufficiently detailed (Wyman, 1977). This technique, like information dowsing, depends upon a mental or extrasensory perception explanation. Map work, like remote dowsing, requires confirmation by field dowsing.

The tools most commonly used in map dowsing are the y-rod or the pendulum. Many specific methods may be used by the dowser, either alone or with an assistant. One technique requires the assistant, out of

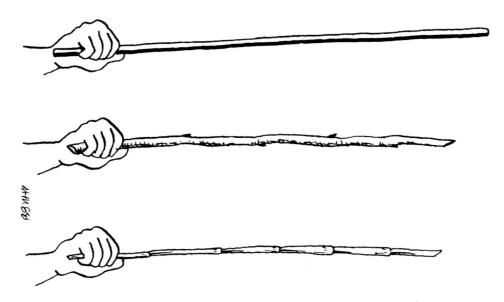

Figure 9.7. The bobber or wand is a flexible pointer made of wood, metal or plastic. (Adapted from Willey, 1984.)

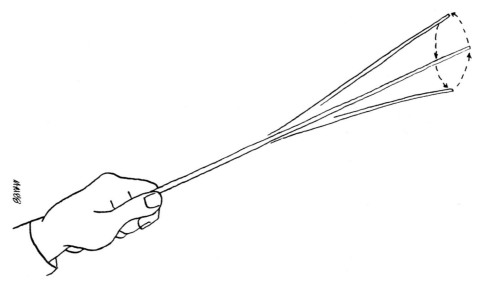

Figure 9.8. Like the Y-rod and pendulum, the dowser supposedly obtains information from the movements of the bobber tip. (Adapted from MacLean, 1976.)

sight of the dowser, to run a ruler slowly over the map, going either north-south or east-west. Responses noted from the dowsing tool are penciled in. The procedure is repeated from other directions until a

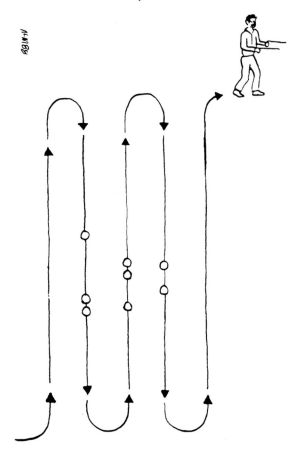

Figure 9.9. Field walking is the traditional technique for finding water. The dowser walks the property and marks where the rods indicate water can be found. A well is then drilled where the signs cluster. (Adapted from Graves, 1976.)

clustering of indicators is assembled. Using another method, the dowser may hold a y-rod in his hands and then move his eyes slowly across the map. Responses from the rod tip will be marked on the map by an assistant (Figure 9.12). In another technique, the dowser moves his pendulum over the map, watching for a response, which is then marked. A fourth technique is for the dowser to wrap a flexible wire around one hand, leaving approximately 4–6 inches protruding as a pointer. He then draws the wire over the map and watches for pendulum indicators (Figure 9.13).

Another technique combines information seeking with map dowsing. First, the map will be sectioned by a grid, then the dowsing tool will be asked whether the target is in one of the large sections. The question will

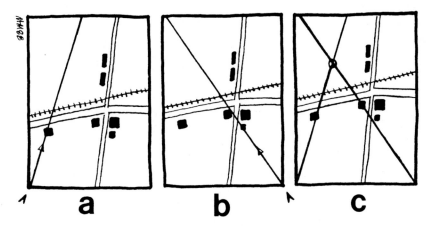

Figure 9.10. Remote dowsing can be done by triangulation. The dowser stands at a corner of the property and takes a bearing on the target (a). The procedure is repeated at another property corner (b). The area where the lines intersect is then searched by field walking (c). (Adapted from Graves, 1976.)

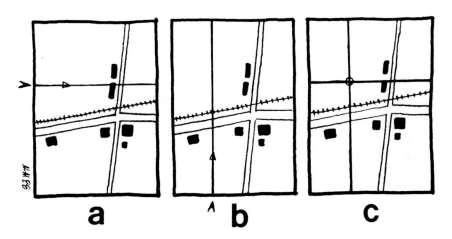

Figure 9.11. Remote dowsing can also be done from perpendicular property lines. The dowser takes a bearing on the target from one boundary (a) and then from a second location (b). A detailed search is then made of the area where the lines intersect (c). (Adapted from Graves, 1976.)

be repeatedly asked until a yes answer is obtained. Then that section will be divided into smaller portions and the question asked again. The process is repeated until the search area becomes a manageable size for field dowsing (Figure 9.14).

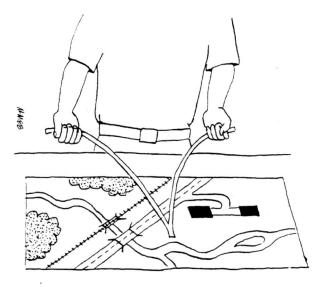

Figure 9.12. Map dowsing may be done with a Y-rod. The dowser moves his eyes over the map while watching for signs of movement from the rod tip. (Adapted from Baum, 1974.)

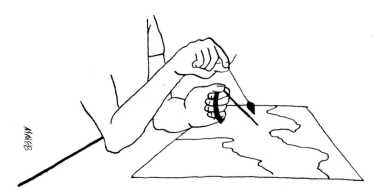

Figure 9.13. Map dowsing may also be done with a pendulum. The dowser moves a pointer across the map while watching the motions of the pendulum. Positive signs are marked on the map and then field walking is done over the "hot" areas. (Adapted from Howells, 1979.)

Regardless of the specific technique, map dowsing is usually done on fairly large-scale maps such as 1:1000 to 1:10,000. The map-dowsing technique has been used in attempts to track missing persons, such as a lost hiker. With the map spread out, the dowser uses his finger or a pointer and, interpreting the pendulum's motion, attempts to recreate the victim's path of travel. Mermet (1959) elaborated on a specific technique for tracing missing persons. He recommended the dowser be

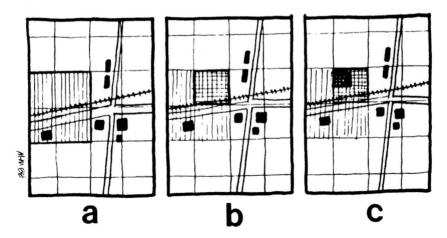

Figure 9.14. Map dowsing can also be done using yes-no questions and a grid sectioned map. The dowser asks "Is the target located here?" If a yes answer is received from the dowsing tool (a), that area is divided into smaller sections and the process repeated (b). Eventually, the area indicated is small enough to search by field walking (c). (Adapted from Graves, 1976.)

given a photograph of the missing person or an object the person recently touched. The dowser should also be given a plan or sketch of where the person was last seen. Lastly, the dowser will need a map of the region on which to recreate the person's movements. Mermet, who described himself as a "radiesthetist," believed that each person emits a unique radiation and that the dowser can tune in to that frequency and follow the person's trail.

Regardless of the specific tool or technique, the same general procedure is used by all dowsers. The first step for the dowser is to learn about the problem or case under investigation. Once he has an understanding of the situation, he can formulate the questions and the procedures he will use. He then takes up his dowsing device and asks the questions. Lastly, he interprets the actions or movements of this tool to answer the questions. Authors who promote dowsing emphasize the importance of properly phrasing the questions and approaching the case with the correct mental attitude. Hitching (1978), quoting William Cookworthy, said that "The rod must be held with indifference," meaning that the dowser must be rested, relaxed, and impartial but clearly focused on the search underway.

Hitching's three principles of dowsing were first that the body reacts physiologically during the dowsing search process. Secondly, the physical reactions of the instrument are just an indicator of the body reactions, and thirdly, that all dowsing is based upon a search question. Therefore, the dowser asks the question, gets a bodily reaction, and the tool indicates the answer in a code specific to the operator. The various tools and techniques of dowsing are not exclusionary. They may be used in combination or sequentially. For instance, the late John G. Shelley, Jr., former president of the American Society of Dowsers, considered himself equally proficient with the y-rod and pendulum. He also used, depending upon the situation, field dowsing, remote dowsing, and map dowsing (Shelley, 1971).

Explanations

Most dowsers claim that the ability to dowse is a "gift" that is found mostly in older men and tends to run in families (Wyman, 1977). Baum (1974) felt that dowsing is an art form found only in certain people. Willey (1984) also believed that it is inherited, an innate ability from birth which cannot later be learned. Hitching (1978:54) believed that forensic dowsing is rarer still and that "in every generation there are only two or three people in the world . . . who can track people and unravel mysteries" through dowsing. He believed that tracing missing persons is the most difficult and elusive of all dowsing jobs and that the ability to do other forms of dowsing, such as finding water, is more common.

Dowsers suggest two possible explanations for dowsing: mental or physical (Tromp, 1949). The mental explanation for dowsing prevails if one believes in the ability of map dowsers, since the dowser is so far removed from his target. Some people believe that dowsing is one form of ESP (extrasensory perception) (McLean, 1976). This is the explanation forwarded by Dr. Joseph B. Rhine (1962) who has worked on ESP phenomena. This "subconscious, supernormal, cognitive faculty" has also been called "cryptesthesia" (Barrett & Besterman, 1968:275). Supporters claim that by this hidden perception, knowledge of the target object enters the dowser's subconscious and somehow produces the physiological disturbances which can then be visualized in the motions of the dowsing tool.

The other explanation is that dowsers do not have perceptions beyond their senses but are simply more sensitive to physical emanations that the rest of us cannot detect. Mermet (1959) described "radiesthesia" as being sensitive to radiations. In addition, he wrote that a good dowser can practice "teleradiesthesia," which is prospection at a distance. Mermet felt that all objects, without exception, are constantly emitting radiation and that the human body detects these radiations. The nervous reaction to that detection is focused in the hands. An object held in the hand, be it a rod or pendulum, manifests the nervous reaction by movements. Those movements are indicators of the level of radiation perceived by the dowser. Baum (1974) concurred that radiations emanate from everything around us, including people, minerals, and water. He claimed the dowser is able to not only detect but separate out the radiations and thus focus his search on the target. Hitching (1978:205) identified the radiations as being electromagnetic in nature: "Since everything above absolute zero degrees temperature emits a small amount of electromagnetic radiation, perhaps this is what a dowser senses and manages to identify." Others have described this alleged sensory sensitivity as a "subconscious smell" which is converted into an involuntary muscle reaction of the hands (Wyman, 1977). Hitching (1978) is likely correct when he said that "most dowsers have given up trying to analyze how it works" except for allegiance to their own pet theories. Or, as Wyman noted, dowsing may simply be self-deception combined with luck and experience at recognizing favorable topographic or geologic conditions.

Problems

All writers and practitioners will admit that dowsing works, at best, only some of the time. A number of excuses are given for the frequent failures. As with psychics, dowsers claim success is most likely when there is a genuine need for their services (Howell, 1979). The failure of dowsers to perform in controlled experiments is often attributed to this lack of genuine human need for positive results.

Dowsers claim that their success can be obstructed by psychological interference or "intrusions of the mind" into dowsing. Graves (1976) identified the types of psychological obstructions which can occur. The first is an attempt by the dowser to consciously control the automatic part of the dowsing process, in other words, attempting to influence or override the dowsing tool. The second possibility is the intrusion of conscious or semi-conscious assumptions and prejudices into the dowsing effort. An example might be disregarding dowsing results when they conflict with common sense or known evidence. Another problem is the intrusion of unconscious assumptions or presumptions such as self-doubt. According to Graves, a dowser who doubts his own abilities or the genuine need of his client is likely to fail, as is a dowser who is physically or psychologically ill at ease.

Supporters claim a dowser can also be wrong about the current location of an object because of "remanence." This is radiation left over after the target object is gone (Graves, 1976). The problem ought to be corrected by asking the precisely accurate question, "Is the target there *now?*" As with most skills, dowsers believe they can improve performance with practice and experience.

There appears to be no scientific evidence to substantiate the accuracy or validity of dowsing (Martin, 1983–84; Randi, 1979; Reese, 1985; Vogt & Hyman, 1979). Dowsing is certainly more common in the popular rather than scientific press, e.g. Wolkomir (1985). Vogt and Hyman (1979) examined the types of evidence commonly used to support water divining. They were: case histories or anecdotes, records of actual cases, field tests, and, lastly, controlled experiments. Case histories are poor evidence because of the well-known problems with human memory, perception, and fidelity. Vogt and Hyman (1979:55) concluded that "There are many reasons, then, why case histories do not qualify as evidence."

Vogt and Hyman (1979:56) found few written records of drilling success rates and that "even when objective records are kept, the case history approach is incapable of providing unequivocal evidence for or against the efficacy of water witching." They found that field tests likewise have been conducted without the necessary controls to make them reliable and "because such controls were lacking . . . the results are inconclusive" (Vogt & Hyman, 1979:58).

Vogt and Hyman (1979:81) found that when properly controlled experiments were conducted, whether in the field or laboratory, "almost without exception, the experiments . . . yield negative results concerning the prowess of the diviner." They concluded that "the evidence for it (dowsing), when assembled and examined, is not merely insufficient; according to current scientific standards, . . . it is appallingly negative" (Vogt & Hyman, 1979:82).

Despite the lack of scientific support for dowsing, there is a reason it might be included in a search plan—it may convince the family, press and supervisors that everything possible is being done; that no investigative opportunity is being overlooked. The use of dowsing is non-destructive to physical evidence or other investigative efforts. It is inexpensive, as most dowsers will work on a volunteer or expenses-only basis. The search supervisor will have to weigh the likelihood of success against the time and effort expended. He will also have to assess the possible negative as well as positive reactions of the public to the use of a dowser.

PSYCHICS

A psychic or "sensitive" has been defined as: "any person who receives information by means other than the five senses and that cannot be explained in terms of established physical principles" (Hibbard & Warring, 1982:16). Psychic powers are usually equated with the possession of extrasensory perception (ESP). Psychics are said to come by their information from intuition, which has been called "the immediate knowing or learning of something but not the conscious use of reasoning" (Emerson, 1974:14).

Just as dowsing has its subcategories, so does ESP. It is often divided into five types. The first is telepathy or passive communication between minds, also called mind reading. The second is clairvoyance, which is seeing or hearing events or objects at a distance beyond the range of normal senses. The third category is precognition or the ability to predict future occurrences. The fourth is dowsing and the fifth is psychometry, also called retrocognition. This is the ability to sense the history of an object or place. Within and across these categories are a host of reported psychic phenomena. These include visions or dreams, impressions gained from holding objects, hearing voices, etc. The critical issue for the investigator is the accuracy of the information obtained, not the nature of the phenomenon. The question of which alleged psi talent is at work is largely irrelevant in practical research (Schwartz, 1978). Psychics are rarely used by police investigators which represent conservative social institutions. To most people, paranormal investigative techniques are equated with occult or bunko schemes. Psychics are most likely to be used as a last resort or in accordance with the wishes of the victim's family.

Psychics may spontaneously contact a department by phone or letter, offering their assistance. These sincere inquiries have to be screened from the cranks that a major case may attract. It is also possible that a perpetrator may provide information to investigators under the guise of being omniscient. Psychics used by the police may be "known"

professionals, amateur psychics with prior experience, or neophytes
having an isolated psychic experience (Hibbard & Warring, 1982). In the
last case, the receiver of the psychic information likely had a close
personal tie to the victim, such as a relative, spouse, etc.

Psychics have also been used in anthropological studies, both in archaeology and cultural anthropology. Psychic or "intuitive" archaeology has
been championed by Dr. J. Norman Emerson (1974, 1976). Sensitives
have chosen excavation sites and they have been asked to predict the
depths and locations where archaeological objects are to be found. Supporters claim that psychics can date artifacts and determine their origins
or histories. Psychics claim they can describe the past life and culture of
site occupants (Van de Castle, 1977). As an example, Emerson's informant "George" gave information about prehistoric Iroquois life from
recovered artifacts or sites. Emerson believed he was able to rule out the
possibility that his psychic had previously studied Iroquois culture or
that he was obtaining information from Emerson through mental telepathy.

In police work, as in anthropology, the evidence for the successful use
of psychics is primarily anecdotal, not scientific (Goldfluss, 1987; Rayl,
1987; Trubo, 1975; Wilson, 1985). Research has failed to substantiate
widespread use or success (Emery, 1988). In 1975, 100 of the largest police
departments in the United States were sent questionnaires about the use
of psychics. Only seven admitted to having used psychics in major
criminal investigations. Among those seven, there were few instances of
success (Guarino, 1975). Psychics, like dowsers, usually fail but at least
their use in an investigation is non-destructive to evidence or other
investigative efforts. Few professionals consider ESP a fact, but then few
are willing to totally dismiss it either. Goldfluss (1987) is a judge who has
predicted that the use of psychics in forensic investigations and trials will
become commonplace. He believed the judicial system will eventually
have to decide the ethical and admissibility standards of such psychic
evidence.

Schwartz (1978) warned that the greatest danger is not from psychics
who fail and admit their failures but from the inflated claims of zealots.
He cautioned:

> What this new sub-discipline (of archaeology) cannot withstand . . . is
> the deadly embrace of over zealous or half-trained true believers.
> These people first promise more than the approach can deliver, and
> compound that misrepresentation by performing their research sloppily,

and finally top the devastation by making outlandish claims for anything their excavations do discover. (Schwartz 1978:291.)

Techniques

Psychics may be used either individually or in a group. The purported advantages of using a group is that information is obtained more quickly and the psychics may potentiate each other's abilities. The disadvantages are that individuals may be influenced by suggestion, interpsychic contamination or personal competition, any of which may disrupt their abilities. Generally psychics are used on only one case at a time.

Psychics may work with no physical props or aids at all. Others claim to receive mental impressions from handling objects associated with the case or from visiting sites involved. Still others work with maps or photographs. Some psychics want close proximity to the investigation, whereas others work from a distance, akin to map dowsers. Most writers claim that psychics work best in person, as opposed to telephone consultations.

Some psychics work completely in the blind about a case. They are allowed to see and handle objects but have no other information about the event or the objects' origins. Another method allows the psychic to receive minimal information about the crime that occurred. For instance, he may be told only the type of crime and the victim's name. A third technique permits the psychic access to all available investigation information. These different approaches may also be used in sequence. The psychic may first be asked for all of his impressions while "in the blind." Then he is given some information and asked for additional facts. Lastly, he is given complete access to the investigation file and is asked to fine-tune or supplement his prior impressions. The less information a psychic has, the less he will be able to tell investigators. The information reported, however, is likely to be more accurate (Hibbard & Warring, 1982). This is confirmed by the researcher-reported phenomenon that early information from a psychic may be the least specific but is generally the most accurate. Of course, vague or general guesses are always more likely to be accurate than specific predictions. A psychic who claims he can pinpoint the location of a body will probably be wrong, but one who predicts the body will be found within the state will probably be right.

Success Factors

Schwartz (1978) believed that the practical use of psychics in archaeology required consideration of six factors. The first is the condition of the psychic, and hence the psychic channel itself. The sensitive must be in good physical condition and feel that he is liked by his co-workers and is engaged in important, meaningful work.

The second factor is the condition of the researcher or non-psychic investigator. He must, in his verbal and non-verbal communication, express confidence in the ability of the psychic. The researcher must have a genuine need for the information requested and should have expertise in both the investigation underway and the use of psychics in general.

Schwartz's third, fourth and fifth factors are the development of a mutually understood language between the psychic and his co-worker. They must have the solution of the case as a common goal and should agree on what information is needed for that solution. There must be some compromise between "psi language" and "cop language." The questions asked should be specific and yet adjusted to the psychic's abilities. For example, if a psychic is asked to locate the body of a homicide victim, the psychic should be asked where the remains of *that* specific victim can be found, not simply to locate bones or any human body. This is similar to the dowser being specifically asked to find potable, accessible water, not just any subterranean water source. The psychic and his co-worker must work together in a partnership, spending time with each other and learning about each other's personalities. Both the psychic and his co-worker may have prejudices that must be recognized so that the unconscious filtering of information is reduced.

Schwartz's last factor is the proper analysis of the psychically obtained data. As an example, Schwartz explained that there might be consistent measurement distortion which he referred to as "psychic astigmatism." A psychic may always report artifacts more deeply than they are actually located. Therefore, the psychic's future predictions must be calibrated. This feedback should help the psychic's subsequent accuracy. Although many authors gave general recommendations for the use of psychics, Schwartz (1978), in his book's appendices, gave specific instructions. These included instructions for pre-field work testing to identify genuine sensitives as well as a detailed fieldwork protocol.

Vaughn (1975) believed that psychics should not be told anything about the case on which they are working. They should simply be allowed to hold an object or be shown a photograph of the victim. Vaughn agreed with Schwartz that the police co-worker must display a keen interest in the outcome of the case without displaying any overt skepticism or suspicion about the psychic's abilities. Vaughn favored the use of open questions such as "What can you tell me about this person?" If the information received is correct, the psychic should be allowed to continue as the questions become more specific, such as "Where is this person now?" If the psychic is wrong from the start, however, he should be stopped, since the proper "psychic connection" has not been formed. Vaughn also suggested using several psychics on the same case but believed they should be given different objects. This, in his opinion, prevents the possibility that the first psychic left inaccurate impressions on the evidence. He also recommended that psychics be employed when the investigation is most actively being worked, not just as a last resort. Since he felt publicity might damage the psychic's ability, he suggested an agreement between the agency and the psychic that neither would release information or discuss the case publicly until it was concluded.

Reiser et al. (1979), on behalf of the Los Angeles Police Department, studied the use of psychics in criminal investigations. He reported that a psychic may generate relatively accurate information on one case but be totally wrong on another, or correct information may only apply to certain parts of a case. He speculated that perhaps displacement occurred, i.e. the psychic received correct information about one case but attributed it to another one. He said a psychic may be accurate on one day but fail on the next. He suggested that personal motivation and active involvement of the psychic in the case may be required before accurate responses can be expected.

Goodman (1977) found that there were four variables affecting the use of psychics. They were: (1) physical and physiological, (2) psychological, (3) spiritual, and (4) engineering variables. By physical and physiological variables, Goodman meant the setting in which the psychic actually works. These included the size of the room, the color of the walls, ventilation, temperature, presence of witnesses, etc. He noted that each psychic had his own peculiarities about working conditions and recommended that those conditions should be provided whenever possible.

The psychological variable was the psychic's mental state. Psychics who are volunteers work best. Goodman recommended that the working atmosphere minimize skepticism and unnecessary testing. In our modern

Western society, being a psychic is abnormal. Thus, the psychic, according to Goodman, needs reassurance and support.

The third variable, psychic factors, was the specific ability of the psychic being used. Psychics may have specialties, such as a narrow prehistoric time period. Many psychics reported the importance of ethics in the investigation; the need for good intentions or purity of purpose. Likewise, psychics working together must be compatible and capable of cooperation.

The engineering variable was the actual procedures used during the investigation. It included practice and training sessions and joint agreement upon the vocabulary and semantics of the questions to be asked. Goodman suggested that the investigator display "toleration of tangents," allowing the psychic to talk freely without narrow restrictions upon the case at hand.

Goodman also suggested that the psychic be taught about the field he is to explore. At least he needs a working knowledge about the investigation underway. Information may help the psychic formulate descriptions and also maintain his interest in the project. As much as possible, according to Goodman, the psychic's work should be made "fun and novel." The co-worker/investigator needs to display an attitude of patience and willingness to help. Goodman also suggested that the investigator himself should practice and learn the psychic techniques of meditation, dream recall, and "imagery generation." He further noted that the psychic is not likely to give accurate information if he works when anxious, tired, or bored.

Hibbard and Warring (1982) made specific recommendations on using a psychic. They suggested that the psychic work at a slow pace in an atmosphere of low pressure, psychological support, and optimism. Psychics claim to work best when they are interested and motivated, so the mood is important to each work session. The investigator, according to the authors, should exude trust and respect without overt skepticism. He must not have a "show-me" attitude. The investigator should hold realistic expectations about what the psychic can do. There is likely to be error and ambiguity in the information. According to Hibbard and Warring, the psychic is only getting impressions about the case and those images may have multiple interpretations. The authors suggested that psychics be used on a regular basis, early in the investigations. Supposedly a "hot" case is a better environment for receiving psi impressions.

Gordon and Tobias (1979) believed that psychics should be recruited before an actual case is underway. They suggested that university or psychic research organizations be asked for referrals. This will help eliminate some charlatans, and the research facility may be able to document ESP skills. This procedure will help a law enforcement agency defend its decision to use the psychic should that decision be questioned later. Gordon and Tobias further recommended that the decision to use psychics be kept confidential, both to minimize pressure on the psychic and to eliminate a skeptical or critical circus atmosphere. They also recommended that officers assigned to work with the psychic be open-minded about ESP phenomena. Conversely, however, the investigation must never be dependent upon the psychic. Gordon and Tobias felt that the officers working with the psychic should have only limited knowledge about other investigative efforts so that they could not accidentally give hints away. They also suggested that all working sessions be tape recorded and transcribed so that information not immediately recognized as important may be rediscovered later.

Gordon and Tobias made specific suggestions about how the investigation, using psychics, should be conducted. They believed each psychic should only receive general information about the crime at first. Additional information should be given to reward success and for confirmation. This supportive feedback will assist the psychic in his work. They felt that the psychic should be assigned specific tasks, such as to draw a composite sketch of the suspect or to locate where the suspect lives. Perhaps the psychic could profile the suspect in terms of age, sex, occupation, education, physical description, etc. If several psychics are used, this baseline information would be useful for comparison. Though they recommended that several psychics be used, they suggested that all of them work on just one case at a time to prevent contamination. They noted that pressure to perform decreased success and that accuracy varied widely. Often, none of the information forthcoming is accurate.

Problems

As noted by most authors, psychics are usually wrong. Sensitives attribute this inaccuracy to a number of causes. A psychic may complain, for instance, that he is accurately reporting information from his "source," but that the source (i.e. dead person or whatever) is sending wrong information. In other cases, the chronology of information may be mixed or transposed. For instance, the location for evidence is accurate, but the evidence has since been moved or has totally decomposed. Additionally, psychics report that they rarely receive specific information about a case, i.e. they cannot learn the name, address or telephone number of a suspect but may only be able to draw a house or circle a general residence area on a map. Unfortunately, the specific information most useful to the police is the information least likely to be provided by a psychic. Reiser et al. (1979) noted, after studying information from 12 psychics, that the information they provided, though accurate, would not be materially helpful in the investigation of the major crimes in question. Some psychics say that their first impressions on a case are likely to be the most accurate and they can't continue to work on a case without a serious decline in accuracy.

Should information from a psychic be both accurate and specific, the possibility of fraud must be considered. One possibility is that someone has leaked information about the investigation to the psychic. Another is that the psychic himself may have some personal involvement in the commission of the crime.

Most authors emphasize that psychics do not perform well under pressure, just as a student's performance may decrease because of test anxiety. "Money and the psychic do not mix" (Schwartz, 1978:306). "Genuine and well-tested psychics repeatedly warn that there must be a genuine desire and need for the information requested" (Hibbard & Warring, 1982:75). The psychic responds best to a humanistic approach, working with an investigator with whom he has established personal rapport. It has been reported that over-questioning may cause a psychic to lose the image or psychic source of information (Goodman, 1977). Most sensitives want to work in a familiar environment without noise or other distractions.

Goodman (1977) divided the problems in the use of psychics into three types. They are problems of accuracy, consistency, and communications between the psychic and the investigator. All of these problems are compounded by physical distance between the psychic and the researcher. According to Goodman, the psychic must be viewed as a link in the communication chain between his psychic source and the police investigator. Anything that disrupts or jams that communication channel stops the flow of information. Goodman felt the link between the psychic and the investigator can be preserved by the use of shared language and working definitions. The link between the psychic source and the sensitive is more difficult to clarify. There will be ongoing problems with time control and locational specificity. Mental associations formed within the psychic's mind may also alter source signals. For example, the image of any apple may somehow become ultimately reported as applesauce (Goodman, 1977).

For the police investigator searching for a body, the important question is whether psychic data can be practically applied to the investigation. The body is either where the psychic or dowser predicts it is, or it is not. To paraphrase Schwartz (1978), the investigator must ask the question of the source, get an answer, and then dig. If the body is indeed found where the dowser or psychic says it should be, then perhaps the reconstruction of the crime is also accurate. Any leads obtained from a psychic or dowser must be compared with evidence independently obtained from other phases of the investigation. Information supplied by parapsychological techniques will have to be independently corroborated for court. Just as a case cannot stand on an uncorroborated confession alone, neither can a case stand on facts supplied by a psychic, no matter how accurate they may appear to be.

Information received from the psychic or dowser must be viewed skeptically. Even the use of parapsychological techniques must be carefully considered, since it may only result in the waste of investigative time, effort and resources. There are no rigorous data to support the value of parapsychological methods to forensic investigators. Reiser et al. (1979:21) accurately sums up the situation regarding the use of parapsychology: "The research data does not support the contention that psychics can provide significant additional information leading to the solution of major crimes." Additionally (Reiser et al. 1979:24), "We are forced to conclude, based on our results, that the usefulness of psychics as an aid in criminal investigations has not been validated." MacInnes (1972:158) discussed the use of parapsychological techniques in search and rescue work and concluded that, "Mediums, clairvoyants and diviners have all been called in at various times to assist in difficult searches. Though interesting and sometimes accurate results have been obtained, such aids cannot be relied upon."

It is clear from the scientific evidence that the use of parapsychological methods should be rejected. Unfortunately, desperate families sometimes demand their use. Under such circumstances, the investigator or search director must control the activity so that fraud is prevented and legitimate search efforts are not obstructed.

Appendix 1

SOURCES OF PLANNING DATA

1. Information About the Victim

Reporting party:	Detain or keep on phone; get phone number, identification, location, auto, photos, maps; return to scene
Reconnaissance:	Maps, geographical viewpoints, helicopter, aerial photography, use backcountry crew or blitz team.
Automobile:	Returned? equipment, notes, maps; leave note to "call police"
Home:	Returned? equipment, notes, maps; leave note to "call police"
Place of work:	Returned? equipment, notes, maps; leave note to "call police"
Friends, relatives, co-workers:	Returned? plans, physical and mental condition, habits, drugs.
Registration cards:	Returned? plans, experience, equipment, who to contact. Contact other parties which may have seen subject.
Wilderness permits:	Contact other parties which may have seen subject or know subject's plans, address.
On scene:	Locate track, equipment.
Clues:	Spot candy wrapper, dog scent articles.
Wanted posters:	Mailed to wilderness permit holders in same area, posted at trailheads and in stores.
Trailheads:	Interview hikers.
Visitor center:	Interview staff, display wanted posters.
Summit registers:	Check for subject and possible witnesses.
Local medical facilities:	Interview staff, check local records.
Local law enforcement:	Separate the overdue from the emergency.
Campgrounds:	Check registers, fee receipts.
Weather records:	Local and regional records.

Source: Modified from *Wilderness Search and Rescue* by Tim J. Setnicka. Copyright ©1980 by Tim J. Setnicka. Presented with the permission of Tim J. Setnicka and the Appalachian Mountain Club, Boston, MA.

2. Information About Incident

What happened?	Fill out lost-person report checklist. Overdue, cries for help, crime, injured, dead, walking wounded, equipment and personnel on scene, instructions by and to victim, reasons why overdue.
Where?	Show maps, photos to witnesses for accuracy. On ground, how far up or down, what route, in water, or bank, what trail, where last seen, headed in which direction, landmarks, distance, type of terrain, route taken before accident, afterwards, washed downstream, how long did witness take to get out? Car parked, was he staying there? Search point last seen; if possible have witness locate it on ground as well as on map.
When?	Last seen, supposed to return, injured, symptoms appeared, fresh tracks or old.
Who?	Name, age, sex, weight, marks. Witness, passers-by, companions, backcountry personnel in area.
Why?	Family problems, drugs, accident, illness.

3. Environmental Information

Weather forecast:	Storm, lightning, rising water.
Marginal forecast:	Call upwind county sheriff or FAA flight service station.
Daylight:	Check dawn and dusk tables in newspapers, almanacs.
Moonlight:	Find out when it rises at the specific locale, what phase, enough to walk or fly by?
Temperatures:	Ascertain valley floor and rim and highlands' temperatures; take differences into account.
Snow, water conditions:	Anticipate changes with time of day and temperature; find out high tides, avalanche conditions.
Rescue reports:	Study local files.
Search and rescue data file:	Study terrain assessments, practices, aerial photos, rescue routes, past rescue histories.
Photographs:	Sort through SAR photo file, aerials, guide books, magazines; contact agencies.
Maps:	Borrow from mountain shops, USGS, USFS, BLM, other parks and agencies, sportsmen.
Guide books, knowledgeable people:	Contact those who live nearby, ski schools, avalanche and forestry workers, hunters, mining companies.
Terrain analysis:	Find out if sloping or level, barriers, escape routes, confu-

sion factors, possible shortcuts, natural attractions, passes or river gorges.

4. Information About Search and Rescue Resource Availability

SAR preplan: Consult resource, means of notification and callout. Check current status of resources, necessary permissions. Activate telephone trees.

Time frame: Estimate period of need honestly. Calculate travel time and organize travel arrangements. Find out if limitations on resource use or time in field.

Politics: Determine if political situation has altered, effects on use of resources and timing.

Base camp: Organize number and person for arriving personnel to call and meet; speedy field deployment factors.

Appendix 2

FORENSIC GEOLOGY CHECKLIST

SITE EVALUATION – OFF SITE

A. Location of Site
   1. Physical location (section, township, range)
   2. Land status
      a. Private (landowner, contact, phone)
      b. Federal (agency, contact, phone)
      c. State government (agency, contact, phone)
      d. Local government (agency, contact, phone)
      e. Other (explain and document)
   3. Accessibility
      a. Roads
      b. 4-wheel drive trail(s)
      c. Footpaths or trails
      d. Utility routes
B. Surface Data Availability
   1. Topographic maps (agency, contact, phone)
   2. Other maps (department, contact, phone)
   3. Geology/soils maps (agency, contact, phone)
   4. Archaeological baseline data (contact, phone)
   5. Air photographs (agency, contact, phone)
      a. Types of photographs available (black and white, color, etc.)
      b. Scale
C. Features In Site Vicinity
   1. Houses
   2. Buildings
   3. Roads
   4. Trails
   5. Communication routes (i.e. railroads)
   6. Overhead/underground utilities
   7. Fences and wells
   8. Other cultural features (i.e. cemeteries)

Source: Modified from *A Short Course in Forensic Geology and Geophysics* by G. Clark Davenport, Heinz W. Seigel and John W. Lindemann, 1986. Presented with the permission of the authors.

    D. Site Ground Surface
        1. Natural, construction fill or landfill
        2. Soil types (general, descriptive)
        3. Drainages (streams, lakes, swamps)
        4. Vegetation (cleared, plowed, cultivated, forested, heavy brush)
        5. Seasonal variation (flooded, snow cover, crops)
    E. Site Over-Flight
        1. Type of flight (visual/photography)
        2. Photographer/observer/pilot

SITE EVALUATION—ON SITE

    A. Foot Reconnaissance
        1. Field check (ground truth) of off-site evaluation
        2. New cultural features (buildings, roads, trails)
        3. Other access
        4. Verification of geology/soil type(s)
        5. Verification of vegetation, cover
        6. Familiarization with entire site
           a. Knowledge of natural conditions
           b. Knowledge of cultural aspects
           c. Walk entire area of interest
    B. Target Selection
        1. Specific areas of potential and/or interest
        2. Specific areas of no potential/interest
    C. Method Applicability
        1. Given the nature of the area and the characteristics of the target, what evaluation methods are most applicable?
    D. Formulation of Operations Plan
        1. Sequence of investigation activities (with minimization of surface disturbance)
        2. Most economic utilization of resources/equipment
        3. Operations plan is dependent on site access
    E. Applicability of Earth Science Technologies
        1. Geological, e.g. surface disturbances
        2. Geochemical, e.g. soil testing
        3. Geophysical, e.g. magnetic surveying
    F. Target Recognition/Definition
        1. Direct (geological)
           a. Topographic anomalies
           b. Vegetation changes
           c. Surface disturbances
           d. Discoloration
           e. Drainage disruption
         2. Indirect (geochemical and/or geophysical)
    G. Target Prioritization
        1. Rank anomalies in order for subsequent investigation

H. Target Evaluation (investigation)
   1. Detailed geophysics
   2. Excavation
I. Analysis of Recovered Evidence
J. Documentation of Entire Search and Recovery

Appendix 3

FORENSIC GEOPHYSICS CHECKLIST

Evaluation Parameters

    A. What is the purpose of the proposed geophysical surveying?

    B. What is the target being searched for?

    C. What are the target characteristics?

        1. Physical dimensions

        2. Physical properties

        3. Expected contrast(s)

        4. Expected depth of burial (limitations)

        5. Any unusual conditions or factors

Site Parameters

    A. Sources of noise

        1. Houses/buildings

        2. Roads

        3. Railroads

        4. Aircraft flight patterns

        5. Powerlines

        6. Underground utilities (map available?)

        7. Pipelines

        8. Fences

        9. Water wells

      10. Radio transmission towers

      11. Site-specific noise (CB or walkie-talkie)

      12. Any other potential noise sources?

    B. Characteristics of near-surface materials

        1. Natural site or landfill

        2. Geological environment

        3. Soil types and profile

        4. Expected characteristics of earth to depth of target—include information on water table

Operational Plan

    A. Selection of Appropriate Geophysical Technique

Source: Modified from *A Short Course in Forensic Geology and Geophysics* by G. Clark Davenport, Heinz W. Seigel and John W. Lindemann, 1986. Presented with the permission of the authors.

1. Based on all the geological/target factors, what are the optimum geophysical methods for use?
2. What is the expected success of each method?
3. Will a site calibration test be conducted?

B. Survey Planning
   1. How will the data be obtained?
      a. Grid pattern
      b. Profiling
      c. Discrete points
      d. What spacing between measurement points will be used?
   2. Where will instrumentation be obtained?
   3. Who will be responsible for running the survey?
   4. How many support personnel will be needed?
   5. What support materials and facilities will be necessary?
   6. Will a calibration site (test area) be necessary?

Documentation

A. What documentation will be required during the investigation?
B. Who will have responsibility for documentation?
C. What filing and storage procedures will be necessary?
D. Has a chain of custody been developed for recovered material?

Appendix 4

SEARCH FACTORS FOR CONSIDERATION

Weather:
    clear
    overcast
    precipitation
Terrain:
    level or gentle
    hills
    mountainous
Ground Cover:
    clear or paved
    open or short crops
    shrubs or high crops
    forest:
        evergreen
        deciduous
Ground Moisture:
    underwater: salt
        fresh
    snow cover
    moist soil
    dry soil
Burial Depth:
    surface
    less than 2 feet
    more than 2 feet
Metal Present:
    none
    trace amounts, e.g. clothing parts
    objects, e.g. weapon
Time Lapse Since Burial:
    less than 2 months
    2 months to 2 years
    more than 2 years
Soil Temperature:
    less than 35° F.
    35 degrees to 60° F.

greater than 60° F.
Search Budget:
  unlimited
  generous
  restricted
Land Use:
  urban
  suburban
  rural
  wilderness
Urgency:
  immediate
  as soon as possible
Manpower Available:
  civilian volunteers
  trained volunteers, e.g. search and rescue teams
  agency staff only
Search Area Size:
  less than 100 acres
  100 to 1,000 acres
  more than 1,000 acres
Soil Type:
  clay and silt
  mixed loam
  sandy
  soil with rocks
Soil pH:
  basic
  neutral
  acidic
Search Authority:
  permission
  warrant or court order
  none

Appendix 5

LOST PERSON REPORT CHECKLIST

Part I: Information critical to immediate decisions and the initiation phases of a search. Record all Part I information at the time of first notice of a lost or overdue person.

Date _____ Time _____

Case incident no. _____ Officer _____

Report taken by _____ phone _____ in person _____

Hours overdue _____

Name of missing person _____

Local address _____ local phone _____

Home address _____ home phone _____

Nicknames _____ Aliases _____

A. Physical   Age _____ Race _____
   description: Height _____ Weight _____ Build _____
                Hair color _____ length _____
                sideburns _____ beard _____ balding? _____
                Eye color _____
                Facial features, shape _____
                Complexion _____
                Any distinguishing marks, scars? _____
                _____
                General appearance _____

B. Clothing: Shirt, sweater style _____ color _____
                Pants   style _____ color _____
                Jacket   style _____ color _____
                Rain gear   style _____ color _____
                Shoes   style _____ size _____
                            sole type _____
                            Is a sample of sole type available? _____
                            where _____

Source: Modified from *Wilderness Search and Rescue* by Tim J. Setnicka. Copyright © 1980 by Tim J. Setnicka. Presented with the permission of Tim J. Setnicka and the Appalachian Mountain Club, Boston, MA.
Note: File separate report for each person. Detailed answers are needed to identify clues when found in the field. Place "none," "NA" (not applicable), or "unsure" in blanks as appropriate.

217

Head gear   style _____ color _____
Gloves   style _____ color _____
Glasses   regular, sun _____ style _____
Any extra clothes, shoes? _____
Scent articles available? _____ where _____

C. Equipment: Pack   ⸱ style _____ brand _____ color _____
                  Tent   style _____ brand _____ color _____
                  Sleeping bag style _____ brand _____ color _____
                  Food: what _____ brands _____ amount _____
                  Water canteen style _____ amount _____
                  Flashlight _____ Matches _____ Knife _____
                  Map _____ Compass _____
                  Ice axe _____ brand _____ covers? _____
                  Snowshoes type _____ brand _____ binding _____
                  type _____
                  Tour skis brand _____ length _____ color _____
                  binding type _____ binding brand _____
                  Ski wax type _____ brands _____ colors _____
                  Ski poles type _____ length _____ color _____
                  brand _____
                  If rental equipment, rental markings? _____
                  Ropes, hardware _____
                  Fishing equipment _____ brands _____
                  Camera _____ brand _____
                  Money _____ amount _____ credit cards _____
                  Firearms type _____ brand _____ ammo _____

D. Trip plans: Going to _____ via _____
                  Purpose _____
                  How long _____ How many in group? _____
                  Group affiliation _____ transportation _____
                  Started at _____ when _____
                  Car located at _____ type _____
                  license _____ verified _____
                  Alternate car at _____ type _____
                  license _____ verified _____
                  Pickup, return time _____ where _____

All in group: Name _____ address _____
                  phone _____ car license _____
                  Name _____ address _____
                  phone _____ car license _____
                  Any alternate plans, routes, objectives discussed? _____

E. Last seen: When _____
                  Where _____
                  By whom _____ present? _____
                  If not, location _____ phone _____

Weather _____

Going which way _____ How long ago _____

Special reason for leaving? _____

How long overdue _____

F. Experience: Familiar with area _____ how recently _____

If not local, experience in what other areas _____

Taken outdoor classes _____ where _____ when _____

Taken first-aid training _____ where _____ when _____

Been in Scouts _____ where _____ when _____

Military service _____

How much overnight experience? _____

Ever been lost before? _____ actions _____

Stay on trails or go cross-country _____

How many long trips before _____

If not regular hike, general athletic interests and ability _____

_____

G. Contacts person would make upon reaching civilization:

Home address _____

phone _____ anyone home? _____

local contact _____ phone _____

friends _____ phone _____

H. Health: General condition _____

Any physical handicaps _____

Any known medical problem _____

knowledgeable doctor _____

phone _____

Any known psychological problems _____

knowledgeable doctor _____ phone _____

Any known external factors that might have affected subject's behavior (family argument, depression, business problems) ____

_____

Taking prescription medication? _____

doctor _____

consequences of loss _____

amount carried _____

Eyesight without glasses _____ spares? _____

I. Actions taken so far:

By (friends, family) _____

Actions taken _____

_____

When _____

_____

Part II. Information that may be significant later in the mission. Can be obtained after initial actions are taken and further information on the subject is necessary.

A. Personality habits:

    Smoke _____ how often _____ what brand _____

    Drink _____ brand _____

    Drugs _____

    Hobbies, interests (fishing, flowers, climbing, photography) ___

    _____

    Works for spare money _____

    Outgoing or quiet; likes groups or lonely _____

    Evidence of leadership _____

    Ever in trouble with law? _____ now? _____

    Hitchhike often _____ accept rides _____

    Any current family or love problems? _____

    Religion _____ serious? _____

    What does person believe in? _____

    What does person value most? _____

    Who is person closest to in family? _____

    in general _____

    Where born and raised? _____

    Any history of depression, running away? _____

    Status in school _____

    Who last talked at length to person? _____

    where _____ subject _____

    Any recent letter? _____

    Give up easily or keep going? _____

    Will person hole up and wait or keeping moving? _____

B. For children: Afraid of dogs? _____ horses? _____

    Afraid of dark? _____

    What training regarding what to do when lost? _____

    What are actions when hurt? Cry? Carry on? _____

    Talk to strangers; accept rides? _____

    Active type or lethargic? _____

    Feelings toward grownups? _____

C. For groups overdue:

    Any personality clashes in group? _____

    Any strong leader types not actually the leader? _____

    What is competitive spirit of group? _____

    What would be actions if separated? _____

    Any persons especially close friends? _____

    What is experience of leader and rest of group? _____

D. Family (to prevent press problems):

    Father's occupation _____

    Parents separated or similar problem _____

    Family's desire to employ special assistance _____

    Name, address, phone of father, mother, husband, wife, son,

daughter to notify if found in good condition (give most appropriate kin for information or contact when found)

Name _____ address _____

phone _____ relationship _____

Person to notify if found in very poor condition or dead (should
be friend, relative, or minister of next of kin)

Name _____ address _____

phone _____ relationship _____

E. Physical evidence available

       Fingerprints on file (footprints?)

       Hair samples

       X-rays: medical and dental

       Recent photographs

       Blood or tissue samples

Appendix 6

SUMMARY OF METHOD
ADVANTAGES AND DISADVANTAGES

FOOT SEARCH FOR VISUAL SIGNS

Advantages:

- Inexpensive if volunteers used
- No damage to subsurface evidence
- Adaptable to any terrain

Disadvantages:

- Difficult to supervise and manage
- Good weather only
- Possible damage to surface evidence
- Searchers need to be trained
- Decreasing thoroughness with time and fatigue
- Cannot be used on snow-covered ground
- Daytime only

AIR-SCENT DOGS

Advantages:

- Inexpensive
- Quick and thorough, even over large areas
- No damage to subsurface evidence
- Minimal damage to surface evidence
- Adaptable to all terrains
- Can be used in most weather conditions
- Ground can be snow covered if body unfrozen
- Day or night
- Can be used after other search methods have failed
- Easy to manage and supervise

Disadvantages:

- Limited availability
- Burial must be fresh or decomposition must be underway
- Not in severe weather (poor scent conditions)

PROBING

Advantages:

- Thorough search
- Minimal surface and subsurface damage
- Inexpensive if volunteers used
- Adaptable to any terrain
- Can be done in combination with visual search
- Searchers more accurate with experience

Disadvantages:

- Slow coverage
- Rest and replacements needed
- Good weather only
- Daytime only
- Only unfrozen ground
- Searchers must be trained

COMBUSTIBLE GAS VAPOR DETECTORS

Advantages:

- Can be done in combination with probe search
- Equipment relatively inexpensive and easy to operate
- Adaptable to any terrain
- Can be done through snow if body unfrozen
- Minimal surface and subsurface damage, no more than probing
- Thorough search
- Easy to supervise

Disadvantages:

- Slow coverage
- Good weather only
- Daytime only
- Active decomposition must be underway
- Requires trained operator

CORING AND DRILLING

Advantages:

- Thorough search
- Drilling may be done through snow and frozen ground
- Easy to supervise
- Can be done in most terrains except very rocky
- Can be done after other search methods have failed

Disadvantages:

- Damage to surface and subsurface evidence
- Very slow coverage
- Requires trained operator
- Good weather only
- Daytime only

SOIL ANALYSIS

Advantages:

- Thorough search
- Can detect very old burials
- Adaptable to any terrain
- Easy to supervise
- Can be used after other methods have failed
- Can be done in combination with coring/drilling
- Can be done through snow or frozen ground

Disadvantages:

- Results not available in the field
- Very slow coverage
- Requires laboratory facilities
- Expensive laboratory examinations
- Damage to subsurface and surface evidence
- Good weather only
- Daytime only

HEAVY EQUIPMENT

Advantages:

- Can be done after other methods fail
- Can be done through snow
- Rapid coverage of large areas

Disadvantages:

- Very destructive to surface and subsurface evidence
- Difficult to supervise
- Expensive equipment
- Trained operator required
- Daytime only
- Good weather only
- Only for gentle terrain with vehicle access
- Light vegetation only (no trees)
- Land reclamation/restoration necessary

GRAVITY SURVEYING

Advantages:

- Minimal surface damage
- No subsurface damage
- Can be used over snow or frozen ground
- Easy to supervise
- Unaffected by groundwater
- Only one technician required

Disadvantages:

- Slow coverage
- Best on flat terrain
- No results available in the field
- Requires trained operator
- Requires data processing
- Requires expert interpretation
- Grave may show insufficient contrast from matrix
- Good weather only
- Daytime only

MAGNETIC SURVEYING

Advantages:

- Detects metal objects and fire residue
- Medium coverage speed
- Some results available in the field
- Easy to supervise
- Minimal surface damage, no subsurface damage
- Can be done over or in water and snow

Disadvantages:

- Grave may show insufficient contrast from matrix
- Interference from metal litter, fences, cars, power lines, buildings, etc.
- Interference from magnetic storms
- Requires trained operator
- Requires data processing
- Requires expert interpretation
- Expensive equipment
- Daytime only
- Good weather only
- Difficult in volcanic rock areas

SELF–POTENTIAL SURVEYING

Advantages:

- Minimal surface or subsurface damage
- Can be done in combination with resistivity
- Medium coverage speed
- Works best in acidic soils
- Relatively inexpensive equipment
- Easy to supervise

Disadvantages:

- Interference from man-made electrical sources
- Grave may show insufficient contrast from matrix
- Affected by groundwater
- Requires trained operator
- Requires data processing
- Requires expert interpretation
- Daytime only
- Good weather only

RESISTIVITY SURVEYING

Advantages:

- Easy to supervise
- Can be done in combination with self-potential
- Can determine lateral position and depth of anomaly
- Relatively inexpensive equipment
- Minimal surface and subsurface damage
- Some field results available
- Can be used as pre-test for ground-penetrating radar

Disadvantages:

- Good weather only
- Slow coverage speed
- Daytime only
- Flat or gentle terrain only
- Grave may show insufficient contrast from matrix
- Affected by groundwater
- Requires trained operator
- Requires data processing
- Requires expert interpretation
- Less useful in cultivated land (fertilizer)
- Interference from metal or electrical sources

ELECTROMAGNETIC (SLINGRAM) PROFILING

Advantages:

- Easy to supervise
- Fast coverage
- Can be used in brush or forest
- Minimal surface and no subsurface damage
- Detects metal objects
- Can be used over dry, hard ground or concrete
- Some results available in the field

Disadvantages:

- Very expensive equipment
- Best on flat or gentle terrain
- Interference from metal or electrical sources
- Grave may show insufficient contrast from matrix
- Requires trained operator
- Data processing required
- Requires expert interpretation
- Interference from electrical storms
- Daytime only
- Good weather only

METAL DETECTORS

Advantages:

- Adjustable to conditions
- Sensitive to *small* metal objects
- Can discriminate metal types

- Immediate results in the field, no data processing required
- Can be used over or under water
- May be used in urban areas
- Can search beneath concrete or pavement
- Easy to supervise
- Minimal surface and no subsurface damage
- Adaptable to any terrain
- Fast coverage

Disadvantages:

- Shallow penetration only
- Requires trained operator
- Insufficient contrast without metal in the grave
- Interference from ground metal litter, *near* metal or electrical sources
- Interference from "black sand" (magnetite)
- Daytime only
- Good weather only

SEISMIC REFRACTION

Advantages:

- Easy to supervise
- Lateral position and depth information possible
- Can be used through concrete or pavement

Disadvantages:

- Grave may show insufficient contrast from matrix
- Requires trained operator
- Only some results available in the field
- Requires data processing
- Requires expert interpretation
- Expensive equipment
- Slow coverage
- Flat or gentle terrain only
- Some surface damage
- Interference from ground vibrations, road traffic, etc.
- Needs proper geologic conditions
- Daytime only
- Good weather only

GROUND-PENETRATING RADAR

Advantages:

- Easy to supervise
- Results immediately available in the field
- Lateral position and depth information possible
- Sensitive to small changes or objects (anomalies)
- Medium coverage speed
- Minimal surface and no subsurface damage
- May be used in urban areas
- Can penetrate concrete and pavement
- Can be used over fresh water
- Adjustable to conditions

Disadvantages:

- Very expensive equipment
- Requires trained operator
- Expert interpretation required
- Flat or gentle terrain only
- Clear ground cover required, no shrubs or trees
- Daytime only
- Good weather only
- Little penetration of salt water or clay
- Soil testing suggested before use

PASSIVE MICROWAVE

Advantages:

- No ground contact or damage
- Elevated viewpoint
- Fast coverage
- Detects differences in temperature and soil moisture
- Detects subsurface conditions
- Adaptable to any terrain and ground cover
- No search warrant required

Disadvantages:

- Very expensive equipment
- No results in the field, requires data processing
- Requires expert operator
- Requires expert interpretation
- Grave may show insufficient contrast from matrix
- Resolution ability poor, unable to detect small anomalies

- Good, clear weather only
- Daytime only
- Difficult to supervise
- Limited availability

SIDE-LOOKING AIRBORNE RADAR

Advantages:

- No search warrant required
- Day or night
- Adjustable to any terrain
- Penetrates most ground cover and snow
- Fast coverage
- No ground contact or damage
- Elevated viewpoint
- Adaptable to nearly any weather conditions
- Adjustable to conditions

Disadvantages:

- Limited availability
- Very expensive
- No results in the field, requires data processing
- Requires expert operator
- Requires expert interpretation
- Grave may show insufficient contrast from matrix
- Poor resolution ability, only large targets
- Difficult to supervise
- Distorted pictorial image
- Only in rural area, affected by surface geometry

INFRARED SCANNER IMAGERY

Advantages:

- No ground contact or damage
- Fast coverage
- Elevated viewpoint
- No search warrant required
- Adaptable to any terrain
- Usually done at night
- Best in dry climates
- Best resolution of remote sensors except for aerial photography
- Sensitive to small temperature differences

Disadvantages:

- Very expensive equipment
- Limited availability
- No results in the field, requires processing
- Requires expert operator
- Requires expert interpretation
- Grave may show insufficient contrast from matrix
- Resolution ability poor, large targets only
- Good, clear weather only
- Detects surface temperature differences only
- Interference from radio waves
- Only penetrates light vegetation cover
- Does not penetrate through snow or frozen ground

VISIBLE COLOR AERIAL PHOTOGRAPHY

Advantages:

- Three-dimensional image possible
- Excellent resolution
- Equipment readily available
- Easy to supervise
- Records visible color brightness, shape, and size
- No ground contact or damage
- Fast coverage
- Elevated viewpoint
- May not require search warrant
- Adjustable to conditions with lenses, film, speed, filters, etc.
- Adaptable to all terrains

Disadvantages:

- Expensive equipment rental (aircraft)
- No results in the field, requires processing
- Requires trained operator
- Requires trained interpreter
- Grave may show insufficient contrast from matrix
- Good, clear weather only
- Daytime only
- Only surface features are seen
- Cannot see through plant cover

COLOR INFRARED AERIAL PHOTOGRAPHY

Advantages:

- Three-dimensional imagery possible
- Excellent resolution
- Good availability of equipment
- Easy to supervise
- Records infrared color, shape, size
- No ground contact or damage
- Fast coverage
- Elevated viewpoint
- May not require search warrant
- Adaptable to any terrain

Disadvantages:

- Expensive equipment rental (aircraft)
- No results in the field, requires processing
- Requires trained operator
- Requires trained interpreter
- Grave may show insufficient contrast from matrix
- Good, clear weather only
- Daytime only
- Only surface features seen
- Slow film speed
- Special film handling
- Cannot see through plant cover

DOWSING

Advantages:

- Inexpensive if volunteer used
- Minimum surface damage, no subsurface damage
- Any terrain
- Any weather
- Any ground cover conditions
- Day or night
- Easy to supervise
- Fast coverage
- Can be used after other methods have failed

Disadvantages:

- Not scientifically proven
- Possible adverse press coverage

- Limited availability
- Requires trained operator
- Frequent failure and false leads, wasted time
- Courtroom inadmissibility
- Possible adverse public reaction

PSYCHICS

Advantages:

- Inexpensive if volunteers used
- Minimum surface damage, no subsurface damage
- Any terrain
- Any weather
- Any ground cover conditions
- Day or night
- Easy to supervise
- Fast coverage
- Can be used after other methods have failed

Disadvantages:

- Not scientifically proven
- Possible adverse press coverage
- Limited availability
- Frequent failure and false leads, wasted time
- Courtroom inadmissibility
- Possible adverse public reaction

Appendix 7

RECOMMENDATIONS

In the course of my research, it became apparent that some of the search methods have proven to be successful in the past and are particularly well suited to a forensic body search. Boyd (1979) recommended three search techniques which were, in order of use, infrared aerial photography, non-intrusive visual search of the ground, and probing in conjunction with a methane gas detector. Both the infrared photography and the gas detection rely on active decomposition of the body. They cannot be used before decomposition has started, while decomposition is suspended by freezing, or after decomposition of the flesh has finished. Despite this limitation, I concur with Boyd that these three search techniques are among the most suitable. To Boyd's list, I would add the use of air-scenting dogs and the geophysical prospecting techniques of ground-penetrating radar and electromagnetic (slingram) profiling.

My recommendation, for a relatively small search area, is initially to take color and infrared color aerial photography from an oblique angle, preferably from a helicopter. As discussed in the aerial photography chapter, the photographs should be taken from a variety of directions, elevations, and under different lighting conditions. For a large search area, this same color and infrared color photography could be done from a light plane to reduce search costs.

Presuming that decomposition is underway, my second recommendation is the use of air-scenting dogs. The search dog and handler will be just as thorough but quicker than human searchers. They will have minimal impact upon the crime scene. Even if the dog fails, subsequent search efforts have not been compromised. Fielding one or more teams of dogs is certainly more economical and manageable than a host of pedestrian searchers.

If the air-scenting dogs do fail, a slow, methodical ground search for visual signs is the next logical step. A small, dedicated search team, carefully searching small grid sections, is preferable to an unmanageable swarm of well-intentioned volunteers. Some of the searchers can be equipped with metal detectors to enhance their search capabilities. The foot search may trample some surface evidence but will not disturb the subsurface conditions.

If the terrain is reasonably level with little or no ground cover, then ground-penetrating radar is the geophysical method of choice for continuous, detailed profiling of subsurface conditions. The fine resolution ability and shallow penetration depth of this system makes it ideal for forensic purposes. If the ground is rougher or has plant cover, then the radar cart is no longer practical. I recommend electromagnetic profiling as a substitute because it is reasonably sensitive, requires no contact with the ground, and can be done anywhere that a man can walk. Both ground-penetrating radar and electromagnetic profiling instruments are expensive and require professional expertise.

Under most conditions, my next suggestion is the use of steel probes wielded by a small team of searchers. The probing effort would be used in conjunction with a methane gas detector. A detailed probe search is slow and tiring but extremely thorough if done in careful accordance with a grid search plan. Imaizumi's (1974) account is a good illustration of the lengthy, tedious but ultimately successful outcome of a probe search.

Unfortunately, none of the methods researched or discussed will work all of the time or under all conditions. Under every condition, however, there will be a few methods that should be tried. At best, all of the techniques will simply indicate a suspicious or promising spot. For confirmations of the grave, "in the end one must simply dig" (Clark, 1970:707).

To summarize, my recommendations for search techniques, in order of use, are as follows:

1. Color and infrared color oblique aerial photography.
2. Air-scenting dog teams.
3. Non-intrusive ground search for visible signs.
4. Ground-penetrating radar and/or electromagnetic (slingram) profiling.
5. Intrusive ground search with probes and methane gas detectors.

These recommendations assume a limited size, rural search area with a shallow, recent grave, hopefully containing some metal. It also assumes good weather for the search, legal authority to be on the premises, and an adequate time limit and budget for the investigation. It also assumes that the search area is reasonably level, with sparse plant cover, and that the soil is neither frozen nor covered with deep snow.

If the weather is inclement, I suggest the search be postponed until it clears. No search techniques work well in heavy rain, wind or snow. If the search cannot be postponed, only the following techniques are worth trying:

1. Air-scenting dogs.
2. Non-intrusive ground search for visible signs, supplemented by the use of metal detectors.

If the terrain is rough or hilly, neither ground-penetrating radar nor electromagnetic profiling are effective. They are also precluded if the ground has a heavy plant cover. The best remaining techniques are:

1. Color and color infrared oblique aerial photography.
2. Air-scenting dog teams
3. Non-intrusive ground search for visible signs, supplemented by the use of metal detectors.
4. Intrusive ground search with probes and combustible gas detectors.

If the ground is frozen or decomposition is probably not underway, then neither air-scenting dogs nor vapor detectors are likely to assist in the search. The remaining techniques are:

1. Color and color infrared oblique aerial photography.
2. Non-intrusive ground search for visible signs.
3. Ground-penetrating radar and/or electromagnetic profiling.

If the search area is covered by a thick layer of snow, the search should be postponed until spring. If it cannot be postponed, it is unlikely that aerial photography, dogs, or ground searches for visible signs alone will be helpful. Electromagnetic profiling is also precluded by the snow cover. The techniques still possible are:

1. Ground search with metal detector.
2. Ground-penetrating radar mounted on a sled.
3. Magnetic surveying.
4. Heavy-equipment plowing to remove the snow cover.

If the burial is relatively old (more than two years), most visible signs may be gone and remaining decomposition may be slight. Under such conditions, the best search methods are likely to be:

1. Color and color infrared oblique aerial photography.
2. Ground-penetrating radar and/or electromagnetic profiling.
3. Intrusive ground search by probing or small-diameter coring.

BIBLIOGRAPHY

Aitken, Martin
    1970 "Magnetic Location" in Brothwell, Don and Eric Higgs (editors), *Science in Archaeology.* New York.
American Society of Civil Engineers (editors)
    1974 *Subsurface Exploration for Underground Excavation & Heavy Construction.* American Society of Civil Engineers. New York.
Baker, W.A.
    1975 "Infra-Red Techniques" in Wilson, D.R. (editor), *Aerial Reconnaissance for Archaeology.* The Council for British Archaeology, London.
Barker, Philip
    1977 *Techniques of Archaeological Excavation.* Universe Books, New York.
Barrett, William and Theodore Besterman
    1968 *The Divining Rod: An Experimental and Psychological Investigation.* University Books, New Hyde Park, NY.
Bass, William M.
    1962 "The Excavation of Human Skeletal Remains" in Spier, R.F.G. *Field Handbook on the Human Skeleton.* Missouri Archaeological Society, Columbia, MO.
Bass, William W.
    1963 "The Use of Heavy Power Equipment in the Excavation of Human Skeletal Material." *Plains Anthropologist.* May, 1963, 8 (20): pp. 122–123.
Bass, William M.
    1987(a) "Forensic Anthropology: The American Experience" in Boddington, A., A.N. Garland and R.C. Janaway (editors), *Death, Decay and Reconstruction: Approaches to Archaeology and Forensic Science.* Manchester University Press, Manchester, United Kingdom.
Bass, William M.
    1987(b) *Human Osteology: A Laboratory and Field Manual of the Human Skeleton, 3rd edition.* Missouri Archaeological Society, Columbia, MO.
Bass, William M. and Walter H. Birkby
    1978 "Exhumation: The Method Could Make the Difference." *F.B.I. Law Enforcement Bulletin.* July, 1978, pp. 6–11.
Baum, Joseph
    1974 *The Beginner's Handbook of Dowsing.* Crown Publishers, New York.
Beck, A.E.
    1981 *Physical Principals of Exploration Methods.* John Wiley, New York.

Berryman, Hugh E.
    1986 "Anthropology as Applied to Forensic Science." *Crime Laboratory Digest.* F.B.I./U.S. Department of Justice, April 1986, 13(2):pp. 38–50.
Bethell, P.H. and M.O.H. Carver
    1987 "Detection and Enhancement of Decayed Inhumations at Sutton Hoo" in Boddington, A., A.N. Garland and R.C. Janaway (editors), *Death, Decay and Reconstruction: Approaches to Archaeology and Forensic Science.* Manchester Press, Manchester, United Kingdom.
Bevan, Bruce W.
    1983 "Electromagnetics for Mapping Buried Earth Features." *Journal of Field Archaeology.* 10:pp. 47–54.
Binford, Lewis R.
    1981 *Bones: Ancient Men and Modern Myths.* Academic Press, New York.
Boddington, A., A.N. Garland and R.C. Janaway
    1987 "Flesh, Bones, Dust and Society" in Boddington, A., A.N. Garland and R.C. Janaway (editors), *Death, Decay and Reconstruction: Approaches to Archaeology and Forensic Science.* Manchester University Press, Manchester, United Kingdom.
Boddington, A., A.N. Garland and R.C. Janaway (editors)
    1987 *Death, Decay and Reconstruction: Approaches to Archaeology and Forensic Science.* Manchester University Press, Manchester, United Kingdom.
Boudreau, John F., Quon Y. Kwan, William E. Faragher, and Genevieve C. Denault
    1977 *Arson and Arson Investigation Survey and Assessment.* U.S. Department of Justice, Washington, D.C.
Boyd, Robert M.
    1979 "Buried Body Cases." *F.B.I. Law Enforcement Bulletin.* February, 1979, pp. 106.
Brannigan, Francis L., Richard G. Bright and Nora H. Jason (editors)
    1980 *Fire Investigation Handbook.* U.S. Department of Commerce, Washington, D.C.
Breiner, Sheldon
    1973 *Applications Manual for Portable Magnetometers.* Geometrics, Sunnyvale, CA.
Breternitz, David A.
    1983 *Dolores Archaeological Program: Field Investigations and Analysis, 1978.* U.S. Department of the Interior, Bureau of Reclamation, Engineering and Research Center, Denver, CO., November, 1983.
Breternitz, David A.
    1984 *Dolores Archaeological Program: Synthetic Report, 1978–1981.* U.S. Department of the Interior, Bureau of Reclamation, Engineering and Research Center, Denver, CO., June, 1984.
Brooks, Sheilagh T. and Richard H. Brooks
    1984 "Problems of Burial Exhumation, Historical and Forensic Aspects" in Rathbun, Ted A. and Jane E. Buikstra (editors), *Human Identification: Case Studies in Forensic Anthropology.* Charles C Thomas, Springfield, IL.

Brues, Alice M.
　1958 "Identification of Skeletal Remains" *Journal of Criminal Law, Criminology, and Police Science.* 48:pp. 551–563.

Bucher, Hans R.
　1989 "Thermal Imaging as a Method to Detect the Invisible." Paper presented at a conference sponsored by the Rocky Mountain Division of the International Association for Identification, Denver, CO, May 19, 1989.

Carneggie, David M. et al.
　1983 "Rangeland Applications" in Colwell, Robert N. (editor), *Manual of Remote Sensing, 2nd edition, Vol. 2, Interpretation and Applications.* American Society of Photogrammetry, Falls Church, VA.

Carr, Christopher
　1982 *Handbook on Soil Resistivity Surveying.* Center for American Archaeology Press, Evanston, IL.

Cherry, Donald G. and J. Lawrence Angel
　1977 "Personalty Reconstruction from Unidentified Remains." *F.B.I. Law Enforcement Bulletin,* August, 1977, 46(8):pp. 12–15.

Clark, Anthony
　1970 "Resistivity Surveying" in Brothwell, Don and Eric S. Higgs (editors), *Science in Archaeology.* Praeger Publishers, New York.

Cochran, Roy C., Jr.
　1986 "Mapping Relic Drainages and Site Locations: An Assessment of the Use of Remote Sensing in the Village Creek Basin" in Klinger, Timothy C., *Village Creek: An Explicitly Regional Approach to the Study of Cultural Resources.* Research Report #26, Arkansas Archaeological Survey, Fayetteville, AR.

Collins, Michael B.
　1975 "Excavation and Recording of Human Physical Remains" in Hester, Thomas R., Robert F. Heizer, and John A. Graham (editors), *Field Methods in Archaeology.* Mayfield Press, Palo Alto, CA.

Colwell, Robert N.
　1976 "The Visible Portion of the Spectrum" in Lintz, Joseph, Jr. and David Simonett (editors), *Remote Sensing of the Environment.* Addison-Wesley, Reading, MA.

Colwell, Robert N. (editor)
　1983 *Manual of Remote Sensing, 2nd edition, Volume 1: Theory, Instruments and Techniques.* American Society of Photogrammetry, Falls Church, VA.

Colwell, Robert N. (editor)
　1983 *Manual of Remote Sensing, 2nd edition, Volume 2: Interpretation and Applications.* American Society of Photogrammetry, Falls Church, VA.

Cook, John C.
　1974 "Status of Ground-Probing Radar and Some Recent Experience" in American Society of Civil Engineers (editors), *Subsurface Exploration for Underground Excavation and Heavy Construction.* New York.

Cooney, Robert A.

1978 "Gas Detection—The First 50 Years." *National Safety News.* August, 1978, 118(2): pp. 53–56.

Cornwall, Ian W.

1966 *Soils for the Archaeologist.* Phoenix House, London.

Cronin, J.F. et al.

1973 "Ultraviolet Radiation and The Terrestrial Surface" in Holz, Robert K. (editor), *The Surveillant Science: Remote Sensing of the Environment.* Houghton Mifflin, Boston, MA.

Davenport, G. Clark, Heinz W. Siegel and John W. Lindemann

1986 *A Short Course in Forensic Geology and Geophysics.* Colorado Bureau of Investigation, Denver, CO.

Dobrin, Milton B.

1976 *Introduction to Geophysical Prospecting, 3rd Edition.* McGraw-Hill, New York.

Dohr, Gerhard

1974 *Applied Geophysics: Introduction to Geophysical Prospecting.* John Wiley, New York.

Dozier, Jeff and Alan H. Strahler

1983 "Ground Investigations in Support of Remote Sensing" in Colwell, Robert N. (editor), *Manual of Remote Sensing, 2nd Edition, Vol. 1: Theory, Instruments and Techniques.* American Society of Photogrammetry, Falls Church, VA.

Dudley, R.J.

1976 "A Simple Method for Determining the pH of Small Soil Samples and its Use in Forensic Science." *Journal of Forensic Science Society.* 16:pp. 21–27, Forensic Science Society Journal, London.

Eastman Kodak Co.

1972(a) *Applied Infra-red Photography.* Eastman Kodak, Rochester, NY.

Eastman Kodak Co.

1972(b) *Ultraviolet and Fluorescence Photography.* Eastman Kodak, Rochester, NY.

Eastman Kodak Co.

1985 *Photography from Light Planes and Helicopters.* Eastman Kodak, Rochester, NY.

Eastman Kodak Co.

1989 Personal Communication.

Ebert, James I. and Robert K. Hitchcock

1977 "The Role of Remote Sensing" in Reher, Charles A. (editor), *Settlement and Subsistence Along the Lower Chaco River: The C.G.P. Survey.* University of New Mexico Press, Albuquerque, NM.

Ebert, James I. and Thomas R. Lyons

1983 "Archaeology, Anthropology, and Cultural Resource Management" in Colwell, Robert N. (editor), *Manual of Remote Sensing, 2nd Edition, Vol. 2: Interpretation and Applications.* American Society of Photogrammetry, Falls Church, VA.

Eddy, Frank W.

1984 *Archaeology: A Cultural-Evolutionary Approach.* Prentice-Hall, Englewood Cliffs, NY.

Eidt, Robert C.
    1977 "Detection and Examination of Anthrosols by Phosphate Analysis." *Science.*
        September, 1977 (4311): pp. 1327–1333.
Eidt, Robert C.
    1985 "Theoretical and Practical Considerations in the Analysis of Anthrosols"
        in Rapp, George and John Gifford (editors), *Archaeological Geology.* Yale
        University Press, New Haven, CT.
Emerson, J. Norman
    1974 "Intuitive Archaeology: A Psychic Approach." *New Horizons.* January,
        1974, 1:pp. 14–18.
Emerson, J. Norman
    1976 "Intuitive Archaeology: Egypt & Iran." *A.R.E. Journal.* (Association for
        Research and Enlightenment) March, 1976 11:pp. 55–63.
Emery, C. Eugene, Jr.
    1988 "An Investigation of Psychic Crimebusting." *The Skeptical Inquirer.* Summer,
        1988, 12(4): pp. 403–410.
Estes, John E. and David S. Simonett
    1975 "Fundamentals of Image Interpretation" in Reeves, Robert G., *Manual of
        Remote Sensing.* American Society of Photogrammetry, Falls Church, VA.
Estes, John E. et al.
    1983 "Fundamentals of Image Analysis: Analysis of Visible and Thermal Infra-
        red Data" in Colwell, Robert N. (editor), *Manual of Remote Sensing, 2nd
        edition, Vol. 1: Theory, Instruments, and Techniques.* American Society of
        Photogrammetry, Falls Church, VA.
Feegel, John R.
    1972 "Exhumation" *Medical Trial Technique Quarterly: 1972 Annual,* pp. 190–197.
        Callaghan and Co., Chicago, IL.
Feegel, John R.
    1973 *Legal Aspects of the Practice of Laboratory Medicine.* Little, Brown, Boston,
        MA.
Firth, J.G., A. Jones and T.A. Jones
    1973 "The Principle of the Detection of Flammable Atmospheres by Catalytic
        Devices." *Combustion and Flame.* June, 1973, 20(3): pp. 303–311.
Fischer, Peter M.
    1980 "The Use of a Metal Detector in Archaeology" in Fischer, Peter M. (editor),
        Applications of Technical Devices in Archaeology. P. Astrom, Goteborg, Sweden.
Fischer, Peter M. (editor)
    1980 *Applications of Technical Devices in Archaeology.* P. Astrom, Goteborg, Sweden.
Fischer, Peter M., Sven G.W. Follin and Peter Ulriksen
    1980 "Subsurface Interface Radar Survey at Hala Sultan Tekke, Cyprus" in
        Fisher, Peter M. (editor), *Applications of Technical Devices in Archaeology.* P.
        Astrom, Goteborg, Sweden.
France, Diane L. and Arthur D. Horn
    1988 *Lab Manual and Workbook for Physical Anthropology.* West Publishing, St.
        Paul, MN.

Garrett, Charles L.
  1985 *The Advanced Handbook on Modern Metal Detectors.* Ram Publishing, Dallas, TX.
Garrett, Charles L., Bob Grant and Roy Lagal
  1980 *Electronic Prospecting.* Ram Publishing, Dallas, TX.
Geberth, Vernon J.
  1983 *Practical Homicide Investigation: Tactics, Procedures and Forensic Techniques.* Elsevier, New York.
GISCO: Geophysical Instrument and Supply Company
undated *Geophysical Instruments* GISCO, Denver, CO.
Goldfluss, Howard E.
  1987 "Courtroom Psychics (Forum)." *Omni.* July, 1987, 9: p. 12.
Goodman, Jeffrey
  1977 *Psychic Archaeology: Time Machine to the Past.* Berkley Publishing, New York.
Gordon, Thomas J. and Jerry J. Tobias
  1979 "Managing the Psychic in Criminal Investigations." *The Police Chief.* May, 1979, pp. 58–59.
Grady, James
  1989 "Aerial Photography and its Use in Archaeology and its Potential Use in Criminal Investigations." Paper presented at a conference sponsored by the Rocky Mountain Division of the International Association for Identification, Denver, Colorado, May 19, 1989.
Graves, Tom
  1976 *The Diviner's Handbook.* Warner Books, New York.
Greene, Marilyn A.
  1982 "Air Scent Dogs in Search and Rescue." *Law and Order.* May, 1982: pp. 46–50.
Greene, Marilyn A.
  1987 Personal communication.
Guarino, Richard
  1975 "The Police and Psychics." *Psychic.* May/June, 1975, 6(2): pp. 9, 14–15.
Gumerman, George J. and Laurence D. Kruckman
  1977 "The Unrealized Potential of Remote Sensing in Archaeology" in Lyons, Thomas R. and Robert K. Hitchcock (editors), *Aerial Remote Sensing Techniques in Archaeology.* Reports of the Chaco Center #2, National Park Service, University of New Mexico, Albuquerque, NM.
Gumerman, George J. and Thomas R. Lyons
  1971 "Archaeological Methodology and Remote Sensing." *Science.* 172: pp. 126–132.
Guralnik, David B. (editor)
  1970 *Webster's New World Dictionary of the American Language, 2nd College Edition.* World Publishing, New York.
Haglund, William D.
  1989 "Scene Investigation and the Recovery of Decomposed Bodies." Workshop

presented at the 41st annual meeting of the American Academy of Forensic Sciences, Las Vegas, Nevada, February 13, 1989.

Hampton, J.N.
1974 "An Experiment in Multi-Spectral Air Photography for Archaeological Research." *Photogrammetric Record,* 8(43): pp. 37–64.

Harp, Elmer Jr.
1975 "Basic Considerations in the Use of Aerial Photography for Archaeological Research" in Harp, Elmer Jr. (editor), *Photography in Archaeological Research.* University of New Mexico Press, Albuquerque, NM.

Harp, Elmer Jr. (editor)
1975 *Photography in Archaeological Research.* University of New Mexico Press, Albuquerque, NM.

Hartz, Nelson W.
1959 "Use of Combustible Gas Indicators." *NFPA National Fire Protection Association Quarterly.* April, 1959, 52(4): pp. 357–365.

Heimmer, Donald H.
1989 Personal communication.

Heller, Robert C. and Joseph J. Ulliman
1983 "Forest Resource Assessments" in Colwell, Robert N. (editor), *Manual of Remote Sensing, 2nd Edition, Vol. 2: Interpretation and Applications.* American Society of Photogrammetry, Falls Church, VA.

Henderson, Janet
1987 "Factors Determining the State of Preservation of Human Remains" in Boddington, A., A.N. Garland, and R.C. Janaway (editors), *Death, Decay and Reconstruction: Approaches to Archaeology and Forensic Science.* Manchester Press, Manchester, United Kingdom.

Hesse, A., A. Jolivet and A. Tabbagh
1986 "New Prospects in Shallow Depth Electrical Surveying for Archaeological and Pedological Applications" in Wynn, Jeffrey C. (editor), *Geophysics in Archaeology,* special issue of *Geophysics.* March, 1986, 51(3): pp. 585–594.

Hester, James J. and James Grady
1982 *Introduction to Archaeology, Second Edition.* Holt, Rinehart and Winston, New York.

Hester, Thomas R., Robert F. Heizer, and John A. Graham (editors)
1975 *Field Methods in Archaeology.* Mayfield Press, Palo Alto, CA.

Hibbard, Whitney S., and Raymond W. Warring
1982 *Psychic Criminology: An Operations Manual For Using Psychics in Criminal Investigations.* Charles C Thomas, Springfield, IL.

Hillard, R. and C. Thomas
1976 "The Combustible Gas Detector (Sniffer), an Evaluation." *Fire and Arson Investigator.* Jan–Mar., 1976, pp. 48–50.

Hitching, Francis
1978 *Dowsing: The Psi Connection.* Anchor Books, Garden City, NY.

Hole, Frank and Robert F. Heizer

1973 *An Introduction to Prehistoric Archaeology, 3rd Edition.* Holt, Rinehart & Winston, New York.

Holter, Marvin R.
   1973 "Passive Microwave Imaging" in Holz, Robert K. (editor), *The Surveillant Science: Remote Sensing of the Environment.* Houghton Mifflin, Boston, MA.

Holz, Robert K. (editor)
   1973 *The Surveillant Science: Remote Sensing of the Environment.* Houghton Mifflin, Boston, MA.

Holz, Robert K.
   1985 *The Surveillant Science: Remote Sensing of the Environment, 2nd Edition.* John Wiley, New York.

Howell, J. Harvey
   1979 *Dowsing for Everyone: Adventures and Instruction in the Art of Modern Dowsing.* Stephen Greene Press, Brattleboro, VT.

Imaizumi, Masataka
   1974 "Locating Buried Bodies." *F.B.I. Law Enforcement Bulletin.* August, 1874, 43(8): pp. 2–5.

Innes, Richard B.
   1973 "An Interpreter's Perspective of Modern Airborne Radar Imagery" in Holz, Robert K. (editor), *The Surveillant Science: Remote Sensing of the Environment.* Houghton Mifflin, Boston, MA.

Jackson, Dan
   1984 "Monitors Keep Eye on Mine Gases." *Coal Age.* September, 1984, 89(9): pp. 90–91.

Johnson, Glen R.
   1977 *Tracking Dog: Theory & Method.* Arner Publications, Westmoreland, New York.

Jones, R.J.A. and R. Evans
   1975 "Soil and Crop Marks in the Recognition of Archaeological Sites by Air Photography" in Wilson, D.R. (editor), *Aerial Reconnaissance for Archaeology.* The Council for British Archaeology, London.

Jorde, Lynn B.
   1977 "Applications of Remote Sensing to Archaeology: Justification, Implementation and Feasibility" in Lyons, Thomas R. (editor), *Remote Sensing Experiments in Cultural Resource Studies: Non-Destructive Methods of Archaeological Exploration, Survey and Analysis.* Reports of the Chaco Center #1, National Park Service, University of New Mexico, Albuquerque, NM.

Jorde, Lynn B.
   1977 "An Evaluation of Some Recent Remote Sensing Projects of the Chaco Center" in Lyons, Thomas R. (editor), *Remote Sensing Experiments in Cultural Resource Studies: Non-Destructive Methods of Archaeological Exploration, Survey and Analysis.* Reports of the Chaco Center #1, National Park Service, University of New Mexico, Albuquerque, NM.

Keller, George V. and Frank C. Frischknecht
   1966 *Electrical Methods in Geophysical Prospecting.* Pergamon Press, New York.

King, Anne
  1983 "Introduction to Gas Detection." *Electronic Technology.* February, 1983, 17(2): pp. 32–34.
Kintigh, Keith W.
  1988 "The Effectiveness of Subsurface Testing: A Simulation Approach." *American Antiquity,* 53(4): pp. 686–707.
Klinger, Timothy C.
  1986 *Village Creek: An Explicitly Regional Approach to the Study of Cultural Resources.* Research Report #26, Arkansas Archaeological Survey, Fayetteville, AR.
Knight, Bernard and Ian Lauder
  1969 "Methods of Dating Skeletal Remains." *Human Biology.* 41(3): pp. 322–341.
Krogman, Wilton M.
  1939 "A Guide to the Identification of Human Skeletal Material." *F.B.I. Law Enforcement Bulletin.* August, 1939: pp. 3–31.
Krogman, Wilton M.
  1943 "The Role of the Physical Anthropologist in the Identification of Human Skeletal Material." *F.B.I. Law Enforcement Bulletin.* Part I in 12(4): pp. 17–40, Part II in 12(5): pp. 12–28.
Krogman, Wilton M.
  1962 *The Human Skeleton in Forensic Medicine.* Charles C Thomas, Springfield, IL.
Krogman, Wilton M. and M. Yasar Iscan
  1986 *The Human Skeleton in Forensic Medicine, 2nd edition.* Charles C Thomas, Springfield, IL.
Lagal, Roy
  1982 *Detector Owner's Field Manual.* Ram Publishing, Dallas TX.
Leonardo, Earl S.
  1973 "Capabilities and Limitation of Remote Sensors" in Holz, Robert K. (editor), *The Surveillant Science: Remote Sensing of the Environment.* Houghton Mifflin, Boston, MA.
Lewis, Anthony J.
  1973 "Evaluation of Multiple-Polarized Radar Imagery for the Detection of Selected Cultural Features" in Holz, Robert K. (editor), *The Surveillant Science: Remote Sensing of the Environment.* Houghton Mifflin, Boston MA.
Levine, Lowell J., Homer R. Campbell Jr., and J. Stanley Rhine
  1984 "Perpendicular Forensic Archaeology" in Rathbun, Ted A. and Jane E. Buikstra (editors), *Human Identification: Case Studies in Forensic Anthropology.* Charles C Thomas, Springfield, IL.
Lillesand, Thomas M. and Ralph W. Kiefer
  1987 *Remote Sensing and Image Interpretation, 2nd edition.* John Wiley, New York.
Limbrey, Susan
  1975 *Soil Science and Archaeology.* Academic Press, New York.
Lintz, Joseph Jr. and David S. Simonett (editors)
  1976 *Remote Sensing of the Environment.* Addison-Wesley, Reading, MA.

Loker, William M.
    1980 "Geophysical Prospecting at the Archaeological Site of Ceren, El Salvador."
        Master's Thesis, Anthropology Department, University of Colorado at
        Boulder.
Loose, Richard W.
    1977 "Airborne TV as an Archaeological Remote Sensing Tool" in Lyons,
        Thomas R. and Robert K. Hitchcock (editors) *Aerial Remote Sensing Tech-
        niques in Archaeology.* Reports of the Chaco Center #2, National Park
        Service, University of New Mexico, Albuquerque, NM.
Lowe, Donald S.
    1976 "Nonphotographic Optical Sensors" in Lintz, Joseph Jr. and David S.
        Simonett (editors), *Remote Sensing of the Environment.* Addison-Wesley,
        Reading, MA.
Lyons, Thomas R. (editor)
    1977 *Remote Sensing Experiments in Cultural Resources Studies: Non-Destructive
        Methods of Archaeological Exploration, Survey, and Analysis.* Reports of the
        Chaco Center #1, National Park Service, University of New Mexico,
        Albuquerque, NM.
Lyons, Thomas R. and Thomas E. Avery
    1977 *Remote Sensing: A Handbook for Archaeologists and Cultural Resource Managers.*
        National Park Service, Washington, D.C.
Lyons, Thomas R. and Robert K. Hitchcock (editors)
    1977 *Aerial Remote Sensing Techniques in Archaeology.* Reports of the Chaco
        Center #2, National Park Service, University of New Mexico, Albuquerque,
        NM.
MacInnes, Hamish
    1972 *International Mountain Rescue Handbook.* Constable, London.
MacLean, Gordon
    1976 *A Field Guide to Dowsing: How to Practice the Ancient Art Today.* American
        Society of Dowsers, Danville, VT.
Mant, A.K.
    1987 "Knowledge Acquired from Post-War Exhumations" in Boddington, A.,
        A.N. Garland, and R.C. Janaway (editors) *Death, Decay and Reconstruction:
        Approaches to Archaeology and Forensic Science.* Manchester University Press,
        Manchester, United Kingdom.
Marbach, William D. and Jeffrey Phillips
    1987 "New Tools for An Ancient Dig." *Newsweek.* November 2, 1987, 110:
        pp. 80–81.
Martin, Michael
    1983–84 "A New Controlled Dowsing Experiment." *The Skeptical Inquirer.* Winter,
        1983–84, 8(2): pp. 138–142.
May, W.G.
    1973 *Mountain Search and Rescue Techniques.* Rocky Mountain Rescue Group,
        Boulder, CO.

McKinnon, Gordon P. (editor)
  1976 *Fire Protection Handbook, 14th edition.* National Fire Protection Association, Boston, MA.
McLaughlin, Jack E.
  1974 *The Detection of Buried Bodies.* Andermac, Yuba City, CA.
McManamon, Francis P.
  1984 "Discovering Sites Unseen" in Schiffer, Michael B. (editor), *Advances in Archaeological Method and Theory, Vol. 7.* Academic Press/Harcourt, Brace, Jovanovich, Orlando FL.
Measures, Raymond
  1984 *Laser Remote Sensing: Fundamentals and Applications.* Wiley Interscience, Somerset, MA.
Mermet, Abbe A.
  1959 *Principles and Practices of Radiesthesia.* Translated by Mark Clement, Thomas Nelson & Sons, New York.
Moffatt, David L.
  1974 "Subsurface Video Pulse Radars" in America Society of Civil Engineers (editors), *Subsurface Exploration for Underground Excavation and Heavy Construction.* New York.
Moore, Richard K.
  1976 "Active Microwave Systems" in Lintz, Joseph Jr. and David S. Simonett (editors), *Remote Sensing of the Environment.* Addison-Wesley, Reading, MA.
Moore, Richard K. et al.
  1983 "Imaging Radar Systems" in Colwell, Robert N. (editor), *Manual of Remote Sensing, 2nd edition, Vol. 1: Theory, Instruments and Techniques.* American Society of Photogrammetry, Falls Church, VA.
Morain, Stanley A. and Thomas K. Budge
  1978 *Remote Sensing: Instrumentation for Non-Destructive Exploration of Cultural Resources.* Supplement No. 2 to Lyons, Thomas R. and Thomas E. Avery, *Remote Sensing: A Handbook for Archaeologists and Cultural Resource Managers.* National Park Service, Washington, D.C.
Morey, Rexford M.
  1974 "Continuous Subsurface Profiling by Impulse Radar" in American Society of Civil Engineers (editors), *Subsurface Exploration for Underground Excavation and Heavy Construction.* New York.
Morse, Dan, Donald Crusoe and H.G. Smith
  1976 "Forensic Archaeology." *Journal of Forensic Sciences.* 21(2): pp. 323–332.
Morse, Dan and Robert C. Dailey
  1985 "The Degree of Deterioration of Associated Death Scene Material." *Journal of Forensic Sciences.* January, 1985, 30(1): pp. 119–127.
Morse, Dan, Robert C. Dailey, James Stoutamire, and Jack Duncan
  1984 "Forensic Archaeology" in Rathbun, Ted A. and Jane Buikstra (editors), *Human Identification: Case Studies in Forensic Anthropology.* Charles C Thomas, Springfield, IL.

Morse, Dan, Jack Duncan and James Stoutamire
    1983 *Handbook of Forensic Archaeology and Anthropology.* Rose Printing, Tallahassee, FL.
Morse, Dan, James Stoutamire, and Jack Duncan
    1976 "A Unique Course in Anthropology." *American Journal of Physical Anthropology.* November, 1976, 45(3): pp. 743–748.
Mueller, Larry
    1986 "Search and Rescue." *Outdoor Life.* March, 1986, 67: pp. 116–120.
Murray, Raymond C. and John C. Tedrow
    1975 *Forensic Geology: Earth Sciences and Criminal Investigations.* Rutgers University Press, New Brunswick, NJ.
Nunnally, Nelson R.
    1973 "Introduction to Remote Sensing: The Physics of Electromagnetic Radiation" in Holz, Robert K. (editor), *The Surveillant Science: Remote Sensing of the Environment.* Houghton Mifflin, Boston, MA.
O'Brien, Kevin P. and Robert C. Sullivan
    1976 *Criminalistics: Theory and Practice.* Holbrook Press, Boston, MA.
Parasnis, D.S.
    1979 *Principles of Applied Geophysics, 3rd edition.* John Wiley, New York.
Pella, Ronald I. and M. Martinelli, Jr.
    1975 *Avalanche Handbook, Agriculture Handbook No. 489.* U.S. Department of Agriculture, U.S. Forest Service, Washington, D.C.
Poulton, Charles E.
    1975 "Range Resources: Inventory, Evaluation and Monitoring" in Reeves, Robert G., *Manual of Remote Sensing.* American Society of Photogrammetry, Falls Church, VA.
Randi, James
    1979 "A Controlled Test of Dowsing Abilities." *The Skeptical Inquirer.* Fall, 1979, 4(1): pp. 16–20.
Ralph, Elizabeth K., Frank Morrison and Douglas P. O'Brien
    1968 "Archaeological Surveying Utilizing a High Sensitivity Difference Magnetometer." *Geological Exploration,* 6: pp. 109–122.
Rathbun, Ted A. and Jane E. Buikstra (editors)
    1984 *Human Identification: Case Studies in Forensic Anthropology.* Charles C Thomas, Springfield, IL.
Rayl, A.J.S.
    1987 "Nightmare Vision (Anti-Matter)." *Omni.* July, 1987, 9: p. 97.
Reedman, J.H.
    1979 *Techniques in Mineral Exploration.* Applied Science Publishers, London.
Reese, K.M.
    1985 "Dowsing for Use in Archaeological Surveys." *Chemical and Engineering News.* March 18, 1985, 63: p. 124.
Reeves, Robert G.
    1975 *Manual of Remote Sensing.* American Society of Photogrammetry, Falls Church, VA.

Reher, Charles A. (editor)
  1977 *Settlement and Subsistence Along the Lower Chaco River: The C.G.P. Survey.* University of New Mexico Press, Albuquerque, NM.

Reichs, Kathleen J. (editor)
  1986 *Forensic Osteology: Advances in the Identification of Human Remains.* Charles C Thomas, Springfield, IL.

Reiser, Martin, Louise Ludwig, Susan Saxe, and Clare Wagner
  1979 "An Evaluation of the Use of Psychics in the Investigation of Major Crimes." *Journal of Police Science and Administration.* 7(1): pp. 18–25.

Ressler, Robert K. (editor)
  1987 *Sexual Homicide: Patterns, Motives and Procedures for Investigators.* Lexington Books, Lexington MA.

Ressler, Robert K. and Ann W. Burgess
  1985 "Crime Scene and Profile Characteristics of Organized and Disorganized Murderers." *F.B.I. Enforcement Bulletin.* August, 1985, pp. 18–25.

Rhine, Joseph B. and Joseph G. Pratt
  1962 *Parapsychology, Frontier Science of the Mind: A Survey of the Field, the Methods, and the Facts of ESP and PK Research.* Charles C Thomas, Springfield, IL.

Rinker, Jack N.
  1975 "Some Technical Aspects of Film Emulsions in Relation to the Analysis and Interpretation of Aerial Photographs" in Wilson, David R. (editor), *Aerial Reconnaissance for Archaeology.* The Council for British Archaeology, London.

Roberts, Kenneth
  1951 *Henry Gross and His Dowsing Rod.* Doubleday, Garden City, NY.

Roberts, Kenneth
  1953 *The Seventh Sense.* Doubleday, Garden City, NY.

Roberts, Kenneth
  1957 *Water Unlimited.* Doubleday, Garden City, NY.

Rodriguez, William C. III
  1987 *Postmortem Animal Activity: Recognition and Interpretation.* Paper presented at the 39th Annual Meeting of the American Academy of Forensic Sciences, San Diego, CA.

Rodriguez, William C. III and William M. Bass
  1983 "Insect Activity and Its Relationship to Decay Rates of Human Cadavers in East Tennessee." *Journal of Forensic Science.* April, 1983, 28(2): pp. 423–432.

Rodriguez, William C. III and William M. Bass
  1985 "Decomposition of Buried Bodies and Methods that May Aid in Their Location." *Journal of Forensic Sciences.* July, 1985, 30(3): pp. 836–852.

Sabins, Floyd F.
  1976 "Geological Applications of Remote Sensing" in Lintz, Joseph Jr. and David S. Simonett (editors), *Remote Sensing of the Environment.* Addison-Wesley, Reading, MA.

Sabins, Floyd F. Jr.
  1987 *Remote Sensing, 2nd edition.* W.H. Freeman, New York.

Sazhina, N. and N. Grushinsky
  1971 *Gravity Prospecting.* Translated by A.K. Chatterjee, MIR Publishers, Moscow, U.S.S.R.
Schiffer, Michael B., Alan P. Sullivan and Timothy C. Klinger
  1977 "The Design of Archaeological Surveys." *World Archaeology.* 10:pp. 1–28.
Schiffer, Michael B. (editor)
  1984 *Advances in Archaeological Method and Theory, Vol. 7.* Academic Press/ Harcourt, Brace, Jovanovich, Orlando, FL.
Schwartz, Stephan A.
  1978 *The Secret Vaults of Time: Psychic Archaeology and The Quest for Man's Beginnings.* Grossett & Dunlap, New York.
Scollar, Irwin
  1972 "Magnetic Mapping of Buried Archaeological Sites." *Endeavor,* 31: pp. 34–40.
Scott, William B.
  1987 "Side-Looking Radars Provide Realistic Images Under Adverse Weather Conditions." *Aviation Week and Space Technology.* September 7, 1987, 127: pp. 93–97.
Setnicka, Tim J.
  1980 *Wilderness Search and Rescue.* Appalachian Mountain Club, Boston, MA.
Sharma, P.V.
  1976 *Geophysical Methods in Geology.* Elsevier, New York.
Shelley, John G. Jr.
  1971 Personal Communication.
Siegel, Heinz W.
  1987 Personal Communication.
Simonett, David S. et al.
  1983 "The Development and Principles of Remote Sensing" in Colwell, Robert N. (editor), *Manual of Remote Sensing, 2nd Edition, Vol. 1: Theory, Instruments, and Techniques.* American Society of Photogrammetry, Falls Church, VA.
Skinner, Mark and Richard A. Lazenby
  1983 *Found! Human Remains: A Field Manual for the Recovery of the Recent Human Skeleton.* Archaeology Press, Simon Fraser University, Burnaby, B.C., Canada.
Snow, Clyde C.
  1982 "Forensic Anthropology." *Annual Review of Anthropology.* 11: pp. 97–131.
Snyder, Lemoyne
  1977 *Homicide Investigation: Practical Information for Coroners, Police Officers and Other Investigators, 3rd Edition.* Charles C Thomas, Springfield, IL.
Sprague, Roderick
  1968 "A Suggested Terminology and Classification for Burial Description." *American Antiquity,* 33(4): pp. 479–485.
Spurr, Stephen H.
  1973 "Types of Aerial Photographs" in Holz, Robert K. (editor), *The Surveillant Science: Remote Sensing of the Environment.* Houghton Mifflin, Boston, MA.

Stanley, John M. and Ronald Green
  1976 "Ultra-Rapid Magnetic Surveying in Archaeology." *Geological Exploration,*
      14(1): pp. 51–56.
St. Joseph, John K.S.
  1966 "Air Photography and Archaeology" in St. Joseph, John K.S. (editor), *The*
      Uses of Air Photography. John Day, New York.
St. Joseph, John K.S. (editor)
  1966 *The Uses of Air Photography.* John Day, New York.
Stewart, T. Dale
  1979 *Essentials of Forensic Anthropology.* Charles C Thomas, Springfield, IL.
Streed, Thomas
  1989 "Dump-site Analysis and Behavioral Characteristics of Psychopathic Killers."
      Paper presented at the 41st annual meeting of the American Academy of
      Forensic Sciences, Las Vegas, Nevada, February 16, 1989.
Swanson, Charles R. Jr., Neil C. Chamelin and Leonard Territo
  1977 *Criminal Investigation.* Goodyear Publishing, Santa Monica, CA.
Swift, Richard L.
  1986 "Gas and Vapor Testing" in Cote, Arthur E. (editor), *Fire Protection Handbook,*
      16th Edition. National Fire Protection Association, Quincy, MA.
Tartaglia, Louis J.
  1977 "Infra-red Archaeological Reconnaissance" in Lyons, Thomas R. and Robert
      K. Hitchcock (editors), *Aerial Remote Sensing Techniques in Archaeology.*
      Reports of the Chaco Center #2, National Park Service, University of New
      Mexico, Albuquerque, NM.
Thackrey, Donald E.
  1973 "Research in Infra-red Sensing" in Holz, Robert K. (editor), *The Surveil-*
      lant Science: Remote Sensing of the Environment. Houghton Mifflin, Boston.
Tromp, Solco Walle
  1949 *Psychical Physics: A Scientific Analysis of Dowsing, Radiesthesia and Kindred*
      Divining Phenomena. Elsevier, New York.
Trubo, Richard
  1975 "Psychics and the Police." *Psychic,* May/June, 1975, 6(2): pp. 8, 10–12.
Ubelaker, Douglas H.
  1984 *Human Skeletal Remains: Excavation, Analysis, Interpretation.* Taraxacum,
      Washington, D.C.
Ulaby, Fawwaz T. and Keith R. Carver
  1983 "Passive Microwave Radiometry" in Colwell, Robert N. (editor), *Manual of*
      Remote Sensing, 2nd Edition, Vol. 1: Theory, Instruments, and Techniques.
      American Society of Photogrammetry, Falls Church, VA.
Van de Castle, Robert L.
  1977 "Parapsychology and Anthropology" in Wolman, Benjamin B. (editor),
      Handbook of Parapsychology. Van Nostrand Reinhold, New York.
Vaughn, Alan
  1975 "Police: How to Use Psychics." *Psychic,* May/June, 1975, 6(2): pp. 22–23.
Vaughn, C.J.
  1986 "Ground-Penetrating Radar Surveys Used in Archaeological Investigations"

in Wynn, Jeffrey C. (editor), Geophysics in Archaeology, special issue of *Geophysics.* March, 1986, 51(3): pp. 595–604.

Vickers, Roger, Lambert Dolphin and David Johnson

   1977 "Archaeological Investigations at Chaco Canyon Using a Subsurface Radar" in Lyons, Thomas R. (editor), *Remote Sensing Experiments in Cultural Resource Studies: Non-Destructive Methods of Archaeological Exploration, Survey and Analysis.* Reports of the Chaco Center #1, National Park Service, University of New Mexico, Albuquerque, NM.

Viksne, Andris, Thomas C. Liston and Cecil D. Sapp

   1973 "SLR Reconnaissance of Panama" in Holz, Robert K. (editor), *The Surveillant Science: Remote Sensing of the Environment.* Houghton Mifflin, Boston, MA.

Vogt, Evon Z. and Ray Hyman

   1979 *Water Witching U.S.A., 2nd edition.* University of Chicago Press, Chicago, IL.

Wait, James R.

   1982 *Geo-Electromagnetism.* Academic Press, New York.

Wallach, Charles and Roy Ricci

   1977 "Security Metal Detection Systems." *Security Management.* July, 1977, pp. 61–66.

Weymouth, John W.

   1976 *A Magnetic Survey of the Walth Bay Site (39WW203).* Midwest Archaeological Center, National Park Service, Lincoln, NE.

Weymouth, John W. and Robert Huggins

   1985 "Geophysical Surveying of Archaeological Sites" in Rapp, George and John Gifford (editors), *Archaeological Geology.* Yale University Press, New Haven, CT.

Willey, Raymond C.

   1984 *All You Need to Know About Modern Dowsing: The Dowser's Handbook.* Treasure Chest Publications, Tucson, AZ.

Wilson, Colin

   1985 *The Psychic Detectives: The Story of Psychometry and Paranormal Crime Detection.* Mercury House, San Francisco, CA.

Wilson, David R.

   1975 "Photographic Techniques in the Air" in Wilson, David R. (editor), *Aerial Reconnaissance for Archaeology.* Council for British Archaeology, London.

Wilson, David R. (editor)

   1975 *Aerial Reconnaissance for Archaeology.* The Council for British Archaeology, London.

Wilson, David R.

   1982 *Air Photo Interpretation for Archaeologists.* St. Martin's Press, New York.

Wolf, David J.

   1986 "Forensic Anthropology Scene Investigations" in Reichs, Kathleen J. (editor), *Forensic Osteology: Advances in the Identification of Human Remains.* Charles C Thomas, Springfield, IL.

Wolkomir, Richard

1985 "Water Witches: Do Dowsers Defy Modern Science or Do They Tap our Secret Spring?" *Omni.* September, 1985, 7: pp. 40–42, 92–94.

Wolman, Benjamin B. (editor)

1977 *Handbook of Parapsychology.* Van Nostrand Reinhold, New York.

Wyckoff, Don G.

1986 *Suggested Outline for Investigating Crime-Related Burial Sites.* Oklahoma Archaeological Survey, University of Oklahoma, Norman, OK.

Wyman, Walker D.

1977 *Witching for Water, Oil, Pipes, and Precious Minerals.* University of Wisconsin, River Falls Press, Park Falls, WI.

Wynn, Jeffrey C. (editor)

1986 Geophysics in Archaeology, special issue of *Geophysics.* March, 1986 51(3), Society of Exploration Geophysicists, Tulsa, OK.

Zatek, J.E.

1970 "Instruments for Measuring Hazardous Atmospheres." *Fire Journal.* September, 1970, 64(5): pp. 76–80.

INDEX

A

Absolute zero, 135, 193
Accelerants, 48
Acid, 60–62
Actinic radiation, 167
Aerial photographs (*see* Photography, aerial)
Agricola, Georgius, 180
Airborne radar (Active microwave), 138,
    144–150, 168 (*see* Side looking airborne
    radar)
Airscenting (*see* Dogs, airscent)
Airspeed, 159, 161, 164, 177
Alkaline, 62
Altitude, 157, 159, 161, 175–177
Aluminum, 112, 114
American Society of Dowsers, Inc., 180, 192
Ammonia, 49, 50, 63
Angle, critical, 121
   normal, 121
   of incidence, 120, 121
   of reflection, 121
Angle rods, 181, 182, 185, 186, 188
Animal activity, 9, 17, 20, 36, 37
Anomalies, 61, 69, 70–72, 75, 76, 78, 79, 83, 85,
    88, 92, 97, 99, 101, 106, 123, 130, 132, 133,
    138–140, 153, 169, 171, 174
Antenna, radar, 126–130, 146–148
Anthropology, 3, 196
Anthropology, cultural, 3, 196
Anthropology, forensic, 3, 4, 6
Anthropology, physical, 3, 4, 6
Anthrosols, 63
Archaeological survey (search), 23, 36, 77, 82,
    91, 102, 123, 125, 131, 155, 157, 172, 196
Archaeology, viii, xi, 3, 5–7, 9
Archaeology, forensic, 5–7, 113
Archaeology, psychic (intuitive), 196–198

Arson, 48
Artifacts, 5, 60, 196, 198
Astigmatism, psychic, 198
Atkinson, R.J., 91
Attenuation, signal, 127
Auger, 55, 57, 65
Avalanche dogs (*see* Dogs, airscent)
Aymar, Jacques, 180

B

Backhoe, 65
Bacteria, 20, 59, 60, 151
Behavior, human, 8, 15–17
Bertillon, Alphonse, 5
Birds, 36, 37
Blitz team, 24
Blooming, 150
Bobber, 181–183, 187
Body disposal, 15–17
Body positions, 7
Bones, 4, 5, 21, 57, 58, 60, 63, 131
Bones, animal, 5
Bones, human, 4, 20, 58
Bouguer map, 75
Broadside shooting, 123, 124
Budget, xiii, 133, 236
Bulldozer, 64
Bundy, Ted, vii
Burial, time of, 5, 6, 9, 10, 20, 21
Burial types, 8–10, 15, 16, 20, 21

C

Calcium, 63
Calibration, gas detectors, 51, 52
Camera types, airphoto, 159, 161, 164,
    165–177

257

L

Laser, 152
Latitude correction (effects), 74, 76, 77, 82
Least effort, 8
LeBorgne effect, 78
Light meter, camera, 161, 168
Light table, 158, 169
Line search, 26–29, 40
Linguistics, 3
Litter, 82, 109, 111, 114
Logistics, 13, 19, 24
Look angle, 146
Loop frame, 104
Lucas, Henry Lee, viii
Luminescence, 58
Lunar correction (effects), 74, 77

M

Magnetic fields, 75–81, 103, 104, 132
Magnetic surveying, 69, 75–86, 101, 132, 226, 227, 237
Magnetite, 78, 114
Magnetometers, 79–82
    fluxgate, 79
    gradiometer, 82
    optical pumping, 80
    proton, 79–82
Magnifying glass, 158, 159, 169
Manganese, 64
Manner of death, 5
Map dowsing, 186–192, 197
Mass disaster, vii
Mass murder, vii, viii, 9
McKinley, A.C., 155
Measured response, 24
Medical records, 5
Mental attitude, 185, 186, 191, 193, 194, 199–202
Mermet, Abbe, 190–193
Metal detectors, 18, 69, 102, 107–117, 133, 228, 229, 235–237
    beat frequency oscillators (B.F.O.), 109, 112
    induction balance (I.B.), 109, 112
    pulsed induction (P.I.), 108, 109, 112
    transmitter–receiver (T.R.), 109–112, 116
    types, 108–112

very low frequency (V.L.F.), 109–112, 114, 116
Methane, 39, 49, 51, 52, 235, 236
Mho meters, 92, 104
Microwave (*see* Passive microwave) (*see* Airborne radar [active microwave])
Millisiemens, 104, 107
Missing person (lost), xi, 11, 13, 14, 180, 190, 192, 206, 217–221
Monkey thoughts, 186, 193
Monopole anomaly, 79, 86
Multi-band, 139, 170
    -bank camera, 164, 165
    -concept, 137–139
    -date, 139
    -directional, 139
    -spectral, 139, 164, 165
    -stage, 138, 139
    -time, 139

N

Nanoseconds, 128
Negative indicators, 31, 32
Newton, Isaac, 71
Nitrogen, 63, 173
Noise, 18, 69, 70, 82, 85, 88, 99, 100, 111, 114, 118
Non-intrusive search, 25

O

Oblique aerial photography, 146, 156–165, 172, 174, 235
Oersted, 76
Ohm meters, 91, 93, 104, 128
Opossums, 36
Osteology, 3

P

Paleontology, 3
Parapsychological methods, 179–203
Passive microwave, 138, 141–145, 230, 231
Pedestrian search (*see* Foot search)
Pedology, 53
Pendulum, 181, 184–186, 188, 190, 192, 193
pH testing, 62
Phosphorescence, 58